D0945022

WITHDRAWN

Power and the People

Supplementary Volumes to
The Papers of Woodrow Wilson
Arthur S. Link, Editor

A list of volumes in this series will be
found at the back of the book.

Power and the People

Executive Management

of Public Opinion in

Foreign Affairs, 1897–1921

ROBERT C. HILDERBRAND

The University of North Carolina Press

Chapel Hill

© 1981 The University of North Carolina Press
All rights reserved
Manufactured in the United States of America
ISBN 0-8078-1432-6
Library of Congress Catalog Card Number 79-28119

Library of Congress Cataloging in Publication Data

Hilderbrand, Robert C   1947–
    Power and the people.

(Supplementary volumes to the papers of Woodrow Wilson)
    Bibliography: p.
    Includes index.
    1. United States—Foreign relations—1865–1921.
2. Public opinion—United States. I. Title.
II. Series: Wilson, Woodrow, Pres. U.S., 1856–
1924.   Papers: Supplementary volume.
E744.H56   327.73   79-28119
ISBN 0-8078-1432-6

For Darlene

Contents

Acknowledgments

Somewhere it is written that no book is easy to write, and this book was no exception to that rule. That it managed to be written at all, in fact, was due to the help and support of many people—my teachers, friends, and colleagues. My thanks to them all.

I owe a special debt of gratitude to Gerald Wolff and R. Alton Lee of the University of South Dakota, who helped me far more than they know. Another former colleague, Miles Fletcher of the University of North Carolina at Chapel Hill, read the entire manuscript and supported me with both his good advice and his friendship.

My editor, Lewis Bateman, handled this nervous author with great tact and patience and let me discover for myself the wisdom that lies in revision.

Two of my teachers at the University of Iowa deserve special mention: Robert Dykstra, who taught me what little I know about the finer points of writing; and Ellis Hawley, who has the uncanny ability of always asking just the right question.

Professor Arthur S. Link of Princeton University read the complete manuscript with characteristic care. He saved me from many errors of fact and interpretation and shared with me his incomparable knowledge of the Wilson years.

I owe the greatest intellectual debt to my mentor, Lawrence Gelfand of the University of Iowa. He spent long hours helping me to make sense out of a topic that some people regarded as impossible and did more than I thought anyone could to ease the pain of writing a dissertation.

This book is dedicated to Darlene, my wife. It is small reward for all that she has given me for so long. This is a debt that truly can never be repaid.

Power and the People

Introduction

What we call the beginning is often the end
And to make an end is to make a beginning.
The end is where we start from. And every
  phrase
And sentence that is right (where every word is
  at home,
Taking its place to support the others,
The word neither diffident nor ostentatious,
An easy commerce of the old and the new,
The common word exact without vulgarity,
The formal word precise but not pedantic,
The complete consort dancing together)
Every phrase and every sentence is an end and a
  beginning,
Every poem an epitaph.

T. S. Eliot, "Little Gidding"

In a time when new disclosures about executive activities seem commonplace, it is no startling revelation that presidents take considerable pains to manage public opinion in foreign affairs. Supported by an immense staff of trained public relations personnel and employing techniques developed by commercial advertisers, today's chief executives take advantage of the various mass communications media to sell their foreign policies to the American people. Such efforts are, indeed, a hallmark of what one historian has recently termed the "Imperial Presidency," and their effectiveness—and danger—became only too apparent during the long travail of war in Vietnam.[1]

But this is the end to our beginning: presidential management has not always been the rule. For thirty years following the Civil War, presidents made little effort to influence the public's view of foreign affairs, confining their activities to occasional personal interventions in ongoing national debates. Although presidential stature insured that even such desultory publicity had some impact on the press and public, these chief executives failed to establish anything like a systematic relationship with the mass media of their day. As a result, their capabilities for managing public opinion were severely limited, awaiting the creation of a more routine and less obtrusive presidential utilization of the press. Not until the administration of William McKinley did a president demonstrate genuine awareness of the advantages of good press relations, and although the next twenty-five years saw a thorough modernization of executive techniques for dealing with the press and public, McKinley's efforts marked the beginning of self-conscious presidential management of public attitudes in foreign affairs.

What was the reason for this change? What transformed a sleepy executive department, expressing little interest in publicity, into a mighty dynamo for generating public opinion? The answers, surely, are varied and complex, encompassing the experience of several presidents, but we may perhaps infer here at least their more visible dimensions. One reason was undoubtedly related to technological change: the late nineteenth century was an era of marked improvement in the nation's mass media of communications, and it was not coincidental that presidents began then to show increased interest in their use. Another was the development of the business of public relations, which produced techniques for mass persuasion as applicable to government as to private industry—and which would ultimately send such notables as Ronald Ziegler to work in the White House. Even more important, perhaps, was the twentieth-century ideology of progressivism. Its emphasis on popular foundations of power clearly enhanced presidential awareness of public opinion, and its concern for sound administration had an impact on the executive's development of news managerial techniques as well. Most important, however, was the rapid expansion of America's role in world affairs. War and empire—and war again—required an ever-increasing degree of public support, and this period's enlargement of presidential influence over the press and public occurred during times of extreme stress in foreign relations.[2]

All of this was, to be sure, part of the larger process of modernization taking hold of the federal government during the late 1890s. That time, according to Arthur Schlesinger, Jr., spawned the idea of the imperial presidency, and Robert Beisner has described it as representing an executive paradigm shift from an old to a new world view. With this in mind, it might be useful to borrow a concept from economics and to view the 1890s as a time of "takeoff" for the modernization of the presidency. Nelson Polsby has applied this idea to Congress in the same period; it appears no less valid for our understanding of the executive as well. For the office of the presidency, the end of the nineteenth century was a time of rapidly expanding power, both at home and abroad—a time when new responsibilities threatened to outstrip administrative capabilities. It should not be surprising, then, that this was also the time when the presidency developed into a complex institution, with staff members undertaking duties divided more distinctly by function than by the transient exigencies of office. One dimension that gained prominence in this way was the management of public opinion; it soon became an important administrative concern as part of the more general institutional takeoff within the executive.[3]

Whatever the reason, there can be no doubt that the years after 1897 saw a marked increase in the chief executive's interest in popular attitudes. This was perhaps most evident in the rapid proliferation of appropriate White House personnel; it also appeared in the growing number of executive press releases made during this period. Another sign of presidential interest could be found in increased use of newspaper scrapbooks, which changed in the late nineteenth century from personal mementos to functional indexes for evaluating public views. Clearly, the executive was developing a new awareness of the press and public—and of his own ability to influence their opinions.

What was the significance of this change? Did increased presidential awareness of public opinion lead to enhancement of the people's role in American democracy? Or was the result a decline in the public's real influence on the policies of the executive? These are, again, questions of some complexity; we can do no more here than to suggest their most probable answers. It should be noted, first of all, that public opinion had had little impact on foreign policy making before 1897, receiving only negligible consideration in the deliberations of presidents and secretaries of state. This might lead us to expect that the public's role was enlarged—it could hardly have been made much smaller—by the executive's new interest.

But there is also reason for us to suppose the opposite. As the president's interest in popular attitudes increased, so did his efforts to guide and influence them, and one outcome was a clear decline in the public's independence. To an extent unimaginable before the end of the nineteenth century, the executive became a dominant force in the leadership of public opinion; it now exercised subtle control over the efforts of Washington correspondents and employed increasingly sophisticated techniques for directing the public's view of international affairs. And although this often took the form of an increase in the amount of information released by the White House—a particular source of pride among progressive presidents—its final effect was to enhance the executive's capability for manipulating public opinion.

Increasing the flow of information also provided the executive with an ideological justification for managing public opinion. This was, predictably, most used by progressive administrations, which found no difficulty in equating the release of desirable information with their goal of expanded public education. Thus Roosevelt's desire for popular support transformed the White House into a "bully pulpit," and Wilson's proclamation of "pitiless publicity" found fruition in carefully orchestrated press conferences. Still, there is no denying that one result of these efforts was a significant enlargement in the public's awareness of foreign affairs, and we shall have to consider whether this salutary development balanced the dangers involved in the president's enhanced control over popular perceptions.

This does not mean, however, that our primary concern is with the perceptions of the public. They are, to be sure, the usual subject of public opinion studies (which this is not), where their exclusive use often produces a serious distortion in attempts to understand the relationship between public and policy maker. Public opinion is a two-way street: impulses moving toward the executive are matched by those directed at the public. And the crux of our story is the president's increased awareness of his ability, through his own words and initiatives, to control the signals that he receives at the White House. From this perspective, it appears that public opinion studies have depicted only the less important half of the relationship between public and executive, leaving unanswered a number of vital questions about presidential perception of popular views. One question relates to the importance of public opinion in policy making: can it sometimes be overlooked in favor of more pressing considerations? Or has the modern chief executive found the old rule of *vox populi suprema lex* too perilous to disregard? The answer to this question changed, as we have noted, throughout the decades following 1890, with increased presidential interest in the public reflecting its growing importance in foreign affairs. It is, perhaps, ironic that executive efforts to generate support fueled an upward spiral of public interest that strengthened at least the appearance of presidential constraints, but it is by no means certain that the chief executive perceived these constraints as any more binding in 1920 than he had thirty years before.

Another question deals with the public's manageability: did the presidents view public opinion as something they could change? Or did they see it as a constant in their foreign policy equation? On this there seems to have been more agreement: all chief executives understood their ability to influence the public's thinking, and all made use of it on one occasion or another. Still, there remained distinct differences in the presidents' perceptions of this power—and of its probity—and we shall want to examine both the causes and the effects of these differences. It is clear, in any event, that the twentieth century saw executives make increasing use of their capacity for directing popular attitudes, a change that reflected some alteration in the presidents' view of the public's manageability.

And finally: did presidents see a positive side to public opinion? Did they attempt to utilize it as an instrument of foreign affairs? Or was it only an impediment to their deliberations? This is, in some ways, the most intriguing of these questions, hinting at a new dimension in the management of public opinion, but it is also the most difficult to answer with any degree of certainty. There existed, as we shall see, some examples of constructive use of the public during this period, especially in time of war, and the idea clearly proliferated—even in peacetime—after 1945. In proclaiming the Truman Doctrine and in conducting relations with the Soviet Union throughout the cold war, the executive has made use of a militant public to buttress the force of its diplomacy. In a time of threatened total war, this has become an essential consideration in the management of public opinion; it is no wonder that today's presidents are as concerned with the creation of a positive image as with the amelioration of negative public attitudes. But we are, characteristically, jumping to the end; let us get on with the beginning.

Chapter 1
In the Ways of
McKinley

 When William McKinley became president in 1897, he inherited an office with immense latent power. Both constitutionally and politically, the president was the nation's one true leader and spokesman, a position that guaranteed him the ability to influence public opinion on national questions. But this ability, like so many other presidential powers, had lain dormant in postbellum America; it was a time when executive authority seemed constantly on the wane—and when presidents exercised little control over public opinion.

This does not mean, however, that Gilded Age presidents had no understanding of their power. On occasion, they did enter the public debate on important foreign policy issues, using their ability to command national attention—what we might call the power of presidential publicity—to facilitate a shift in opinion. And they did seem, at times, to be developing an appreciation for the potential value of public opinion management. This was particularly true of Garfield, who wrote, for instance, that public opinion had now been rendered "all pervading" and constituted "more than ever a strong bond of nationality." It was also true of Cleveland, whose successful use of his publicity power was best described by the editor of the *New York World* in 1896. "The President has recently tested his capacity for rousing the country," he wrote, and the result was "the blaze which swept across it after the Venezuela message."[1]

But such behavior was the exception rather than the rule. Nineteenth-century presidents used their ability to influence the public only rarely—and never completely. Even when reacting to a crisis, they seemed unable to convince themselves that it was proper to use their power to its fullest. Nor did they think that they ever had to do so. This presidential confidence came in part from their faith in the judgment of the people, in what Hayes called the public's "second thought"; it also came from an understanding of their ability to influence that judgment. This was most clearly expressed by Edwards Pierrepont, writing in 1873 to Grant's secretary of state. "The coun-

try have such confidence in the President and his cabinet," wrote
Pierrepont, "that they will cheerfully follow wherever you may
jointly lead"; and the president could also rest assured that his own
views "are the views or *will become the views of our best men.*"
Sharing this attitude, presidents in the Gilded Age saw little to fear
from public opinion.[2]

Partly as a result of their lack of concern, these presidents failed
to develop advanced techniques for dealing with the press and public. In general, they relied upon interviews with one or two favored
reporters—a carryover from the days of the partisan press—and
upon publication of their messages to Congress. They did not develop methods for the routine release of information; nor did they do
much to attach correspondents to the executive office. They did
pioneer the compiling of newspaper scrapbooks as an aid in assessing public opinion, but they never seemed quite certain just how
these should be used. In short, these presidents did not see the press
as a mass medium that could be manipulated by controlling the flow
of information to its reporters, and they took no steps designed to
make this possible.[3]

Thus, throughout this period, presidential forays into the realm of
public opinion remained desultory and sporadic, relying almost entirely upon the power of presidential publicity to present singular
messages to the American people. These chief executives created no
program for the day-to-day molding of opinion; they merely reacted
to difficulties as they arose. They continued to view Washington
correspondents as a meddlesome encumbrance to the administration of foreign affairs, resisting steadfastly their efforts to transform
the White House into a primary source of news. This was, to be
sure, in keeping with presidential needs during this period. The
White House did not consider public opinion a factor in making
decisions on foreign policy because it did not see that most of its
decisions required public support. When this situation changed, as
it would during the McKinley administration, the president would
begin to search for ways of exerting daily influence over the press
and public.[4]

This change came about as a result of America's greatly expanded
world role at the end of the nineteenth century. At that time, the
Spanish-American War—and its imperialistic backwash—produced
a foreign policy that involved military action in places as distant as
China and the Philippines. Such a policy required clear public
support, and the McKinley administration responded not only by
demonstrating an increased awareness of public opinion but also by
developing improved techniques for influencing it as well. The time

had passed when presidents seemed content to see White House correspondents gather news serendipitously; in the future they would make a daily effort to assist reporters and to influence their stories.

McKinley laid the foundation for these changes in the first few months of his administration, when he assembled an executive staff more skilled in handling the press than any of its predecessors. At its head stood John Addison Porter, who held the newly created post of secretary to the president. No mere amanuensis, Porter performed duties similar to those of previous presidents' private secretaries but exercised the prestige and authority of a cabinet member. In increasing the status of his top assistant, McKinley was responding to a number of administrative pressures, including the need for an authoritative voice in communicating with White House reporters. Porter supplied this voice so well that he developed into a prototype for the presidential press secretary, despite the fact that his other responsibilities limited the time that he could spend with correspondents. Still, Porter always found time for the press, and he became the first secretary to meet daily with the Washington newspapermen. At ten o'clock each evening he conducted a press briefing, generally consisting of a prepared statement of the day's events accompanied by a series of press releases and a question-and-answer period. In this way, Porter exercised a more subtle and consistent influence on the press than any previous secretary, and he soon increased his office's control over the flow of White House news. To be sure, this control remained far from total, but it gave the McKinley administration some capacity for exploiting the usefulness of Washington correspondents.[5]

Also playing an important part in the new administration's press relations was George B. Cortelyou. As Porter's assistant, Cortelyou became responsible for drawing up many White House press releases, for distributing news when the secretary was otherwise occupied, and for overseeing compilation of the president's newspaper scrapbooks. In addition, Cortelyou generally went along on McKinley's speech-making tours and handled all press relations for the trip. It was in this capacity that he first became known to reporters as the person to contact for information; he supplied them with timetables, press releases, and advance copies of the president's addresses. As McKinley soon discovered, Cortelyou proved well suited for these tasks. He combined gregariousness with competence in the performance of administrative duties, so that when Porter retired he was the obvious choice for the job. He ultimately became, in the words of one newspaperman, "very nearly the ideal Secretary to the President."[6]

An expansion of the White House staff also facilitated McKinley's relations with the press. In March 1897, the president's staff comprised only six typists and clerks, one of whom was detailed to handle the first lady's correspondence; by the end of the year, his entourage had grown to eighteen. Even this proved insufficient, however, when the responsibilities of war and empire added to administrative duties, so that by 1901 the White House staff grew to more than eighty assistants. One reason for this expansion was the added clerical work of preparing and distributing press releases; one result was more time for dealing with Washington correspondents.[7]

The situation was different at the State Department, however, where press relations failed to improve following McKinley's inauguration. Although slightly enlarged, the department's size remained too small to allow much time for working with reporters. This limitation was magnified by the coming of war with Spain, when the department's antiquated methods were applied to tasks they were not designed to accomplish. In addition, McKinley's ancient secretary of state, John Sherman, developed a reputation for garrulousness with reporters that irritated the White House secretariat; small wonder, then, that his relations with Porter and Cortelyou were often strained. The result was that the State Department did not contribute much to the administration's handling of the press.[8]

McKinley did much himself to compensate for deficiencies within his administration. During long service in the House of Representatives, the new president had learned the value of maintaining cordial relations with the press, and he brought to the White House long-standing friendships with many Washington reporters. He won additional goodwill early in his administration when he set a day for meeting all members of the press corps, attended the Gridiron Club dinner, and issued correspondents their first invitations to attend the New Year's receptions at the White House. At the same time, he also let it be known that his administration would be less secretive than its forerunners and that "the reporters are at liberty to call upon him or his cabinet for information on public affairs." Correspondents soon perceived an atmosphere in the White House that was both relaxed and responsive to their needs; they responded with vast increases in the flow of copy from that source. In so doing, they transformed the White House into an important center of news, paving the way for presidential dominance after the onset of the Spanish-American War.[9]

For all his interest in the press, McKinley proved a lackluster subject for correspondents. He lacked the flair for publicity—the ability to place himself in the spotlight—required of a first-rate newspaper personality, and he showed no adeptness at playing up his personal role in handling the affairs of state. This was due in part to the president's unfailingly stiff demeanor, which not only prevented his coming alive in the stories of reporters but made him appear posed and unnatural in photographs as well. So self-conscious, in fact, did McKinley feel about being photographed that he always stood in the same position and formed the same expression on his face, and it is not surprising that he strictly forbade the kind of candid photographs that later filled the pages of newspapers and magazines. McKinley's newspaper image was also hampered by traditional presidential fear of lese majesty, which combined with his reserved personality to limit both his usefulness to the press and his own ability to gain publicity.[10]

McKinley's concern for the press reflected his interest in public attitudes. Newspapers formed his chief guide to public opinion, and he read several of them daily. He also instructed his secretaries to prepare scrapbooks of clippings for his daily use—entitled "Current Comment"—that included items culled from newspapers in every section of the country. For McKinley, these scrapbooks provided a necessary index of publicity needs and successes, and they informed him of areas where enhanced presidential influence was most needed or could do the most good. This does not mean, however, that McKinley was dependent entirely upon newspapers for such information; he also consulted men throughout the country for their perceptions of the public's attitudes. Ultimately, of course, McKinley was his own judge of public opinion, and he believed—like most politicians—that he was an astute one.[11]

The new administration's skill in dealing with the press and public received a severe test from the situation in Cuba. Like his predecessor, McKinley seemed determined to end the revolution, even though he realized that war might be the outcome of his endeavors. Such a situation required considerable public support, but McKinley knew that he had, as Mark Hanna told the *Washington Post*, "public opinion and endless persuasive abilities at his disposal." In fact, the president's primary concern was that the public had too much desire to intervene. Just as public zeal for intervention had plagued the efforts of the Cleveland administration, McKinley feared that it would hinder his own attempts to settle the rebellion diplomatically. Still, he did not regard this kind of public opinion as a very serious problem—it was a hindrance that he, like Cleveland, was confident he could overcome.[12]

It should not be supposed, however, that Cuba dominated the

early months of the McKinley administration. The new president spent most of his time on political questions and apparently did not regard the Cuban situation—certainly no major issue in his election —as having much political significance. Accordingly, he neglected to include any direct reference to Cuba in either his inaugural address or his early recommendations to Congress, and he failed to formulate a Cuban policy during his first two months in office. But more than McKinley's political instincts told him to downplay the Cuban situation; he received similar information from his indexes of public opinion as well. His "Current Comment" scrapbook included only two Cuban references before June 1897, and his mailbags contained only three letters on the island during the same period. The president's clippings and mail, like his thoughts, dealt with questions of patronage and jobs, both matters of greater political importance than revolution in Cuba.[13]

In the summer of 1897, McKinley finally turned his attention to Cuba, only to find that it commanded virtually no public interest. By then, even the few clippings and letters of the preceding months had disappeared from view, and there existed little if any public pressure upon the president to take steps to end the rebellion. It was at this time, in the absence of articulate public concern over the island, that McKinley formulated the Cuban policy that led to war with Spain. His objective was a conciliation of the warring parties, which he hoped to achieve by placing increasing pressure on the Spanish to grant concessions to the rebels. There was, to be sure, an element of risk in McKinley's design: with each application of pressure the president moved steadily closer to intervention; he might reach a point where the Spanish were unwilling to make further concessions and he was left no option but to intervene. Still, the president was aware of this danger and sincerely hoped to avoid the war with Spain that it implied. He had, at any rate, no reason to doubt that any result would receive the support of the American people.[14]

Thus confident, McKinley began to tighten the screws on the Spanish. On 26 June he had the secretary of state present a note to the Spanish minister outlining his Cuban policy. In it, the president presumed an American role in the rebellion, arguing—quite undiplomatically—that he conceived that he had "a right to demand that a war, conducted almost within the sight of our shores and grievously affecting American citizens and their interests throughout the length and breadth of the land, shall at least be conducted according to the military codes of civilization." At the same time, he stated acceptable terms for the conflict's resolution, including improved living conditions for the Cubans and reform of the island's colonial government. These were not, certainly, demands that the Spanish could easily accept, and the tone of their presentation made it clear that McKinley was already willing to run the risk of war to settle the rebellion.[15]

This willingness was also evident in McKinley's instructions to his new minister to Spain, Stewart Woodford. Once again, the president threatened intervention unless the Spanish put down the rebellion and granted reforms in Cuba. He instructed Woodford to advise the Spanish government that Congress and public opinion might force the president to take stronger measures than he desired and to point out that unwanted intervention might be the result of any delay. In this, however, McKinley was clearly disingenuous; the real demands that Spain had to meet were not the public's, or Congress's, but his own.[16]

These demands soon took the form of an ultimatum. On 18 September Woodford met the Spanish foreign minister, read him the president's instructions, and "suggested, in bringing our interview to an end, but without pointing out any formula, that the Spanish government should give to me before the first of November next such assurance as would satisfy the United States that early and certain peace can be promptly secured." The alternative to this assurance, as the Spanish minister was certain to understand, might be American intervention in Cuba. McKinley, too, realized this implication, informing Woodford of his determination, should the Spanish fail, to "be free to take such action . . . as may be dictated by the situation."[17]

By October, then, McKinley had issued an ultimatum and moved to the verge of war with Spain over its handling of the Cuban insurrection. Still, the outcome of McKinley's policy depended on the Spanish government: only its willingness to acquiesce in American demands could prevent the two nations from clashing. And there the situation would remain until war settled the issue six months later. Throughout this period, when McKinley hammered home his position to the Spanish, he labored under little public pressure to intervene in Cuba. The public's interest in the island seemed at its ebb—a fact apparent in the president's mailbags and scrapbooks, if not in his relations with Spain.[18]

While thus engaged, McKinley maintained public silence on the question of Cuba. He made no attempt to utilize the president's ability to attract publicity, allowing public opinion to drift on the issue of intervention. Above all, he hoped for a free hand in his negotiations with the Spanish; he could see nothing to be gained from speaking out to offset the complications it might create. Indeed, because he remained unsure where his policy might lead, McKinley could not be certain if publicity would take the public in the proper direction. It was better, he thought, to let the public follow its own course—he could always influence it later.[19]

Even Spain's reply to the September ultimatum did not stir McKinley to break silence. In part, this reflected his ambivalence about the Spanish plan; it shows that he was still uncertain about the proper course for public opinion. Ultimately, McKinley realized, the question of American intervention would be determined by the success or failure of the Spanish autonomy scheme, and he decided to await the results of this endeavor. But this did not mean that the president held out much hope for its success. Spain's response had stopped short of granting the Cubans autonomy, and its demands on the United States, which accounted for more than half the note, created a tone something less than compliant. Still, the Spanish had shown some willingness to meet American demands for reform, and McKinley—albeit dissatisfied—would keep his doubts to himself.[20]

Not until December, when he delivered his annual message to Congress, did McKinley make public pronouncement of his Cuban policy. By then, the new Congress was threatening to pass resolutions for intervention in Cuba; McKinley hoped that his statement would cool congressional ardor. The president also realized the importance of his message as a guide to public opinion. It was with this in mind that he started to compose it a month in advance, endeavoring, according to Cortelyou, "to express himself in simple language to appeal to the people." No matter how simple his language, however, McKinley's policy remained ambiguous, as he continued to set a course that hoped for peace while threatening intervention. The result, predictably enough, was vague and unclear, containing both elements of the president's approach and counseling, above all, an attitude of watchful waiting. After pointing out that the United States had tried everything in Cuba but annexation, recognition, and intervention, McKinley firmly rejected the first two and ruled out the third until Spain "be given a reasonable chance" to make good its November concessions. Yet, the president continued, the Spanish must not forget that the United States had "never in any way abrogated its sovereign prerogative of reserving to itself the determination of its policy and course" or that intervention remained possible in the event of the policy's failure in Cuba. Such a message did not, surely, satisfy congressional hotheads, but it did stop far short of calling for a noninterventionist public opinion.[21]

If McKinley suffered from congressional criticism, however, he could take solace in the newspaper response to his message. On the day after its transmission, Porter telegraphed his chief—McKinley was in Ohio—to give him a summary of editorial opinion. The press, according to the secretary, approved heartily the president's message, applauding in particular McKinley's firm but not bellicose tone. A similar view appeared in the president's newspaper scrapbooks, which contained almost entirely laudatory clippings on the message. From the perspective of the White House, at least, there could be no doubt of McKinley's success in using his annual message to win public support for his cautious policy in Cuba.[22]

With the public under control, McKinley turned his attention to Cuba, where events in January 1898 were threatening to undermine his diplomacy. In the two months since Spain's declaration of the autonomy decrees, the president had seen his reservations about them justified, as one by one the Cuban groups had rejected their provisions. The final stroke fell on 12 January, when pro-Spain elements in Havana—abetted by the Spanish army—rioted to protest autonomy. This new development made two things clear to the McKinley administration: the autonomy plan had never been a practicable solution to the problems of Cuba; and the war, with its danger of American intervention, remained still far from conclusion. Shaken, McKinley declared privately that autonomy had failed and began to make preparations for the storm that he now was certain lay ahead. The president realized that the Cuban riots marked the turning of a corner in his relations with Spain, a corner that he had tried to avoid and that would lead, ultimately, to war.[23]

During the next three weeks, McKinley came to doubt the sincerity as well as the success of autonomy. This new doubt stemmed from the de Lôme letter, which offered tangible proof of Spanish duplicity in negotiations with the United States. In his famous letter, intercepted and made public by Cuban sympathizers, the Spanish minister emphasized his hostility to negotiations with the Cuban rebels, even on the basis of autonomy. Angered, the McKinley administration interpreted these remarks to mean that Spain had never intended to fulfill its promise of a Cuban settlement, and Sherman informed Woodford that de Lôme had to be recalled, at least in part, for the "want of candor which appeared to underly" his proposals. Now McKinley could see clearly that his diplomacy was built on a shaky foundation—no wonder it was crumbling all around him.[24]

Evidence of McKinley's disillusionment with Spain came in his decision to release the consular reports on the *reconcentrados*. This material, uniformly hostile to Spain's attempts at pacification, made clear to the American people what McKinley already knew: the

Spanish reform program was a failure. In releasing these reports, the president indicated for the first time his desire for a more interventionist public opinion; he now endeavored, in the face of an almost hopeless diplomatic situation, to make sure of his support at home.[25]

Such support was made certain by the explosion of the *Maine*. McKinley knew that the battleship's destruction must have a decisive impact on public opinion; in fact, it rendered superfluous any efforts of his own to prepare the public for war. With tenders of service coming to the White House with every delivery of mail, the president could be certain that a decision to fight would not lack public approval. Still, McKinley was not yet ready to make such a decision; he hoped instead that the *Maine* disaster might supply the additional leverage he needed to win a Cuban settlement. Thus armed, he was prepared to give the Spanish one more chance. But if they failed—and by now he must have been almost certain they would—the result would have to be intervention.[26]

Although it added a new dimension to Spanish-American diplomacy, the *Maine* explosion was not alone in determining the success or failure of the ongoing negotiations. When McKinley instructed Woodford to inform the Spanish of the appointment of a naval board of inquiry, he also let him know that "whatever the report may be, it by no means relieves the situation of its difficulties." Other things, including "the policy of starvation, the failure of Spain to take effective measures to suppress the insurrection," and "the insulting and insincere character of the de Lôme letter," were responsible for the real gravity of the situation. McKinley would, to be sure, employ the *Maine* disaster to increase Spain's discomfiture, but his most important concern remained a final settlement of the Cuban problem. As a result, Spain could not avoid American intervention simply by acquitting itself of the *Maine* explosion; it would also have to answer for its failure to satisfy McKinley's previous demands. And because these demands—made over the preceding nine months—could be met only by ending the insurrection, they placed Spain in the straitest of circumstances. Hoping for peace, McKinley was pressuring the Spanish into war, not as a result of the *Maine* explosion but as the culmination of his original Cuban policy.[27]

As he began his final round of negotiations, McKinley adopted a renewed strategy of silence on the issue of war with Spain. Aware that public opinion must be influenced by his every word, the president decided to let it drift, withholding the one man's opinion around which it was certain to crystallize. Such strategy seemed well suited to McKinley's needs, which included, above all else, time to work his diplomacy. The president could also predict the direction of the public's drift, and he saw little reason to guide a public opinion that was moving—parallel to his own diplomacy—inexorably toward war. With hostilities appearing increasingly likely, McKinley did not want to dissipate the public's desire to fight any more than he wanted to endanger his diplomacy by inflaming popular sentiment, and he spent the next two months allowing public opinion to build its own momentum.[28]

Allowing the public to set its own course for war was in keeping with McKinley's usual administrative style. Because he often remained aloof from the debates that raged around him, McKinley sometimes appeared to outsiders as weak and impressionable. In fact, his aloofness was a subtle form of persuasion, which his closest advisers knew he used skillfully to bring them to his own point of view. Cortelyou learned of this technique after a particularly animated cabinet meeting, when McKinley, who had said little during the debate, produced a slip of paper on which he had previously written the cabinet's ultimate decision. Elihu Root detected this same ability: "He had a way of handling men so that they thought his ideas were their own. I have talked with him again and again before a cabinet meeting and found that his ideas were fixed and his mind firmly made up," only to see him apparently persuaded by the cabinet into accepting his own position. When McKinley avoided participation in the debate over war with Spain, he was employing this familiar technique. He would work outside the limelight, directing the debate and no more than hinting at his own opinion; yet he was sure to have his own way in the end.[29]

On 16 February, the day following the *Maine* explosion, McKinley established the pattern for dealing with public opinion he would follow for the next two months. By nine o'clock, he had authorized Secretary of the Navy John D. Long to tell the correspondents that there was no "cause for alarm" and "no indication of anything but an accident. Judgment should be suspended until a full investigation is made." In this way, McKinley avoided releasing a public statement of his own, using Long's comments to inform the public of his attitude toward the explosion. He also had his secretaries see to it that reporters were given copies of all telegrams from Havana as they came in through the day, insuring that newspapers would have plenty of reliable copy on the disaster. And finally, he made evident his own concern over the tragedy by issuing—through the newspapers—an order to fly all flags at half-mast until further notice. If McKinley showed no desire to provoke the country into war over the *Maine*, neither did he wish to dam the flood of patriotic sentiment he knew the incident would unleash.[30]

As president, McKinley could be certain that the public's patriotism would lend support to his policies. In a crisis situation, like the one precipitated by the *Maine* explosion, public attitudes rally behind the president, and McKinley's advisers assured him that the current situation was no exception. Newspaper publisher Whitelaw Reid, in one of his regular reports to McKinley, submitted that he had "never seen a more profound or touching readiness to trust the President." And Senator Henry Cabot Lodge, whose desire for war gave him reason to offer a negative viewpoint, wrote McKinley that he was "more unanimously supported than any other President in a crisis situation." In light of this information, McKinley's decision to issue a public flag order takes on new significance: it emphasized the need for patriotism in the crisis and enhanced his position as symbolic head of the American people, thereby broadening his popular support at a critical juncture in his negotiations.[31]

In the following weeks McKinley continued to work behind the scenes for a favorable public opinion. He stepped up efforts to gain control of the flow of White House news, increasing markedly the number of press releases given to correspondents. For the first time in any administration, he ordered information and statements released routinely to the press throughout the day, guaranteeing reporters a regular supply of usable material. This eased the tasks of White House correspondents, but it also offered several advantages to the McKinley administration: it provided a ready audience for any information that the president desired to make public; it allowed the administration to place its own interpretation on that information; and it heightened the dependence of correspondents upon the White House staff. In addition, McKinley's secretaries recognized the importance of the three wire services by giving their representatives special consideration. They were always first to receive copies of press releases, and it is no wonder that the news services usually supported the administration. In his success with the correspondents, McKinley did not have to rely upon public pronouncements to influence popular opinion—he was transforming the White House press corps into an instrument of the indirect persuasion he used so skillfully in handling administrative matters.[32]

McKinley's mastery of the correspondents was apparent in his handling of the *Maine* court of inquiry, which he contrived—in addition to uncovering the explosion's cause—to buy time for his own diplomacy. McKinley knew, of course, that the public's ultimate reaction must depend upon the report of this investigation, and he sent a naval commission, directed by Captain W. T. Sampson, to Havana for what promised to be a lengthy inquiry. And to make certain that the public would respond with patience, the president instructed his spokesmen to request it to withhold judgment until the commission's report had been completed.[33]

In the month before the report was made public, McKinley took pains to see that it remained the focus of popular attention, ordering statements about it from cabinet members and enticing White House correspondents with hints of its imminent release. Although designed to direct the public's view of the explosion, administration comments reflected the president's own ambivalence about the outcome of his Spanish diplomacy. After a 1 March cabinet meeting, Secretary Long informed reporters that it appeared doubtful whether the Spanish had played a part in the *Maine*'s destruction. Long was clearly expressing McKinley's desire to downplay the likelihood of war; yet he was rebuked one day later by Secretary of War Russell Alger—another presidential spokesman—who told the correspondents that his colleague's statement had been personal rather than official. With the possibility of war looming on the horizon, McKinley did not want the public to become too complacent about the responsibility of the Spanish.[34]

When he finally received the *Maine* report, McKinley instructed his secretaries to guard it carefully. This was more than usual precaution. The president realized the report's importance, and when it leaked out anyway he showed his anger by ordering the Washington manager of the Associated Press "raked over the coals" and forced to sign a "cast iron" statement that the information was not obtained from a White House source. The president had good reason to be incensed: Cortelyou had, as he wrote in his diary, "spent considerable time preparing for the press the interviews of the Court of Inquiry and the message of the President to accompany them," only to have a forecast of the commission's findings made public without the administration's interpretation. McKinley acted quickly, however, sending his message to Congress and releasing the report only three days after he received it, and succeeded in reaching most reporters with his view of the court's conclusions. He also presented his ideas in a presidential message to Congress, which stopped short of proclaiming the disaster a reason for war but which made it clear that war could be averted only if Spain altered the conditions that had made the explosion possible in the first place. McKinley made no effort to placate the public ire he knew the commission's report would engender; he was content to see the public continue its drift toward war.[35]

Another aspect of McKinley's influence on public opinion was his ability to propose legislation. He put this to good use in early March, when he called Republican House leader Joe Cannon to the executive mansion and asked him to submit a bill granting the president, "for national defense, fifty million dollars." Such a measure was, certainly, designed to serve several purposes, not least of which was to arm for war with Spain, but McKinley also knew that it could not fail to have an impact on public opinion. Continuing to tread a middle ground between peace and war, the president did not want the bill made into an occasion for jingoistic excesses. Still, he was certain that the public would get the point without them and must have been reassured to note that, in the words of one observer, "before it was over it seemed as though a hundred Fourths of July had been let loose in the House." If the bill would stir Congress to such new heights of patriotism, it could hardly fail to have a salutary effect on public opinion.[36]

As the weeks wore on, McKinley saw his efforts rewarded with public attitudes that suited his needs almost perfectly. His newspaper scrapbooks grew fat with editorials lauding his firm but prudent diplomacy—and expressing a willingness to go to war should it fail. These clippings, numbering in the hundreds, formed McKinley's chief gauge of public opinion, and they assured him of the public's continued support whatever the outcome of his negotiations. The president's mail yielded a similar conclusion, with letters of support pouring in from all sections of the country. Although tenders of service indicated that the public would not shy away from war, most letters simply "commended his firm policy and his determination to wait until he was convinced that he was right before going ahead." In fact, the majority of McKinley's correspondents were certain he was following a course of "peace with honor" and wrote only to offer their support. "On a most conservative estimate," according to Cortelyou, "ninety percent of the entire correspondence that has come to the office since the beginning of the concluding negotiations on the Spanish-Cuban question has been an endorsement of the President's course," favoring war only "as a necessity and for the upholding of the national honor." Because McKinley would have no difficulty making "national honor" the basis of any decision for war, he had nothing to fear from even the most pacifistic of these letters. His mail, like his scrapbooks, promised a public opinion that was almost completely permissive.[37]

In addition to Cortelyou, a number of other advisers told McKinley of his support among the public. Whitelaw Reid, touring the country to gather information for the president, assured him that the "more intelligent classes" favored his policies and that even "conservative public sentiment will sustain purchases of ammunition and . . . war-ships." McKinley also heard from John M. Walden, bishop of the Methodist Episcopal church, who after offering the president his own support informed him that his views represented those of "a quiet but influential class," from which he heard only praise of McKinley's policies. House Speaker Thomas B. Reed forwarded a similar letter, this time from *Cincinnati Gazette* editor J. H. Woodward, detailing the results of a personal opinion poll. As the writer informed Reed, he found no one who favored war with Spain, unless there was no other alternative, a judgment his respondents remained content to leave with the president. Woodward's poll was, to be sure, grossly unscientific, but its results lent credence to what McKinley learned about public attitudes in his scrapbooks and mail.[38]

McKinley's success in directing public opinion can also be seen in the Iowa press. As a midwestern, "isolationist" state with supposedly fixed ideas on foreign affairs, Iowa serves as a good test of the president's ability to influence newspaper editors with his statements and policies. It is possible to determine how—and if—this worked in 1898 by casting editorial fluctuations during the period of the *Maine* crisis against the background of McKinley's endeavors. The importance of editorials must be considered with two propositions in mind: first, although they cannot be said to mirror public opinion, they have often been perceived by government officials as if they did; and second, because the ideas presented in them probably had some effect on the reading public, their alteration might indicate changes in public attitudes. Thus, a study of Iowa newspapers can hope to discover how one state's public opinion might have appeared to officials looking for the views of their constituents. It can also hope to assess the direction in which this opinion was moving over a period of time. Without being able to identify the exact content of popular perceptions, then, it might be possible to determine, on the basis of editorial information, the extent of McKinley's influence over the public.

To make such a test, this study analyzes editorials from all available newspapers published during the crisis and compares their fluctuations with changes in administration policy. In so doing, it is possible to avoid the methodological pitfalls into which previous investigations of McKinley and the public have stumbled. The first of these is the use of a severely limited number of sources. Joseph Wisan, for example, utilized only the New York City press in developing his view of public attitudes, and other historians, endeavoring to avoid the geographical limitations of Wisan's work, have also been highly selective in their study of "representative" newspapers from various sections of the country. Even George Auxier's more thorough regional study, which included an extensive investigation of newspaper opinion, employed a limited number of sources selected from states in the Midwest. A second pitfall is the serious bias that selectivity has imparted to these studies in favor of the urban press, as any differences between city and country have gone undetected by historians drawing conclusions solely from the urban population. By studying the Iowa press, then, it is possible to gain insight into the views of small towns as well as cities and to achieve a more balanced image of popular opinion.[39]

Iowa editors responded angrily to first reports of the *Maine* explosion. A majority (see Table 1) favored war with Spain over the disaster, claiming the defense of American honor and dignity—essential ideas of nationalism—as sufficient reason to fight. To most it seemed likely that Spain was responsible for the ship's destruction; they were determined, should that prove to be the case, that the result must be war. "If it is found," wrote the editor of the *Des Moines Leader*, "that Spanish treachery demolished the *Maine*, the United States would be warranted, in fact compelled to maintain her honor in waging war on Spain." The response of the *Dubuque Daily Times* was more poetic if less thoughtful. "Just think of it, 253 brave men sent to an untimely death by Spanish assassins! Arise ye men in whose breasts the fire of patriotism burns and demand satisfaction, and let this be not less than the annihilation of the Spanish dogs!" During the first two weeks of the crisis, the fire of patriotism burned hotly in Iowa editors, who called for war in almost every issue.[40]

Table 1
Initial Reaction to the *Maine* Explosion

For war	51.1%
For war with reservations	28.9
Against war slightly	17.8
Against war strongly	2.2
	100.0%
N	45

Note: Because so many of the newspapers dealt with in this study were published weekly, the "initial" reaction covers the first two weeks of the crisis.
Source: See bibliography of Iowa newspapers, herein.

During the next two weeks, Iowa editors lost most of their reservations; they came to favor war almost unanimously (see Table 2) by 15 March. As Figure 1 illustrates, most editors who had formerly experienced serious doubts now discovered reasons for moving into the prowar camp. One reason was a redefinition of conditions under which the Spanish might be considered culpable. At first, editors assumed that the ship had been exploded deliberately by the Spanish, but second thoughts, based on Spain's obvious desire to avoid war, left this assumption doubtful. Undaunted, the press redefined Spanish responsibility to include any explosion not internal to the ship. The Spanish could not, clearly, have prevented an internal explosion, and they could not be held accountable if that proved to have been the case. But the editors now argued that any external detonation, whether deliberate or accidental, was the responsibility of Spanish authorities. "Spain is responsible," asserted the *Council Bluffs Nonpareil*, "even if it was private citizens who destroyed the *Maine*. Law should be considered, but not hair-splitting." Determined to take the large view, most editors now fitted the *Maine* explosion into the context of Spain's difficulties in Cuba. "All this misery," according to the *Davenport Daily Democrat*, "is due to the inhuman policy of General Weyler," and Spain had more to atone for than the destruction of an American battleship. And finally, many editors expressed increased appreciation of American might, contending that military superiority would make fighting the Spanish a lark.[41]

Table 2
Editorial Opinion during
Second Two Weeks of Crisis

For war	55.5%
For war with reservations	31.1
Against war slightly	13.4
Against war strongly	0.0
	100.0%
N	45

Source: See bibliography of Iowa newspapers, herein.

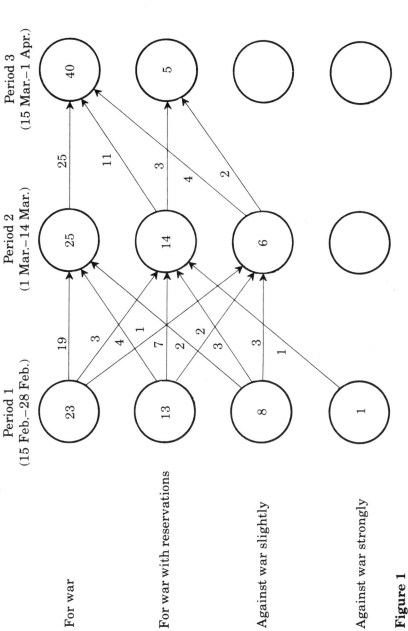

Figure 1
Editorial Opinion and Opinion Changes, Iowa Newspapers, 15 February to 1 April 1898.

These arguments became even more compelling during the third two weeks of the crisis, as Iowa editors lost any remaining doubts about the desirability of war. They now called for hostilities almost without reservation (see Table 3); when war was finally declared at the end of the second month, they accepted it gleefully.[42]

To a remarkable extent, local editorial arguments reflected elements of administration policy. Redefinition of Spanish responsibility followed the announcement of the Sampson investigation, which centered its inquiries on the location of the explosion. Although external detonation hardly proved Spain caused the disaster, it appeared so to editors who knew only the general terms of the navy's investigation. Similarly, editorials placing the *Maine* disaster in the context of Spain's Cuban difficulties mirrored the reality of McKinley's diplomacy. And finally, the editors' appreciation of American arms increased only after the president requested and received his $50 million emergency military appropriation. The strength this measure implied may have had some effect upon the Spanish; it certainly did upon Iowa editors. In weeks following its passage, the press took on a tone of confidence in America's ultimate victory and found the risk of war much easier to accept.

Still, editorial desire for war preceded McKinley's request for a declaration, prompting some historians to see newspaper pressure as playing a part in his decision. Iowa editors did call for action from their president, and they did show some impatience with his conservative diplomacy. But this was surely the way of the cautious McKinley: he made very certain of his support before taking the

Table 3
Editorial Opinion during Third
Two Weeks of Crisis

For war	88.9%
For war with reservations	11.1
Against war slightly	0.0
Against war strongly	0.0
	100.0%
N	45

Source: See bibliography of Iowa newspapers, herein.

country into war. Nor was editorial impatience a sign of the president's inability to control newspaper opinion. McKinley remained the symbol of national unity and purpose, and Iowa editors tempered their prowar arguments with willingness to follow his direction. On 31 March the *Weekly Northern Vindicator* put it thus: "President McKinley's thoughtful and conscientious course in determining the final action of the administration upon the Cuban question is being generally commended by citizens and newspapers, irrespective of party." And two weeks later, after the president's message to Congress, it noted, "The President is receiving many congratulations on the wise, patriotic statesmanship displayed in his message." Such remarks were typical of the Iowa press and indicate the strength of presidential authority in time of serious national crisis.[43]

McKinley realized, of course, that there were those who disagreed with his policy of negotiation—they were every bit as vocal as his supporters—but he did not believe that they represented the public consensus. Chief among the president's detractors was the sensationalist press, which had been screaming for intervention in Cuba since 1895 and which pulled out all stops in the weeks following the *Maine* explosion. The yellow journals were wasting their ink on McKinley, however; he rarely saw anything of their efforts. Not only did he neglect as a rule to read either the *New York Journal* or *New York World*, but clippings from their columns were almost entirely absent from his scrapbooks as well. This might have been only the administration's response to criticism, but Cortelyou contended that the president was shown "everything, whether in the shape of mail, telegrams, or newspapers, that can indicate the drift of public opinion" and that he was not shown the yellow newspapers because they were "the products of degenerate minds" and "misrepresent public opinion." As such, the sensationalist press played little part in the administration's evaluation of public attitudes, a part best expressed, according to Cortelyou, by the fact that it served as the butt of many White House jokes.[44]

No matter what he thought of them, however, McKinley knew that yellow journals had some influence on the public. With their innovative—if unsophisticated—techniques and rapidly expanding circulation, they threatened to produce a consensus demanding speedier action than he was prepared to take. Still, this threat seemed insignificant to McKinley, who saw their influence as more than balanced by the many newspapers—even in New York City—that supported his diplomacy. Then, too, the president felt little threatened by the readers of the yellow press, who lacked the political influence to

harm his policy. And finally, McKinley regarded any problems resulting from the yellow journals' fulminations as clearly the lesser
of two evils; in his situation, an opposition pressing for war was far
less dangerous than a resolutely pacifist one. As the president himself saw it, he could well afford to ignore the sensationalist press,
and he chose to do so almost completely.[45]

A more serious problem was posed by Congress, where interventionists were trying to push McKinley—as they had his predecessors—into taking a stronger position on Cuba. The president knew,
of course, that this attitude was at least partly a response to interventionist elements in the public, and his concern over a premature
mandate for war stemmed primarily from his awareness of constitu-
ent pressure on Congress. Still, McKinley remained certain that
his congressional critics would find it difficult to wrest from him
the reins of foreign policy; he could count on the support of many
powerful senators and congressmen. The president was, in fact,
sufficiently sure of himself that even at the height of his difficulties
with Congress he told Currency Comptroller Charles G. Dawes he
would call it back into session if it tried to adjourn. And right to the
end, when he disagreed with leading interventionists over recognition of Cuban independence, he controlled enough votes to have his
way. To whatever extent McKinley felt harried by his detractors in
Congress, he was never in danger of being dominated by them—
and he certainly never considered allowing them to determine his
foreign policy.[46]

As far as Cuba was concerned, McKinley's policy had been determined months before, in a time of relative quiet. One by one, his
demands had gone unmet, and now even the *Maine* disaster had
failed to bring the Spanish around. By early April McKinley knew
that they must pay the consequences. Still he did not call for war,
hoping desperately that something would allow him to avert the
inevitable. Finally, he set 6 April as the date for his war message to
Congress, but—grasping at the thinnest of straws—he used Havana
consul Fitzhugh Lee's fears for the safety of Americans in Cuba to
put it off for five more days. Perhaps he hoped that the Spanish
would capitulate in that time. They did not, and McKinley saw
so little hope in the concessions they did grant that he could do
nothing more than append them to his reluctantly bellicose message
to Congress.[47]

If the president's message seemed less than a ringing call for war,
however, it still had a powerful effect on Congress and the press,
neither of which had any difficulty deciphering its meaning. McKinley was warmly congratulated on all sides, with disapproval coming

only from what Cortelyou called the "blatherskite sheets." This was one occasion, however, when the president did not deserve editorial commendation; he had—uncharacteristically—missed a good chance to rally the nation in support of the coming war with Spain. The reason for this failure may have been his knowledge that the public would understand anyway—he had, after all, been guiding it with understatement for several months. But the situation had changed, and there was no longer need for subtlety, unless McKinley was somehow still hoping that a Spanish capitulation would save him from the logic of his own diplomacy. Or perhaps the president was simply too depressed—or fatigued—to give much thought to his role as leader of national attitudes. Whatever the reason, McKinley's 11 April message was the one time in the Cuban crisis when he failed to deal deftly with public opinion.[48]

Sometime during the next two weeks, however, McKinley regained his command of the situation. On 25 April he informed Congress of the nation's readiness for war, once again establishing himself as the undisputed leader of public opinion. He ordered copies of the message prepared hastily for the press, who had them, as Cortelyou put it, "within a few minutes after Major Pruden left for the Senate." Perhaps unhappy with the outcome of his Spanish diplomacy, McKinley still had a war to fight—and he would fight it as commander in chief of national opinion as well as of the armed forces.[49]

Chapter 2
The White House
at War

 April 1898 saw Washington transformed into a frenetic center of activity. As it turned energetically to the countless new responsibilities—and opportunities—afforded by war with Spain, the usually sluggish capital became, for the first time since the Civil War, the sustained focus of world attention. At no place was this more profoundly felt than the White House, where the president and his staff, adding the conduct of war to their already considerable duties, addressed problems both new and substantial. All at once McKinley faced the wartime tasks of commanding the armed forces, keeping a wary eye on the governments of Europe, and exercising control over public opinion at home. Aware that failure in any of these areas might jeopardize the war effort, the president paid careful attention to each of them, often working late into the night surrounded by maps, advisers, and friendly newspapermen. By the time of the armistice, three months later, he had succeeded in each area, altering the president's relationship not only to the governments of the world but to the American people as well.[1]

Perhaps more than anything else, war with Spain forced McKinley to strengthen his control of public opinion. Before the actual outbreak of hostilities, he had regarded public support as something of a luxury, satisfying himself with the results of his indirect methods of persuasion. Now, however, the requirements of war made public support a necessity and called for methods considerably more direct. Early in May, for example, when the public was learning of Commodore George Dewey's triumph in the Philippines, McKinley sent a special message to Congress proclaiming victory and heightening the public's already frenzied response to the battle. At the same time, he publicly ordered General Nelson Miles to capture Havana. Although the president knew that shortages of materiel would prevent the immediate success of Miles's campaign, his decision to issue his order publicly indicates that he had something more than the military situation on his mind. Pleased with Dewey's success in the Philippines, McKinley now hoped that his Havana order would prevent the development of public restiveness over lack of similar results in Cuba. It did, at least for the time being, and he enjoyed the popularity of a successful leader in wartime.[2]

While increasing his direct impact on the public, McKinley also strengthened his relationship with the press. Presidential secretary Porter's evening press briefings continued during the war, as did the practice of issuing press releases to reporters throughout the day. With war adding to the importance of White House news, the president and his staff thus won increased favor from correspondents for continuing their access to information. But McKinley did more than enlarge upon old practices. He also broke precedent by allowing reporters to set up shop in the White House, providing accommodations for them in an outer reception room of the mansion's business section. Besides bringing the reporters near the presidential offices, where they could be reached at a moment's notice, this arrangement drew journalists away from "Newspaper Row," as the great north portico's east side was called, where they had previously gathered to question White House visitors. In this way, McKinley was attempting to shift reporters' focus from his visitors, who might tell them anything, to his own office, where the flow of information could be controlled. And if some correspondents continued to pump McKinley's visitors for candid remarks, more were lured by the president's steady and reliable information to the door of the executive office.[3]

Not all McKinley's innovations were designed to win support from the press, however. Concerned about the dangers of newspaper publication of military activities, he invoked strict censorship at Key West, Florida, on 23 April. And shortly thereafter, when on-the-scene censorship proved insufficient, he placed an additional censor in New York City, where the wire services—and the yellow journals —were located. Press reaction to McKinley's order was predictable, and more than one angry telegram was delivered to the White House protesting the inconveniences it caused correspondents. For all their protests, however, the news services remained stymied by McKinley's efforts, which were so successful in guarding troop movements that Cortelyou could write in May that few "authentic details of what is going on reach the public."[4]

Besides reducing its quantity, McKinley's censorship also centralized the release of military information. In fact, because few additional efforts were made by the army and navy to secure their movements from enemy intelligence, centralization may have been McKinley's primary reason for issuing the order. When, for example, General William Shafter's flotilla sailed to attack Santiago, it spent five and a half days within sight of the Cuban coast, neglecting even to extinguish the ships' lights at night. Such military laxness in maintaining even elementary security must have made redundant any information Spain might glean from the American press, but it did not affect the benefits McKinley gained from centralizing the flow of wartime information. For one thing, centralization allowed him to control which aspects of the military situation were made public, making it possible for him to emphasize success in the Philippines while overlooking the bottleneck in Florida. For another thing, because there was no censorship of material originating in Washington and because, as Cortelyou put it, other "sources of information are more closely guarded," the order enhanced the White House as a news center and allowed McKinley to increase further his influence with the correspondents. Despite its cost in newspaper irritation, then, McKinley's censorship order succeeded in centering public attention on Washington, where he was in control.[5]

Whatever ill feeling censorship generated, it did not poison McKinley's relationship with the wire services. On 17 May the board of directors of the Associated Press adopted a resolution advising its general manager "to loyally sustain the general government in the conduct of the war" and directing him to avoid publication of "any information likely to give aid to the enemy or to embarrass the government." This support reflected in part the patriotic climate of the war, but it also demonstrated, at a time when his censorship was under heavy fire, the strength of McKinley's hard-won influence with the press.[6]

McKinley needed this influence, at least early in the war, to dilute newspaper criticism of the army. Unlike the navy, which had benefited from presidential interest as far back as Arthur and, more recently, from the so-called $50 million bill, the army remained far from prepared to engage the Spanish in early combat. Furnished with the rawest of recruits and taxed with planning and supplying amphibious operations it knew nothing about, the War Department quickly demonstrated its incompetence. Public criticism centered on Secretary of War Alger, who was unwilling—or unable—to remove the dead weight from his department. As reports of supply shortages, troop backups, and dangerously unsanitary camp conditions filtered back from the front, newspapers coined a new term, "Algerism," to denote the most extreme kind of ineptitude. McKinley could do little to ease his secretary's situation, using public silence to indicate at least tacit support for the beleaguered Alger and relying upon censorship and the goodwill of the press to keep criticism to a minimum. These tactics proved effective during the war; although Alger would cause McKinley considerable difficulty in months to come, the desire of most of the press not "to embarrass the government" protected the administration until the armistice was signed.[7]

While the army's failures kept McKinley engaged in affairs at home, the navy's success presented him with a new problem on the other side of the world. Dewey's victory at Manila Bay—accomplished with surprising ease—unleashed images of vast American possibilities in the Orient, images that McKinley found at once dangerous and alluring. Eventually the president would have to decide the fate of the Philippines; for the time being, however, it was enough to insure that the decision remained solely in his own hands. On 2 May, five days before Dewey's success received official confirmation, McKinley authorized a military expedition to seize the islands from the Spanish. Spain was not the only problem, however; its control of the Philippines was already being challenged by an insurgent army, led by Emilio Aguinaldo, which threatened to preempt any American claim to the islands. McKinley was aware of this danger, and his instructions to General Wesley Merritt, whose command departed San Francisco on 25 May, emphasized his desire for a free hand in the Philippines. As he informed the general, his primary responsibility was the establishment of American sovereignty—any relations with Filipino leaders must be based on their acknowledgment of that fact. And although McKinley hinted that this arrangement would be only temporary, holding out hope for a government more to the Filipinos' liking, he made it clear that while American troops remained in the islands authority would not be shared with the insurgents.[8]

Keeping close watch on events in the Philippines, McKinley also took action to gain a free hand at home. Although word of Dewey's victory produced visible public interest in the islands, with a number of newspapers calling for eventual annexation, McKinley knew that the first flush of victory must soon give way to sober second thoughts about such a proposal. Only through assiduous effort could he assure the public's approval, and McKinley was not yet prepared to commit himself to such a program. Nevertheless, he would not rule out taking the Philippines, and he carefully avoided any word or action that might close the door on such a decision. Thus, while he encouraged public rejoicing over the victory at Manila, he kept his own counsel on the subject of the islands' disposition, allowing the Philippines to return temporarily to their former obscurity. For the time being, at least, he remained content to have the public forget about the islands—he would bring them up again when he was ready.[9]

It is difficult to say exactly when McKinley decided to keep the Philippines. Some scholars have contended that he did not make up his mind until late autumn 1898, after a speaking tour of the Midwest convinced him of the public's desire for retention. They have argued, further, that McKinley accepted annexation reluctantly, surrendering finally to the will of a public whose opinions he had done little to create.[10] More recently, historians have questioned this interpretation, contending that McKinley's actions in the summer of 1898, especially concerning the negotiation of the armistice with Spain, indicate he made his decision well before the beginning of his westward trip. Unconvinced by his stated reluctance to accept the public's mandate, they have argued that McKinley, in the words of Paolo Coletta, "added to and led the imperialistic clamor."[11] There can be little doubt that this newer view is the correct one, for McKinley's rationalizations about the Philippines, preserved primarily by Herman Kohlsaat, correspond poorly with his behavior. Had he really thought, "if Old Dewey had just sailed away when he smashed the Spanish fleet, what a lot of trouble he would have saved us," he would not have sent an army to complicate the problem further, and had he really, as he claimed, been unable to locate the Philippines on the map at the time of Dewey's victory, he could hardly have planned the invasion of the islands five days earlier. As early as May, then, McKinley had thoughts of acquiring the Philippines, thoughts that became more definite as, through the summer, he pursued a course that moved the United States steadily toward annexation of the islands. Still, in the absence of direct evidence for dating McKinley's final decision, it can only be said for certain that he made up his mind to keep the Philippines sometime during the summer of 1898.[12]

While so doing, McKinley made good use, both publicly and in the cabinet room, of his talent for indirect leadership. Step by step, he allowed the American commitment to deepen in the Philippines, strengthening the position of the annexationists but refusing to take part in public or private debates of the question. At the same time, he scrupulously avoided bringing the issue to a decision, holding off a vote in the cabinet until after the Spanish armistice request in July and, even then, directing debate from the chair as an ostensible moderator. He managed to maintain the appearance of neutrality while guiding the public and cabinet around the pitfalls of an early decision, which he was certain would provide for the retention of something less than all the islands. The danger of haste and McKinley's response to it are summed up in an exchange between the president and Secretary of State William R. Day. "Mr.

President, you didn't put my motion for a naval base," observed the secretary after a grueling cabinet session in late July. "No, Judge, I was afraid it would be carried!" replied McKinley, who had no intention of being tied to such a narrow commitment in the islands. A similar fate befell Day's suggestion for keeping only Luzon; Mc-Kinley buried it. Within a week, the cabinet approved unlimited expansion in the Philippines, leaving its details to the discretion of an apparently undecided McKinley.[13]

If he seemed indecisive in the cabinet room, however, McKinley was nothing but resolute in negotiating the armistice. Shortly after his meeting on 22 July with Jules Cambon, the French ambassador who presented the Spanish plea for peace, McKinley noted: "As to the Philippines, I am of the opinion, that with propriety, and advantage they can be the subject of negotiation."[14] He maintained this position through the armistice talks, refusing to compromise on his decision to make the islands a subject for later negotiation and enforcing his demands by holding the "city, bay, and harbor of Manila" until the peace conference could meet.[15] When the Spanish response of 7 August expressed chagrin at American aspirations in the Philippines, McKinley would do no more than reiterate his earlier position. "The Madrid government may be assured," he wrote, "that up to this time there is nothing determined *a priori* in my mind against Spain; likewise, I consider there is nothing decided against the United States." The Spanish capitulated three days later, realizing, as Cambon put it, that McKinley was "as firm as a rock," and the protocol was signed on 12 August.[16]

Through the summer McKinley kept close watch on public opinion, making, at least to Cortelyou, "frequent comments upon the suggestions for peace [it] brought to his attention." At that time, however, he made no effort to influence the public directly. This changed in early August, when with the armistice under negotiation he instructed his White House secretaries to issue a press release outlining the terms of his initial note to Spain. As the thirty or forty correspondents on duty must have realized, this release indicated the administration's intention to keep some territory in the Philippines; it also informed the public that the general question of the islands had been decided. And when the protocol was signed ten days later, McKinley made certain no one missed the point by ordering the release of another statement of terms. In months to come McKinley would enlarge these public statements, expanding in public his view of America's role in the Philippines, but for now he wanted only to inform the public of the existence, not the details, of that role.[17]

No matter how deft his use of press releases, however, McKinley still failed to take full advantage of the publicity afforded by the armistice. Days before the signing of the protocol, several newsmen and photographers applied to Cortelyou for permission to attend the ceremony. McKinley refused, contending that their presence might mar the dignity of the proceedings, thus denying himself the additional publicity that photographers in particular could have provided the event. Perhaps, like other nineteenth-century presidents, McKinley was ignorant of the public relations value of photographs. But considering his awareness of the uses to which such things as press releases could be put, it is more likely here that his fear of diminished dignity outweighed his desire for improved publicity. At any rate, McKinley's refusal to admit photographers to the signing reveals the personal limits he placed upon the use of publicity in his administration.[18]

With the question of the Philippines still hanging fire, it is small wonder that much of McKinley's—and the public's—attention focused on the selection of peace commissioners to negotiate with Spain. Everyone, or so it must have seemed to the president, had (or was) a candidate for the commission, as both pro- and antiexpansionists touted like-minded individuals for the job. As usual, McKinley listened graciously to advice from all quarters. And, as usual, he made up his own mind. Secretary Day, retiring from his post at the State Department, seemed the obvious choice for chairman, even if he was still dragging his feet on the issue of expansion. McKinley more than countered Day's moderation, however, by appointing three avowed expansionists to the commission: Minnesota's Senator Cushman Davis, Maine's Senator William Frye, and *New York Tribune* publisher Whitelaw Reid. And, always attentive to the demands of propriety, McKinley also found room on the commission for an antiexpansionist and Democrat, Delaware's Senator George Gray. In all, the commission contained a majority of strong expansionists, a composition that reflected McKinley's determination to keep the Philippines for the United States and that informed the press and public, albeit subtly, of the change in his position.[19]

Despite public hints that he was becoming an expansionist, McKinley continued to be wary, even in private, of appearing to move too fast. On 16 September he summoned the commissioners to the White House for a farewell dinner and a final conference on the peace terms. After asking each for his views on the Philippines and listening attentively to their comments, he refused to make a firm commitment of his own. He did remark, however, that he thought the people demanded full retention of the islands, which should have given at least Day and Reid, who were familiar with the president's style, a certain indication of his position. McKinley closed the meeting by reading his formal instructions to the commissioners, informing them that they "cannot accept less than the cession in full right and sovereignty of the island of Luzon." Luzon was only a minimum, of course, and the president's tone implied that larger demands were in the offing. How else could the commissioners interpret such remarks as "the march of events rules and overrules human action" and the Battle of Manila Bay "brought us new duties and responsibilities which we must meet and discharge as becomes a great nation"? There was no mistaking where such reasoning must lead even the cautious McKinley, who, they realized, was as susceptible as the next man to the pull of "destiny."[20]

It was soon apparent that McKinley's minimums had a way of growing. New positions engrossed old ones like the cartoonist's hungry fishes, each one swallowing the one next smaller and, in turn, being swallowed by a larger one still. At first he appeared to want only concessions in the Philippines, but this gave way to possession of Manila, then to all of Luzon, and finally to the complete group of islands. With each change of mind he also added to the aura of inevitability surrounding his demands, presenting himself as nothing more than a passive participant in an ineluctable "march of events." Having previously referred to Hawaiian annexation as "manifest destiny," he now appeared to have no more control over the fate of the Philippines, where each step seemed to demand the taking of the next. Making good use of his talent for dissimulation, McKinley guided the public from one position to the next, moving always closer to full retention of the islands.[21]

Through September, McKinley stuck publicly to the position outlined in his armistice agreement with Spain; he left the final disposition of the Philippines for the peace conference to decide. By then, however, he had made his decision to keep all the islands and was only waiting for the right moment to make public his design. Exercising his usual caution, he chose to put off making an announcement until the last possible minute, endeavoring in the meantime to prepare the public for his decision. Although this was nothing new for McKinley, who had dissembled to advantage on a number of previous issues, the present situation did pose special problems: time was short and public support vital. Already negotiations were underway in Paris, where soon the diplomats would turn to the question of the Philippines and force McKinley to state his final position. He had perhaps until the end of October, no longer, to win the public's support for total retention; after that it would be impossible for him to mask his intentions. This lack of time was made worse by the importance of the public's opinion, which rivaled even that embracing political support for war with Spain. Although McKinley remained ignorant of the full situation in the Philippines, he knew that keeping the islands would be fraught with difficulties, perhaps requiring indefinite garrisoning of troops. But already the public was growing restive about the lack of discharges, prompting McKinley to comment on 9 September that "the people want us to hold everything but the soldiers, forgetting that without them we could not hold anything." These problems called for extraordinary measures, and they forced McKinley out of his usual pattern and onto the stump. With a congressional election due in November, the president decided to combine politics with the promotion of his Philippine policy and take a "swing around the circle."[22]

Anxious for large audiences, McKinley accepted invitations to address the Trans-Mississippi Exposition in Omaha on 12 October and the National Peace Jubilee at Chicago one week later. In addition, and more in keeping with his wonted campaign style, he instructed his secretaries to arrange a special train for a whistle-stop tour of the Midwest before and after his major engagements. From Ohio to Nebraska and back again, he would address small-town midwesterners on the Philippines, pushing the islands to the forefront of campaign issues as he won converts to his own position. McKinley assigned the trip's details to the meticulous eyes of Porter and Cortelyou, who saw to it, among other things, that publicity was thoroughly planned. Reporters received permission to accompany the official party, and space was made available for them on the special train. As usual, they were placed under the tutelage of the helpful Cortelyou, whose position on McKinley's journeys closely approximated that of today's press secretaries and whose relations with the correspondents had never been warmer. He prepared, often in advance, copies of each presidential message for the journalists; he also wired these as bulletins to major newspapers under the auspices of the Associated Press. Such efforts reflected the importance McKinley placed on reporters; they show that he was concerned with a much larger audience than the midwestern electorate.[23]

Preparations completed, McKinley left Washington in early October, carrying west his views on expansion in the Philippines. He began cautiously enough, seeming to use the westward leg of his journey as a sounding board for public opinion. But caution came naturally to McKinley: it was his politician's desire not to get his feet wet before testing the water rather than a wish to be guided by the public that accounted for his reticence. He knew that the public could hardly fail to respond to his message, based as it was on such concepts as honor and duty, but he also knew that it would be best to develop his ideas gradually. Besides, moving slowly would allow him to give the impression of being influenced by the public's response to his remarks, and he was never one to pass up a chance to pose as follower of the people. Never was his talent for dissimulation more acute, however, than when he seemed to waver at Tama, Iowa, on his way to Omaha. "We want to preserve carefully," he said, "all the old life of the nation,—the dear old life of the nation and our cherished institutions—," only to finish by declaring, "but we do not want to shirk a single responsibility that has been put upon us by the results of the war." In weeks to come he would be much more explicit about the nature of America's "responsibility"; for the time being, it was enough to introduce the term.[24]

Demonstrating an artist's sense of symmetry, McKinley chose Omaha, the turning point of his journey, as the stage for his first really forthright speech. In his address before the peace celebration on 12 October, he cast aside all pretense of indecision and became a determined molder of public opinion. Leaving little room for misunderstanding, he told the crowd that "Divine favor seemed manifest everywhere. In fighting for humanity's sake we have been signally blessed. . . . The war was not more invited by us than were the questions which were laid at our door by its results. Now, as then, we will do our duty." Finally, he asked the audience for its opinion, phrasing his question in a way that he knew would admit only one answer: "Shall we deny to ourselves what the rest of the world so freely and so justly accords us?" Not remarkable, surely, was the crowd's response, a resounding no, for it was being worked by a master. Highlighted by the president's visit, the Omaha "jubilee" became more of a victory than a peace celebration, the tenor of which was caught perfectly by McKinley's jingoistic speech.[25]

His caution gone, McKinley retained throughout his journey the new tone established in Omaha. Traveling east across middle America—Iowa, Illinois, Indiana, and Ohio—he set forth in ringing terms his reasons for retaining the Philippines. At Chariton, Iowa, he stressed the blessings that retention would bring the Filipinos: "Territory sometimes comes to us when we go to war in a holy cause, and whenever it does the banner of liberty will float over it and bring, I trust, blessings and benefits to all the people." The next day, at Springfield, Illinois, hometown of Abraham Lincoln, he evoked a Lincolnesque fusion of idealism and national unity: "having gone to war for humanity's sake, we must accept no settlement that will not take into account the interests of humanity. As we stood together in war, let us stand together until its settlements are made." On 18 October in Chicago, he eloquently suggested that American destiny was once again manifest: "My countrymen, the currents of destiny flow through the hearts of the people. Who will check them, then; who will divert them, who will stop them?" Seeming to gain momentum with every speech, he saved his strongest comments for the final days of the tour. By the time he reached Tipton, Indiana, on 21 October, he prepared to tell his listeners how they felt about the Philippines: "As I look into your earnest faces I know that you would have this nation help the oppressed people who have by the war been brought within the sphere of our influence." Finally reaching Columbus, Ohio, he closed his journey with a call for the acceptance of new international responsibilities: "We know what our country is now in its territory, but we do not know what it may be in the near future. But whatever it is, whatever obligation shall justly come from this strife for humanity, we must take up and perform as free, strong, brave people, accept the trust which civilization puts upon us." His case argued, McKinley headed for Washington, confident that the public would support his decision to keep the Philippines.[26]

Despite such obvious proselytism, McKinley still refused to state openly his resolve to retain the islands. No doubt his silence came partly from concern over damaging negotiations in Paris; more important was his desire to avoid appearing inflexible at home. Aware that difficult times were ahead in the Philippines and that the public's second thoughts would be weaker and slower to develop if the initial decision appeared to be its own, he never surrendered his carefully cultivated image as follower of the people, even when, as at Tipton, he told his audience what they wanted him to do. At no time on his midwestern trip did McKinley actually follow public opinion, of course; he merely realized that appearing to follow was often the most fruitful way to lead. And if, as A. W. Dunn has written, McKinley really used crowd reaction to gauge public sentiment on the Philippines, he did so more to test his own success than to determine the course he should follow.[27]

Not everyone was misled by McKinley's pose as follower of public attitudes. Numerous editorials told the American people what his speeches portended for the Philippines, emphasizing for their readers that his remarks "made it clear" what such things as "humanity and manifest destiny" demanded of the United States. Other editors, like Joseph Medill of the *Chicago Tribune*, who wrote to McKinley in the midst of his tour, informed the president that he "may as well openly say what he means with regard to the Philippines" because "the people and press" realized that he intended to keep all of the islands. Such revelations did not disappoint McKinley, however; like the reaction of his audiences, they demonstrated that his message was coming across loud and clear.[28]

Back in Washington, McKinley had a chance to ponder the fruits of his midwestern passage. He had already heard from Secretary of State John Hay that his efforts had been "splendidly successful"; now he could see the same conclusion in his scrapbooks and mail. As never before, the president's letters and clippings seemed to favor retention of the Philippines, leading him to conclude, as he wrote Day in Paris, that "the well-considered opinion of the majority would be that duty requires we should take all the archipelago." So successful had McKinley's tour been, in fact, that Hay could wire in his final instructions to the commissioners that "the sentiment in the United States is almost universal that the people of the Philippines, whatever else is done, must be liberated from Spanish domination." Forced by circumstances to alter his style and go directly to the people, McKinley had managed to create a public opinion that seemed prepared, for the time being at least, to support his decision on the Philippines.[29]

While McKinley was dealing successfully with the electorate, his commissioners in Paris attempted to exert an influence of their own. In this they followed Whitelaw Reid, whose newspaper background made him especially cognizant of the uses of publicity. Shortly after arriving in France, Reid pressed C. Inham Barnard, the *Tribune's* Paris correspondent, into the commission's service and instructed him to keep abreast of newspaper comment on the peace conference. Barnard did so for the next three and a half months, preparing daily press summaries and clipping books of editorials from both European and American newspapers. As an ardent expansionist, Reid found Barnard's clippings, which mostly favored American control of the Philippines, useful for convincing such wavering commissioners as Day, but he aimed most of his own publicity at public opinion back in the United States. In early October he attempted to obtain a statement on the Philippines from Admiral Dewey; he believed the admiral favored retention of all the islands and thought his views would "carry great weight with the public."[30] In addition, although assuring McKinley that "as a rule we have not talked to the newspapers at all," he dictated a long interview explaining the administration's reasons for keeping the Philippines, attributing the information to an "unofficial person." Convinced that "for effect here and at home" the interview should be withheld from publication until "a day or two before the Philippine question was raised here, and a week before your elections," he kept it a secret from all but one of his fellow commissioners and found a "discreet method" of sending it across the Atlantic. For all his trouble Reid probably contributed little to McKinley's success with the public. Still, his concern for publicity added a new—and soon to be important— dimension to the activities of commissioners attending international conferences.[31]

It must have been with a mixture of satisfaction and misgiving that McKinley read Day's 10 December account of the treaty's signing: satisfaction, because his commissioners had succeeded in wringing every last concession from the Spanish; and misgiving, because he still faced a stiff fight for the treaty in the Senate. Day had been correct a few weeks earlier, when he wired the president, "whatever treaty we get here, I suppose, will meet with considerable opposition in the Senate," but his subsequent success in Paris had added greatly to the strength of that opposition. Already, Senator George Vest had introduced a resolution denouncing the islands' acquisition as unconstitutional; he seemed certain to find plenty of support when the treaty became known to the Senate. In McKinley's favor, of course, was the public support generated by his midwestern trip, with which he hoped to bring pressure on recalcitrant senators. At least once before, the senators had tried to employ public pressure to force McKinley's hand; now he intended to turn the tables.[32]

To this end McKinley resolved to mount another speaking tour, this time through the South. As a Republican president, he was traveling into the heart of enemy territory; yet he felt certain that his own popularity—and that of his message about the Philippines—would overcome traditional southern hostilities. Besides, where better could he go to convince Democratic senators that playing politics with the treaty would be foolhardy? Accordingly, he accepted an invitation to address the Atlanta Peace Celebration in mid-December, again scheduling a series of whistle-stop speeches along the way. Repeating the technique so successful in October, McKinley dotted his remarks with references to American duty and responsibility; as before, he heard them greeted with resounding cheers. The climax came in Atlanta, where his address to a joint session of the Georgia state legislature received such thunderous applause that the great dome of the capitol seemed to rock. Buoyed by the southern response, McKinley returned to Washington with renewed confidence in the treaty's success. He had taken his policies into Dixie, the Democrats' stronghold—and he had carried the day.[33]

Although only the opening salvo, McKinley's southern trip may have won the battle for the treaty. It appears to have made an impact upon at least one Democrat, and he was the most important one of all—William Jennings Bryan. Arriving in Washington at about the time of McKinley's triumphant return, Bryan brought a message to Democratic senators: no political advantage could be gained from defeating the treaty; they should vote for ratification. All too aware of McKinley's successes, first in the Midwest and now in the South, Bryan feared for the very life of a Democratic party that opposed the terms of peace. He knew that McKinley could make their opposition look traitorous, that his party would bear the onus for continuing the war. To avoid this, he argued, the Democrats must vote with the administration; after that, any problems the Republicans encountered in the Philippines—and he thought there would be many—would be their own. In the end, Bryan helped persuade seventeen Democrats and Populists to vote for the treaty; any two of them could have defeated it.[34]

Even with Bryan's unexpected support, however, the treaty faced a serious challenge in the Senate. Not only did the necessary two-thirds majority remain a doubtful prospect, but opposition senators, including both obdurate Democrats and antiexpansionist Republicans, threatened to contest McKinley's control of public opinion as well. Although enjoined to secrecy on the treaty itself, the Senate found ample excuse to debate openly its most important provision— the acquisition of the Philippines—in a spate of resolutions on the question of new territories. Of these the most dangerous was the Vest resolution, to which the Senate devoted the lion's share of its public debate on the treaty. Vest, backed by such diverse senatorial types as the urbane George Frisbie Hoar and the outspoken rustic "Pitchfork Ben" Tillman, argued that the Constitution—as well as American tradition—forbade the acquisition of territory for purpose other than eventual statehood. Speaking to the galleries, all the Vest resolution's backers—and Hoar in particular—proved most effective in mixing traditional rhetoric about freedom and self-government with sarcasm about descendants of the Founding Fathers who "strut about in the cast-off clothing of pinchbeck emperors and pewter kings" and who seemed as "excited by the smell of gunpowder and the sound of guns of a single victory as a small boy by a firecracker on some Fourth of July morning." Ultimately, of course, these resolutions had little chance of success; they were primarily sounding boards for antiexpansionist arguments.[35]

A close surveillance of public opinion convinced McKinley to bring increasing pressure against his Senate opponents. He too found ways to circumvent the secrecy injunction, and he used his position as president to offset his adversaries' publicity. As early as 30 October, he had instructed Secretary of Agriculture James Wilson to leak his order to keep all the Philippines; now, utilizing the same technique, he made public additional information about both the treaty and the islands. For McKinley, the issue of public opinion was settled decisively on 4 February 1899, when he learned that fighting had erupted in Manila. As he told Cortelyou: "This means the ratification of the treaty; the people will understand now, the people will insist upon its ratification." And just to make sure they did, he told Cortelyou to inform correspondents already gathering at the White House "that the insurgents had attacked Manila," leaving no doubt as to the Filipinos' blame. When, two days later, the Senate approved the Treaty of Paris, it did so amid the excitement—and heightened pressure—of a new war.[36]

But if war out of Manila helped settle one public issue for McKinley, it also presented him with another, more difficult one. No matter how "foolish" the Filipino insurgents had been to instigate hostilities on the very eve of the treaty vote, their action seemed certain in the long run to highlight the strong points of the anti-expansionist position. Singing the praises of American beneficence in the islands, McKinley had succeeded in neutralizing the effect of these points on the treaty fight. But now it was the United States, not Spain, that faced a bitter colonial war, a circumstance that turned topsy-turvy the logic of McKinley's position. In this new context his contention that America was the agent of freedom and democracy appeared absurd; yet he would have to justify the war to the American people—and to himself—in just those terms.[37]

He wasted little time doing so, accepting invitations to speak in Boston on 16 and 17 February. As McKinley's first public pronouncements since ratification by the Senate, these addresses proved—as planned—the subject of national attention for what they promised to tell of administration plans for the Philippines. And their importance was enhanced by the ever-present Cortelyou, who saw to it that reporters "were given such information as was of interest to them."[38] The president offered the first and more important of his two speeches at the Home Market Club, where he felt he could count on a friendly reception from assembled businessmen. To applause that was sometimes "too great to continue," he defended the Philippine acquisition as the only practical alternative, dismissing immediate self-determination for the Filipinos as the dream of visionaries.[39] Here he also struck a new note, employing such remarks as "it is not a good time for the liberator to submit important questions concerning liberty and government to the liberated while they are engaged in shooting down the rescuers" to express a contempt for the *insurrectos* that was not evident in his earlier speeches. Not all his words were sharp, however. In the end they were mellifluous, closing his address with the benign vision of a Philippines that, under American tutelage, would become "a land of plenty and of increasing possibilities," its people "redeemed from savage indolence and habits, devoted to the arts of peace, in touch with the commerce and trade of all nations, enjoying the blessings of freedom, of civil and religious liberty, of education, of homes, and whose children and children's children shall for ages hence bless the American republic because it emancipated their fatherland, and set them in the pathway of the world's best civilization." It was these conjuring words that newspapers noted, and often quoted, in referring to McKinley's address, encouraging him to a new interpretation of humanitarianism for the Philippines.[40]

The next day, however, speaking before a reception given by the Boston Commercial Club, McKinley made clear his awareness of another option. Boston recently had seen the creation of the New England Antiimperialist League, an organization adamant in its opposition to the Philippine acquisition, and the city continued to be the national hotbed of antiexpansionist action. With his tour having come to resemble a "triumphal procession," McKinley might have chosen to overlook the Bostonian undercurrent of dissent, but he took the opportunity afforded by his visit to score points on the opposition. One of the most successful arguments of his midwestern tour had been the need for national unity until the peace treaty could be signed; now, with the country involved in new hostilities, that approach promised to be even more useful. Thus, appealing at once to their pride and patriotism, he told Bostonians that "whatever the difference of opinion in Massachusetts, ... I have discovered that when there [is] a crisis, national or otherwise, Massachusetts stands together for national credit and national honor."[41]

In the following months McKinley returned often to each of these arguments, as he made loyalty, humanitarianism, and the uncivilized character of the *insurrectos* the themes of his campaign in behalf of the Philippine War. A summer speaking tour took him back to the North, where he endeavored to attach no less a national symbol than the stars and stripes to his policy in the islands. At Springfield, Massachusetts, he uttered lengthy platitudes on the meaning of the flag, piously observing that "it does not stand for despotism—it stands for peace and progress and liberty and law and kindly government wherever its sacred folds float." One place it floated, of course, was over the Philippines, and McKinley made it clear that he intended it to remain there despite the activities of insurgent nationalists. "Rebellion may delay, but it can never defeat its blessed mission of liberty and humanity," he told a crowd at Cliff Haven, New York. The rebels' worst depredations were not against the flag, however; they were against American soldiers in the field. For this subject McKinley reserved his strongest language, depicting the insurgents as little more than savages: "Our kindness was reciprocated with a Mauser. The flag of truce was invoked only to be dishonored. Our soldiers were shot down when ministering to wounded Philipinos [*sic*]. The dead were mutilated." Turning next to Aguinaldo and the other "cruel leaders" of the rebellion, McKinley suggested they had "needlessly sacrificed the lives of thousands of their best people, at the cost of some of the best blood," only "for the gratification of their own ambitious designs."[42]

But McKinley did not reserve all his criticism for the Philippine nationalists; he also assailed their sympathizers at home. October found him once again on the stump, retracing his midwestern trip of the previous autumn and lambasting domestic opponents of the war. His speeches during the summer had come increasingly to stress patriotic, as opposed to humanitarian, aspects of administration policy; now they seemed to do so almost entirely. Whistle-stopping his way from Illinois to the Dakotas and back to Indiana, he repeatedly dismissed the insurrection as a "rebellion against the sovereignty of the United States." As such, its defeat demanded the support of all patriotic Americans; opposition was a kind of treason. Yet there were those who opposed "adding to the glory of the United States," who wanted to "scuttle" in the face of Filipino opposition; these McKinley compared to opponents of the Louisiana Purchase and the copperheads of the Civil War. Referring often to the valor of midwestern military units, he contrasted their efforts with those of the antiimperialists: while the soldiers fought fearlessly, the antiimperialists deserted in the face of the enemy; while the soldiers served their country, the antiimperialists aided their foes. There would be less trouble with the Filipinos, he implied, if only the people at home would see their duty as clearly as the soldiers in the Philippines.[43]

With local elections approaching in November and with McKinley himself standing for reelection in a year's time, these thrusts at antiimperialist spokesmen seemed aimed directly at the Democratic party. This was true, insofar as many leading antiimperialists were also Democrats. But McKinley's purpose was not primarily a partisan one; more important was continuation of public support for the war in the Philippines, upon which hinged the future of McKinley's expansionist policies. Surrendering the islands was unthinkable; it would make the United States the "laughing stock of the world." Yet an unfavorable public opinion might require McKinley to withdraw American soldiers, creating a power vacuum that Aguinaldo and his troops were sure to fill. This danger prompted McKinley, who had campaigned from his front porch in 1896 and who would do so again in 1900, to take his case directly to the people. Such strong measures had not seemed necessary in the troubled weeks before the Spanish-American War, or even once the actual fighting had begun; his use of them now indicated the peril he perceived in the Philippine situation.[44]

There was more to McKinley's perception than fear, however: he also saw in the Philippines an opportunity to educate the American people for their new responsibilities. Convinced that the spirit of "isolation" under which the United States had labored since the Mexican War did not befit the nation's new status as a "world power," he attempted to create a public consensus to complement his vision of a great and expansionist America. Speaking on 2 March 1900 to the Ohio Society of New York City, he presented America's expansion as humane and benevolent—quite unlike the imperialism practiced by European nations. In this speech, as in many others, he imbued expansionism with respectability, developing the Philippine issue into a springboard for defending what he believed to be the policy of the future. With one eye on success in the Philippines, the other on America's expansionist direction, McKinley glanced only obliquely to the election of 1900.[45]

Although the Philippine insurrection was certain to continue past November 1900, its conduct was not affected by the presidential election. To whatever extent—and it appears to have been slight—McKinley's pleas reflected concern over his reelection, he gave no sign of scaling down his Philippine commitment for that purpose. The election did pose some constraints, however. In dealing in June with the so-called Boxer Rebellion, a matter of less importance, McKinley seemed considerably more susceptible to political pressure; he appeared, in fact, to formulate policy with the electorate in mind. In sending troops to China, even for the purpose of rescuing beleaguered legations, McKinley laid himself open to renewed charges of imperialism that threatened to resuscitate the acrimonious Philippine debate. Yet the siege of Peking left him little choice, especially if he hoped to continue America's pretension to the role of a major—and moral—force in Chinese affairs. By the end of August, the joint expeditionary force had succeeded in capturing the capital city, and McKinley prepared to remove American troops. As he informed Secretary of State Hay: "we want to avoid being in China for a long time and it must be a long time if we stay there for the diplomatic negotiations." Hay demurred but eventually agreed to reduce the force to a legation guard. In this case, at least, politics superseded policy.[46]

Timing was the primary reason for this reversed ordering of priorities. To some extent McKinley found the China question especially difficult because it arose in the context of the Philippine War, but overall this was considerably less significant than its proximity to election day. Given sufficient time, McKinley felt confident of his ability to convince the electorate of his policy's righteousness, even in a situation as controversial as the Philippines. In the short run, however, public opinion remained much less predictable. Thus, when McKinley sent troops into China only five months before the election, he could not be certain of the impact it would have on the polls. Still, five months might have given him enough time—he had insured acceptance of his Philippines policy in less—had he not already established a campaign strategy of holding himself aloof from public exposure. Under such circumstances, he saw the eleventh hour as a poor moment for a potentially divisive departure in foreign policy and chose to withdraw the troops from China as quickly as possible.

Throughout the Philippine insurrection, McKinley remained on good terms with the working press; their support found ample reflection in the president's scrapbooks. In newspapers he regularly followed, at least, editorials praising McKinley and reviling his enemies (both at home and in the Philippines) generally accompanied reports of his speeches. One issue endangered this support—the imposition of military censorship, which threatened, as it had during the war with Spain, to come between the president and even his warmest editorial admirers. On 9 July 1899 American correspondents in Manila cabled home a round robin, complaining of censorship in the Philippines. Published in the United States eight days later, their dispatch charged General Elwell Otis, United States commander in the islands, with deliberately attempting to prevent transmittal of war news to the American public, not for reasons of military necessity but for a concern that the truth would "alarm the people at home." According to reporters, Otis had allowed only censored, and therefore misleading, press dispatches to leave the Philippines, suppressing even casualty reports in order to hide high rates of Americans killed, wounded, and sick. As a result, they argued, the American people had no idea of the real military situation in the islands, which was by no means as well in hand as Otis had reported in official releases.[47]

The correspondents' complaints provoked a storm of criticism over the administration's handling of the war. Remembering McKinley's earlier censorship order, many journalists associated the president as well as Otis with preventing publication of war news. Moreover, because Otis's official dispatches were released in Washington, their stigma was readily attached to officials of much higher rank than general; it was thus, as the *Cleveland Plain Dealer* pointed out, impossible to tell for certain whether Otis misled the administration or the administration misled the public on its own. Whoever was at fault, it remained clear that the censorship issue, with its negative implications for freedom of the press, seemed capable of uniting newspapers of the most diverse points of view. Among McKinley's detractors could now be found such proexpansionist journals as the *New York Tribune* and *New York World*; it remained for a handful of important editors, among his dozens of regular supporters, to defend McKinley by contending that only he, not the public, understood the military situation and that the press should trust his judgment on the need for censorship.[48]

Faced with such criticism, McKinley might have found it necessary to reevaluate all of his press relations. To a degree true of no other issue, censorship had the potential for undermining those relations; it threatened to make a mockery of his—and Cortelyou's—policy of openness in the White House. No matter how useful both he and reporters had found increased contact in the past, it could never survive, much less flourish, in the atmosphere of mistrust engendered by censorship. Nevertheless, McKinley remained unwilling to eliminate press restrictions in the Philippines, choosing instead to wait out the storm. Following a cabinet meeting on censorship, McKinley issued a press release refusing to interfere with Otis's handling of war correspondents. This statement gave the impression that the policy of censorship had been imposed by the general himself; he alone appeared responsible for its abuses. To remove himself even farther from the picture, McKinley also allowed Secretary of War Alger to take responsibility for any official misrepresentation of the war. Alger, an embarrassment to the administration for over a year, was finally cajoled by McKinley into resigning in early July. Alger's resignation had nothing to do with censorship in the Philippines, but it was made public two days after the round robin appeared in the press. Many newspapers jumped naturally to the conclusion that Alger had been fired—and, as they saw it, rightfully so—for complicity in Otis's activities. When McKinley did nothing to dispel this impression, journalists apparently assumed its correctness, and many accepted it as a presidential attempt to placate their ruffled sensitivity to censorship. Within a week, the issue no longer commanded space in the daily newspapers, and it had little lasting impact on McKinley's relations with the press.[49]

That these relations remained good was due in no small measure to the efforts of Secretary Cortelyou, who managed throughout to keep himself—and McKinley—on the friendliest of terms with White House reporters. Since the early days of the administration, Cortelyou had courted the favor of the press, supplying the warmth generally lacking in their relations with the informative but too often supercilious Porter. When, in early 1900, illness forced Porter to resign his post of presidential secretary, Cortelyou was finally able to combine the power of that office with his own talent for dealing with the press. Most important, however, was his capacity for what a later generation would call press relations, which, according to historian Margaret Leech, "did much to regulate the hit-or-miss methods of news-gathering at the White House." Cortelyou's abilities, long useful to McKinley, became indispensable for a presidential secretary in the difficult days of the Philippine War.[50]

Also valuable to McKinley were the press relations established by Secretary of State Hay. On taking office in September 1898, Hay inherited "an antiquated, feeble organization, enslaved by precedents and routine inherited from another century, remote from the public gaze and indifferent to it." For this Hay's immediate predecessors—Sherman and Day—were largely to blame; they, like other nineteenth-century secretaries, had shunned rather than facilitated relations with the press. Although the new secretary, aristocratic in demeanor and more at home in London than Washington, seemed hardly the figure to ingratiate the department with reporters, he won their favor—and transformed State Department press relations—by innovating the regular press conference. These conferences developed out of Hay's concern over public unrest during the Philippine War; it was at this time that he made frequent meetings with four or five reporters a part of his weekly routine. In this way he could defend his policies, often explaining background and motive in great detail, while enjoining the journalists to secrecy whenever he found it prudent to do so. Following the lead of the White House, the Department of State was becoming, at the end of the nineteenth century, an important source of information—and influence—for the press.[51]

In the end, of course, McKinley won his battle for the Philippines. Perhaps he never doubted that he would; for although the issue presented him with the greatest challenge of his administration, he seemed never to lose his faith in the people's willingness to be led.

His many speeches on the subject reflected this faith—they rarely failed to give the audience an opportunity for registering approval of his leadership. McKinley never doubted that his role as president was to lead, and he clearly understood the weight lent by his office to his words. Thus, when most in need of public support, he maximized his personal persuasiveness by taking his message directly to the people. This technique never failed him; no wonder he could be so sanguine as to write a troubled Hay that "the clouds would pass" and that "for the public welfare we must not be swayed by the tumult of the hour." At the same time, it might be added, McKinley worked behind the scenes to create an executive department that wielded, through its daily contact with the press, a more unobtrusive influence on public views. Succeeding in both areas, he opened up a new dimension in the president's relations with the American people.[52]

Chapter 3
The Power of the
Press Release

 Within a few hours of his return from McKinley's burial at Canton, Ohio, President Theodore Roosevelt summoned local representatives of the three major press associations. When all were seated in his office, he informed the journalists— Barry of the *New York Sun* Press Association, Boynton of the Associated Press, and Keen of the United Press—of "the relations that should, and will, exist between the White House and your organizations." Starting on a positive note, Roosevelt announced that Boynton and Barry, with whom he had had previous dealings, would continue to have his confidence, and at their insistence, he extended his trust to Keen as well. But, he admonished them, such relations could last only as long as the reporters did not violate his confidence. He cited the case of a correspondent who had once earned his displeasure and who was now barred from the White House: anyone failing to live up to his trust would receive the same treatment. With this threat dangling and with his administration's press relations firmly established, Roosevelt terminated his first "little talk" with the journalists.[1]

In years to come, Roosevelt would have many such little talks with news correspondents, but none would be more characteristic of his style in dealing with the press. By calling top reporters together he had seized the initiative—indeed, he had seized the upper hand—making sure that he alone would set the terms of his relationship with the press. He had likewise made clear that he did not intend to leave the procedure of gathering White House news to chance; he was already displaying the thoroughness that would characterize his administration's handling of the press. And finally, with information flowing readily from his offices to journalists willing to obey his rules, TR had given himself the ability to control both reporters and the material they collected.[2]

Although clothed in different style, many of Roosevelt's techniques were carryovers from the McKinley administration. In time, of course, the new president would enlarge both their power and dimension, but such things as press releases, briefings, and advance copies of speeches—the mainstays of Roosevelt's influence with reporters—were innovations of his predecessor in the White House. More important than any technique, however, was Roosevelt's decision to retain Secretary Cortelyou, the man who had overseen their development—and had made them work—during the McKinley years. With Cortelyou in his outer office, Roosevelt assured himself of good press relations; the secretary's expertise in disseminating White House news combined with his understanding of correspondents to make certain that, as one reporter put it, "everything ran as smoothly as an eight-day clock." As vice-president, TR had witnessed Cortelyou's skilled handling of the press, both on the road and in the White House; small wonder, then, that the new president insisted the secretary stay on as chief of the executive offices and, at least in the early days of his administration, leaned heavily upon his special abilities.[3]

As Cortelyou soon discovered, he faced a different task with Roosevelt than he had with McKinley. Outgoing and energetic, the new president seemed determined to handle his own press relations, a situation that made the secretary's job both easier and more complex. In many ways, TR's willingness to meet reporters made him the ideal subject for Cortelyou's efforts. But it also increased markedly the president's visibility, and this added to the secretary's concerns. Now, as never before, he found it essential to verify every presidential remark, authenticate every fact, and check every quotation, as, increasingly, he was called upon to interpret, explain, and elaborate on Roosevelt's pronouncements. Cortelyou proved equal to the task; "there were never," according to newspaperman Edward Lowry, "'unfortunate slips' when Mr. Cortelyou was in the White House Executive offices." Eventually, Roosevelt promoted his secretary to a cabinet post, demonstrating beyond doubt the esteem in which he held him. In the meantime, Cortelyou succeeded in maintaining the good press relations established under McKinley and in adapting them to the changed conditions of the Roosevelt administration.[4]

Because Cortelyou worked behind the scenes, however, it was not his but Roosevelt's personality that dominated the administration's publicity. In newspaper terms of the time, the new president was a "natural"—today he would be termed a "media personality"—because he had a way of dramatizing events that never failed to catch the attention of reporters. Speaking or acting, he was always good copy. He not only understood, to a degree true of no previous president, the value of publicity, but he was also willing to beguile correspondents in order to earn it. He also seemed to know "by instinct," said Archie Butt, his military aide, "what would be of interest to the public," a talent that persuaded the reporters to trust his evaluation of what was news. And finally, he maintained friendly personal relations with many in the White House press corps and appeared, at least, to enjoy their company—perhaps for the same reason he enjoyed that of the tough-minded cowboys he had known out west. At any rate, Roosevelt's friendliness, along with his personal élan and love of publicity, allowed him to leave his own stamp on the reporting of White House news.[5]

Besides a gregarious personality, Roosevelt also brought to the presidency considerable experience in dealing with the press. To some degree, of course, this must be true of all presidents; few aspirants to such high office can avoid all contact with reporters. But Roosevelt had gone beyond mere contact to the creation of useful press relations while in his previous offices. As governor of New York, for example, he had met twice daily with local correspondents, "to make them feel," as he put it, "that they were part of his work." More recently, as assistant secretary of the navy and vice-president, he had displayed an awareness of publicity that allowed him to win valuable friends among Washington reporters.[6]

Possibly even more important than Roosevelt's personality and background was his progressivism, which gave his perception of public opinion an ideological component lacking in previous presidents. Through most of the nineteenth century, foreign policy makers had seen little threat in the rather mild vicissitudes of public opinion; even McKinley, for all his efforts to influence the public's views, never doubted their essential soundness. By the end of the century, however, changes in American society were undermining this traditional faith in the public, as the development of a mass society, informed by an unsavory and often corrupt yellow press, appeared to endanger the administration of both foreign and domestic policy. For Roosevelt, this threat took the form of "hysteria" in the public and press. "I suppose there is a certain hysterical element in our people; probably in all peoples," he wrote Secretary of the Navy Charles Bonaparte. "But it is so evident in our own people that to my mind it is one of the most serious dangers to be confronted in any great foreign or domestic crisis." Partly a response to the threat posed by the transformation of America into a perceived mass society, progressivism offered Roosevelt a rationale for dealing with the menace he now perceived in public opinion.[7]

The progressive view of public opinion appeared in *Social Control* by Stanford sociologist Edward A. Ross. What was needed, according to Ross, was the replacement of "social influence," or purposeless, undirected mob control, with "social control," or purposeful domination to fulfill the life of the community. Public opinion might, he argued, "become a respectable agent for the righteous protection of the social welfare" in three ways: first, by "a general improvement in character and intelligence"; second, by "a general acceptance of principles of law and right"; and third, by "the ascendency of the wise." With these changes Ross saw no reason why the crowd must always be a "beast"; if structured properly into "an organic combination of the people," it might serve a useful purpose in a democratic society. "Such a guidance being possible," Ross concluded, "the remedy for the abuses of public opinion is not to discredit it but to instruct it."[8]

Writing to Ross, Roosevelt agreed that "public opinion, if only sufficiently enlightened and aroused, is equal to the necessary regenerative task and can yet dominate the future." This qualified optimism formed the core of Roosevelt's—and the progressives'—view of public opinion; it was also manifest in TR's many campaigns to win political support for his foreign policies. These campaigns, in fact, provided the key to Roosevelt's optimism, for the pernicious influence of the masses could only be overcome, and public opinion made into a force for political reconstruction, if the people's faculty for becoming "enlightened and aroused" was prodded by a determined leader. Roosevelt characteristically projected himself into that role, although he realized that he could not hope to succeed without assistance from the press. For this reason, he took every opportunity to remind journalists of their responsibility in a democratic society; as he put it, they "do the most toward shaping the thought of the people." Although such exhortations were often self-serving, Roosevelt found in progressive moralism a source of great energy—and considerable support—in dealing with press and public.[9]

It is in a sense ironic that Roosevelt's progressivism, through which he expressed a desire to increase the public's control of the political process, should have made the management of public opinion seem more necessary to him than to previous presidents. This irony reflects an unresolved contradiction within the progressive faith itself: if the public was to have more political power, its views would have to be controlled to insure that it made the proper decisions; yet such control could only negate the increased impact of the public on the political process that was the progressive's goal. Not surprisingly, Roosevelt never felt the sting of this contradiction; he always saw his efforts as "educating" public opinion or as "waking up the country to what is necessary" and experienced no difficulty reconciling them with the progressive desire for an informed body politic. Nevertheless, especially in the area of foreign affairs, about which, Roosevelt contended, "the average American citizen does not take the trouble to think carefully or deeply," his progressivism called for an increased control of public opinion at least commensurate with the public's enlarged influence in national politics.[10]

In another sense, however, public opinion management remained an integral part of the progressive creed, which displayed concern for efficient management in all areas of government. As Samuel Haber has pointed out, the impact of progressivism on American life "was less a matter of rooting up and destroying than of management, control, and regulation." By applying such principles to press relations and the dissemination of White House news, Roosevelt made the control of public attitudes part of a more general movement—characteristic of progressivism—away from the traditional theory of administrative laissez-faire.[11]

Like many progressives, Roosevelt believed that centralization made for better management and tighter administrative control. Just as in business, where combination promoted efficiency, the executive branch could benefit from uniting the reins of authority in a single pair of hands; thus, nothing seemed more cardinal to Roosevelt's theory of government than that its "efficiency . . . depends upon its possessing a strong central executive." He attempted, accordingly, to concentrate the release of all executive news in White House offices and to direct personally, as much as possible, the publicity of his entire administration. Central to this was the control of information about cabinet meetings, which provided correspondents with much of their knowledge about administration interests and designs. For as long as reporters could remember, they had learned about cabinet affairs from exiting department heads, who, whether loose-tongued or inspired, had taken a few minutes after sessions to discuss issues receiving consideration. Early in his administration, however, Roosevelt put a stop to this practice, announcing after a cabinet meeting that "hereafter the work of the cabinet will be announced by Secretary Cortelyou" and that "cabinet officers will not be pursued . . . for details of the business considered by the cabinet, and will allow everything to be given out at the White House." True to his progressive ideals, TR explained this by contending that it would prevent the publication of "misleading news" and would therefore result in a more accurately informed public opinion. Predictably, these restrictions proved short-lived, and the cabinet returned almost completely to its old procedure within a year.[12]

Roosevelt did not give up, however; by 1905 he was again dissatis-fied with the correspondents' practice of questioning cabinet mem-bers. Supported by his new secretary of state, who was also made nervous by talkative department heads, he interrupted a cabinet meeting to reinstate his previous ban on chatting with the press. This time his directive proved more effective. Cabinet members refused to answer reporters' questions about the meetings for the next two years, and cabinet news was funneled almost exclusively through White House offices. As one might suppose, the effect of this order was to diminish the cabinet as a source of news and to enhance the presidential secretary's position as the correspondents' infor-mant. Roosevelt found both results desirable, and when in 1907 his ban again fell into disuse, he clamped it quickly back on the cabinet and insisted it remain in effect until the end of his administration.[13]

While centralizing news of cabinet meetings, Roosevelt also at-tempted to control the flow of information about various executive activities. Although he did not make it a standing rule for depart-mental press releases to be approved by the president, he did de-mand this procedure in a number of specific instances. During his first year in office, for example, he warned Secretary of Agriculture James Wilson against "allowing any publication or statement in the newspapers in connection with our economic troubles with Ger-many" until after consulting him in full. In other cases, Roosevelt desired to free rather than to dam the flow of information, as when he requested Assistant Secretary of State Francis Butler Loomis to issue a press statement about the treatment of Jews in Russia, but either way his goal remained the centralization of press information pertaining to the executive departments.[14]

If he did not always trust the judgment of cabinet officials, Roose-velt was also concerned about leaks within the White House itself. He argued, in a presidential memorandum, that "the chance for damage by a foolish or treacherous clerk is very great." "The recent experience in the War Department," he continued, "where unautho-rized publications have caused serious detriment to the service," indicated the need for establishing strict regulations and for insur-ing that anyone placed in the executive mansion to do telegraphic or any other sort of clerical work must be "of a special and confidential type." For Roosevelt, the control of White House news—the key to his influence with the press—was too important for information to be released without his or his secretary's direct approval.[15]

Roosevelt preferred, of course, to handle publicity himself. It was this that earned him the love of Washington newsmen—as well as praise from historians—and that set his administration's publicity clearly apart from McKinley's. From his first days in the White

House, TR made a habit of calling in reporters whenever he had an important policy or piece of information to discuss. On occasion, this practice produced something approximating a presidential press conference, with Roosevelt summoning as many as forty or fifty correspondents to his office. But more often these meetings were smaller affairs, where the president opened up—often off the record—to a handful of reporters he knew he could trust. Among the famous members of this privileged group were Mark Sullivan, John J. Leary, Oscar K. Davis, Charles Willis Thompson, Lincoln Steffens, and Sydney Brooks, with other less-known reporters included on various occasions. In time, these men developed an affection for Roosevelt that closely resembled hero worship, and they rarely disappointed the president in sending favorable reports to their newspapers.[16]

Some members of this "newspaper cabinet," as TR called them, also received individual attention. One of these was the *New York Times*'s Oscar Davis, who was, as he later wrote, "in the habit of seeing the President two or three times a week, for private talks." According to Davis, Roosevelt was always accessible early in the evening while he signed his daily correspondence, and the journalist generally chose that time to drop in on him. "He had an amazing facility," Davis remembered, "for carrying on conversation while he was going over the mail." Another of Roosevelt's favorites who received individual treatment was the muckraker Lincoln Steffens. TR gave him "the barber's hour"—every day at 12:40—for his personal consultations. As Steffens recalled them, these meetings showed Roosevelt's love of talk more than his desire to answer questions. The journalist generally managed only two queries—one when he entered, followed by a monologue, then another when the president was silenced by the shaving of his lower lip. Coming from anyone else, such behavior might have made reporters doubt the value of impromptu meetings, but Roosevelt was so adept at holding their interest that they always returned for more.[17]

Roosevelt also went out of his way to help his favorites gather news throughout the administration. One recipient of this attention was Steffens, who sought the president's assistance in compiling a series about the federal government for the McClure Newspaper Syndicate. TR responded with an open letter "to any officer or employee of the Government," asking that he "please tell Mr. Lincoln Steffens anything whatever about the running of the government that you know (not incompatible with the public interests) and provided only that you tell him the truth—no matter what it may be—I will see that you are not hurt." Steffens never did benefit from this "carte blanche," as he called it, however, because most officials thought that talking to reporters at all violated "the public interests." In fact, the chief beneficiary seemed Roosevelt himself; his generosity disarmed Steffens, whose articles on the administration proved pallid by usual muckraking standards.[18]

The key to Roosevelt's success with newsmen was his extreme candor, what correspondent Isaac Marcosson called his "almost incredible frankness" in interviews. In dealing with his "fair-haired" reporters, TR always made it clear that he trusted their judgment and discretion. He had a talent for making newspapermen feel that they were being taken into his confidence, and they invariably responded with stories favorable to his administration. As reporters saw him, Roosevelt lacked the deviousness of other news managers; he always, according to Charles W. Thompson, treated newspapermen in a "straightforward" fashion. Reporters liked him for this, and, Thompson concluded, they liked him all the more because he was so "confoundedly human." In 1901 correspondents had not yet grown accustomed to enjoying personal relations with presidents; they would have to get used to it with Roosevelt in the White House.[19]

It should not be supposed, however, that Roosevelt was always completely open with his favorites among the press. On the contrary, he never told them more than he wanted them to know, and he never, according to Thompson, gave an interview unless he "directed the form the interview should take." TR may have given the impression that he was impulsive in his remarks to journalists, but nothing could be farther from the truth. He might tell various reporters more or less of his opinions, depending upon how much he trusted them, but he always governed his remarks by the publicity needs of his administration.[20]

Roosevelt also made it clear that his trust required greater responsibility on the part of reporters. One thing he would not tolerate was abuse of his confidence, especially where this involved direct quotation of his remarks. As Oscar Davis noted, "any violation of that terminated a correspondent's usefulness to his paper, so far as the White House was concerned." It also got him elected to the Ananais Club, TR's designation for reporters he could not trust. In this, as in so many things, Roosevelt seemed a man of extremes. He trusted each journalist completely until he broke his confidence, then lost all faith in his honesty. "It was," Davis concluded, "all or nothing with him."[21]

There can be no doubt that Roosevelt's publicity benefited from his easy relations with reporters. His friendliness and ebullience allowed him to develop a loyal following that he could count on for favorable treatment in the press. He also used this group to make important announcements and put out what reporter J. Frederick Essary called "feelers" through them. But he did not, in this way, truly advance the cause of presidential news management. In fact, his efforts here represented only an improved version of traditional press relations, with friendliness—what TR called the "Oyster Bay atmosphere"—replacing partisanship as the touchstone of confidence. As such, Roosevelt's techniques did facilitate increased news dissemination, but only on a scale that remained limited. It had been the goal of the McKinley administration—and still was the goal of Secretary Cortelyou within the Roosevelt administration—to make the release of information more routine and bureaucratic, to rationalize the flow of White House news to all reporters. Roosevelt's personal relations seemed a step in the opposite direction, back toward the nineteenth-century use of occasional presidential publicity. And TR, of course, played favorites, which is hardly a very bureaucratic way to do anything. Taken on its own terms, this was the greatest weakness of Roosevelt's personal handling of the press; his favoritism angered many reporters who found themselves outside the inner circle, resulting in complaints of a privileged press that would remain for Wilson to answer with the introduction of all-inclusive news conferences.[22]

The real heart of Roosevelt's efforts to manage executive information was the press release, which he employed to provide all White House correspondents with an almost continuous supply of carefully prepared administration news. Although issuing press bulletins had been made routine during the McKinley administration, it remained for Roosevelt to set them in the modern form of a statement detailing presidential action or policy. He also developed new purposes to which they might be put. Press releases were now used to present advance information on presidential journeys, including the itinerary, meetings, and speaking engagements planned for each trip. Now, too, bulletins alerted reporters well in advance to addresses the White House considered important, allowing Roosevelt to insure attendance by representatives of wire services and important newspapers. Handouts were also employed to deny, sometimes vehemently, what Roosevelt termed "misleading statements" appearing in the press, a use that gave him the opportunity to neutralize potentially damaging information. Releases likewise informed reporters of White House regulations, as when the president let them know it would be a waste of time to question cabinet members. And finally, press releases became the primary source of presidential quotations when Roosevelt abolished the practice of quoting from his little talks. The result was a more solid footing for the relationship between the president and press, with the news release serving as a formal medium of communication between the two.[23]

It also remained for Roosevelt to realize the power of threatening to withhold press releases. As he informed the wire service heads on his first day in office, TR intended to hold back executive press bulletins from correspondents who stepped out of line, and he went to this extreme at least twice during his years in the White House. He exceeded even this in December 1904, when he banned an entire newspaper, the *Boston Herald*, from utilizing executive newsgathering facilities. Accusing its reporters of lying about the content of official news releases, Roosevelt closed to the *Herald* all "sources of information" under his authority and set loose a storm of editorial criticism of his high-handedness. If newspapermen remained willing to accept the consignment of an occasional correspondent to a kind of journalistic limbo, they reacted quite differently to withholding information from an entire newspaper, which they perceived as a form of prior censorship. Roosevelt realized he had gone too far and, wishing to avoid further deterioration of his press relations, reinstated the newspaper with executive offices. And although he pointedly avoided taking such a step again, the president saw in the editors' reaction a confirmation of the influence he could gain by threatening to deny them information.[24]

For Roosevelt as for McKinley, however, it was the release of information rather than its denial that constituted the real strength of his influence with press and public. Roosevelt, as David S. Barry noted, "was greatly impressed with the power exerted upon the minds of the people by the news articles published in the newspapers"; he frequently used press releases to gain some control over their contents. By releasing information, he focused journalistic attention on issues—or aspects of them—of his own choosing. At the same time, he managed to present his own interpretation of these topics, which many correspondents simply passed on to the public. Thus, when dealing with a controversial matter, or one he felt required public education, Roosevelt stepped up the flow of newsworthy information and looked for it to have a salutary effect upon his relations with the public.[25]

Of such instances, perhaps none was more controversial than the events leading to the construction of the Panama Canal; certainly none elicited more thorough presidential publicity. From the start of his administration, Roosevelt had been frustrated in efforts to clear

the way for a canal; thus, when Colombian officials broke off negotiations about an American lease of the isthmian site during the
summer of 1903, considerable speculation existed that the president
might send troops to seize the area. In fact, the president was
pondering just such a plan, informing Secretary of State Hay on 17
August that "we may have to give a lesson to those jackrabbits." Two
months later, still incensed over Colombia's rejection of the Hay-
Herran Treaty, Roosevelt wrote a similar proposal into a rough draft
of his annual message to Congress, arguing that the United States
should, "without any further parley with Colombia enter upon the
completion of the canal which the French company has begun." At
about that same time, however, he was learning—despite his later
protestations to the contrary—of Panama's intention to secede from
Colombia, and he began to formulate a different strategy. This was
the course he pursued when the revolution occurred on 3 November:
he protected the rebels and recognized their government—and insured Panamanian willingness to negotiate a canal treaty.[26]

Before dispatching warships to the isthmus, however, Roosevelt
laid the groundwork for public acceptance of his decision to intervene. As recently as 7 October, he had admitted privately that, "as
yet, the people of the United States are not willing to take the
ground for building the canal by force," and he could not be certain
that indirect military interference would fare any better with the
public. He thus solicited the help of his many journalist friends,
who, led by Lawrence Abbott of the *Outlook*, produced something
of an editorial groundswell for the secession of the canal zone.
But Roosevelt also worried about his aggressive image and asked
John D. Long, his old boss at the Navy Department, to tone down
remarks about Roosevelt's activities as Long's young assistant at
the outset of the war with Spain, remarks that the president feared
made him seem to be a lion at a time when it suited his purposes to
look like a lamb. And, finally, he began piecing together his rather
elaborate public justification for the action he would take in the
isthmus. By the time the revolution got underway, which it did
according to schedule, Roosevelt was prepared to deal with public
opinion on the issue. He was, in fact, confident, as he informed his
son Kermit on the day following the revolution: "Of course, I may
encounter checks, but I think I shall put it through all right."[27]

Within hours of the uprising in the canal zone, Roosevelt began
feeding information about it to White House correspondents. In a
press release dated 3 November, the day of the revolution, he informed the press of the existence of "rather serious disturbances at
both Panama and Colon" and of the dispatching of several vessels to

"keep the transit open." Although Roosevelt was here already beginning to construct his apologia for intervening in the isthmus, he did not want this release published as a policy statement. In fact, because he wished to be certain that his hands appeared clean, he had the bulletin stamped, "not to be used as a statement from the White House," and forbade even the attribution of news of the revolution to official sources. In this way, he saw to it that reporters had information of the Panamanian uprising, phrased in accordance with his designs, without making the White House appear unduly interested in the situation.[28]

After three days of thus employing press releases, Roosevelt prepared to defend his decision to intervene. On 6 November he invited a number of leading journalists, including John C. Davis of the *Philadelphia Ledger* and Lawrence Abbott of the *Outlook*, to a White House luncheon on Panama. He also issued, later that same day, a six-page statement from Secretary of State Hay, detailing American policy in the isthmus and defending the administration's actions as in "the strictest accordance with the principles of justice and equity." Basing his justification on a paper written by international law expert John Bassett Moore of Columbia University, Roosevelt contended that the United States had been obliged to take action by an 1846 treaty with New Grenada, which called for American intervention to keep the isthmus open for transit. To honor this obligation, he continued, and to protect the valuable Panamanian trade highway, he had found it necessary to prevent military action in the area. He also claimed his behavior was in strict accordance with international law: he played no part in the uprising and recognized the new government of Panama only after the revolution was clearly successful. Years later, in one of his "bully" moods, Roosevelt would assert that he "took" the canal zone. But in November 1903 and in months to follow, he wanted to make certain that no public— or congressional—doubt interfered with his plans for the isthmus.[29]

Temporarily, at least, it appeared such doubt might develop anyway. On 9 November Senator Henry Teller commented that he did not believe the country would approve the president's course in Panama. Even Roosevelt, writing privately to Theodore Jr., announced that "Senators, businessmen, and everybody else" had become "panic-struck" and "raised a wild clamor" for "foolish and cowardly action" in the isthmus. Most striking were the appearance of a few articles in the muckraker style, which reporters rarely applied to foreign affairs and which threatened to offer more effective criticism of administration policy than the usual fulminations of the opposition press.[30]

Roosevelt responded in characteristic fashion, vehemently defending his role in Panama. In a number of public statements and letters to opinion leaders, he not only protested himself innocent of wrongdoing but claimed that "all good Americans" should support his actions. He also leaked a copy of the message to Congress he had been preparing in October, which called for the seizure of the isthmus but which Roosevelt somehow contended proved his restraint and moderation in dealing with the revolution. Later, he returned to his initial defense, basing his 4 January Panama message to Congress on the justification established in his 6 November press release. By February, when the Senate voted on the new canal treaty with Panama, Roosevelt's press clippings reflected a favorable editorial opinion, and the treaty passed easily.[31]

As Roosevelt understood, however, the treaty was only the first of many difficulties facing the canal. Actual construction of the waterway would take several years to complete, and there would remain the danger that shortages of funds, renewed criticism, or flagging popular interest might cause it to be left uncompleted. Roosevelt thus continued to be concerned about the public's view of the canal; he endeavored throughout his administration to win it friendly coverage in the newspapers. In periodic press releases beginning during the summer of 1904, he spoke reassuringly about progress in the canal zone. Even this seemed insufficient, however, when construction had not begun by early 1906. Roosevelt decided then to make public, almost simultaneously, a letter from a worker in the isthmus acclaiming the great progress being made there and a report from Secretary of War William Howard Taft, detailing in several pages the architects' proposals for the canal. Once the digging was finally underway, TR continued to answer the canal's critics by releasing letters from individuals on the scene that, among other things, supported the president's promise that each American was "getting" his "money's worth in the digging of the ditch."[32]

Roosevelt's canal publicity campaign also included a presidential journey to the isthmus. A visit there by Secretary of State Elihu Root had been a great success, achieving, as Roosevelt put it, "all and more than all I dared hope" in the area of public opinion. Now the president completed his own plans for a November 1906 trip to the canal site. Nothing, as Roosevelt realized, could generate more publicity than a presidential visit, and he saw to it that the journey's arrangements provided for plenty of press coverage. Once in Panama, he further demonstrated his talent for publicity, fueling correspondents' interest with such stunts as eating with the workers and operating a steam shovel, and spread his own contagious enthusiasm for the project. At the same time, he also gathered information for his fight against the canal's opponents in the United States, information that he used effectively in his special message to Congress—and to the public—one month later. He had, or so he contended, investigated personally each of the usual charges made against the canal and found that complaints of slow or low-quality work and of poor food for the workers were all absolutely "unfounded."[33]

Ten years after the revolution, TR wrote in his autobiography that on the question of the isthmus he had "in advance discounted the clamor of those Americans who have made a fetish of disloyalty to their country." To whatever extent this was true in the making of policy, it did not prevent the president from constructing an apologia sufficiently elaborate to reach even his most virulent detractors or from continuing to labor for the canal throughout the remainder of his administration. In the long run, moreover, he succeeded in adding the canal's usefulness and feasibility to the verities of American international politics.[34]

As his Panama justification made clear, Roosevelt did not blink at using press releases to present his actions in the best possible light, even when he was compelled to shade something of the truth in order to do so. This predilection for mendacity was perhaps most apparent in the bulletins he issued at the time of his 1906 intervention in Cuba, which displayed vividly his concern for appearance at the expense of reality. By September 1906 two years of political instability had left Cuba a shambles, and American attempts to conciliate the Palma government with rebellious liberal elements had come to nothing. Roosevelt, annoyed, invoked the Platt Amendment "to intervene," as he put it, "for the maintenance of a government adequate for the protection of life, property and individual liberty" and sent United States troops to the island.[35]

In thus stating his reasons for intervention, Roosevelt was doubtless telling the truth, yet he also took great pains to make the action appear less significant than it actually was. Cuban intervention was likely to produce editorial protests, and Roosevelt telegraphed Secretary of War Taft, in charge of affairs there, that "not only for the sake of the Cubans but for the sake of meeting our opponents at home" he ought to leave "as little room for attack as possible." Taft should, Roosevelt continued, "avoid the use of the word intervention in any proclamation or paper . . . emphasizing the temporary character of the landing and the hope that our keeping sailors, marines or troops on the island will be but for a short time until a permanent government has been formed." Even more important than duration was the extent of the intervention, and Roosevelt informed his emissary that "I should like to avoid taking possession *in appearance* of the entire island if this is possible."[36]

Two days later, Roosevelt was again on the wire to Taft, giving him the final order to call in marines and to issue the previously outlined proclamation. In so doing, the president added, Taft should "if possible emphasize [the] fact that you are landing only at [Cuban President Estrada] Palma's request." Another telegram followed, stressing once again the importance of putting intervention in the proper terms. "Remember," Roosevelt warned, "that we have to do not only what is best for the island, but what we can get public sentiment in this country to support." What this meant Roosevelt had already made clear: a temporary and partial occupation by marines, not identified as an intervention and requested by President Palma. It did not matter that such a statement comprised little more than a series of half-truths; Roosevelt was concerned here only with appearance, and he knew well the ability of press releases to give the semblance of fact to impalpable falsehood.[37]

Almost a year later, Roosevelt wrote a long letter to Taft on the subject of public opinion, citing Cuba as an instance where careful public relations had succeeded in carrying "our people with us." In a somewhat pessimistic mood, the president went on to remind his secretary of war of the limits imposed on the executive by popular sentiment and to complain that it was sometimes necessary "to recognize that the convictions of the great mass of our people" are "unalterable." In extreme cases, this might limit the ability of the president to make policy. But usually, as in the case of Cuba, it required only a careful formulation of statements that, when made public in the form of handouts to the press, would give at least the impression of bending to the public's "convictions."[38]

Not all popular opinions remained unalterable, of course; these were the target of many "educational" campaigns conducted by the chief executive. For the most part, Roosevelt designed these efforts to awaken the United States to its enlarged role in world affairs, as when he issued press releases about such questions as the treatment of Jews in Russia, support for the International Red Cross, and famine relief in eastern Europe. Most important, however, was public appreciation of the instrument for enlarging America's role, and Roosevelt reserved his most concerted campaign for his efforts on behalf of the navy.[39]

Of all subjects holding the president's mercurial attention, none was treated with the kind of all-consuming passion he bestowed on the United States Navy. He worked hard for the construction of a new fleet and presented its necessity to the public in a number of speeches and press releases. He extolled the virtues of a large and powerful ocean force, employing his talent for publicity to insure construction of a first-rate fleet of battleships. "We need to educate our people slowly up to the need of the navy," he told the New York Sons of the American Revolution in 1905. "We had quite a time for several years in persuading excellent people of good intentions, but with not entirely clear minds," of the desirability of naval construction. Such people, Roosevelt realized, included many senators and congressmen, and he was determined to create public attitudes that might compel votes for his new battleships. Thus, during a December 1903 debate on naval appropriations, he issued press releases stating his desire for their increase and pointed out that the United States had more ships on paper—in the process of being built— than actually in commission. Again, under similar circumstances in 1906, he "expressed himself," according to the *Washington Star*, hopeful that "no backward step will be taken in the policy of maintaining a navy that will discourage war" and threatened, if such a step was taken, to make public a report revealing potential wartime deficiencies in the supply of naval ammunition.[40]

Roosevelt also took advantage of numerous opportunities to speak publicly on the necessity of a large navy. In one instance, he used an address at Annapolis, Maryland, on the reinterment of the remains of John Paul Jones to draw parallels between the War of 1812 and the present state of naval unpreparedness. On another occasion, in a speech delivered at the Naval War College, but directed at a larger audience, he attacked those who wished to maintain only a defensive and coastwise navy, arguing that none of America's larger policies—in Cuba, Panama, or the Philippines—could be carried out without superior naval support. And because he realized that the interior of the country was most likely to be skeptical, he made occasional speechmaking forays to the Midwest. There he argued that "the navy is not primarily of importance only to the coast regions"; it is, he continued, "every bit as much the concern of the farmer who dwells a thousand miles from sea water as of the fisherman who makes his living on the ocean, for it is the concern of every good American who knows what the meaning of the word patriotism is." President at a time of rapidly expanding national horizons, Roosevelt intended to make sure that the navy—an integral part of that expansion—did not remain a matter of purely sectional concern.[41]

No matter how convincing the president's rhetoric, there remained much to fear from bad publicity for his favorite project. This ap-

peared to Roosevelt in April 1904, when a fatal explosion during
maneuvers of the U.S.S. *Missouri* cast doubt on the safety of the
new navy. Concerned that the accident might be used against the
creation of a modern and well-trained naval force, the president
issued a press release expressing his regret over the incident and
explaining the need for target practice. "Under the conditions of
modern warfare," he argued, "in order efficiently to prepare for war,
risk must be run similar in kind, though not in degree, to the risk
run in battle; and these men have died for their country as much as
if the ship had been in action against the enemy." Although newspaper response followed the tone set in Roosevelt's bulletin, some
criticism developed, prompting him to argue, in several additional
press releases, that the navy had performed well throughout the
crisis on the *Missouri*. His efforts' effectiveness, in Roosevelt's opinion at least, was demonstrated a year later, when the president
reassured Secretary of the Navy Charles Bonaparte that there was
no reason to become "rattled" over a similar disaster.[42]

More bad publicity resulted from the case of Willard H. Brownson,
who resigned as chief of the Bureau of Navigation following a disagreement with the president. Aware that dissension in the navy's
ranks threatened to give ammunition to its critics, TR apparently
considered taking steps to suppress the issue. He quickly realized
that this would be impossible, however, and released Brownson's
resignation to the press, explaining that it had been "inadvertently
omitted" from an earlier group of correspondence. With the issue
now in the open, Roosevelt took pains to minimize its importance
and to defend his part in the dispute. And when a few journalists
persisted in making something of the affair, he castigated them
openly.[43]

On other occasions Roosevelt went beyond efforts to sidestep bad
publicity, manufacturing incidents designed to generate a favorable
press for the new navy. He did this, for example, when he requested
the Oyster Bay naval review of September 1906, which he hoped
might popularize his program of naval construction by displaying
the efficiency and progress of the fleet. Roosevelt realized, as he
wrote Elihu Root, that the naval review would probably "be the
subject of hysterical attack in many of the newspapers," but he
believed that its overall effect would prove beneficial to his public
relations campaign for the new navy. The problem, as he saw it, was
the public's lack of awareness; he therefore intended to impress the
fleet's capabilities firmly on the minds of the people.[44]

Publicity also played a part in Roosevelt's decision to send the
fleet around the world in the winter of 1907–8. Other objectives

were no less important, of course, such as his desire to demonstrate the navy's effectiveness to the Japanese and the need for training in Pacific maneuvers; yet Roosevelt contended in his autobiography, where he did not as a rule disguise his aggressiveness, that his "prime purpose was to impress the American people." He informed Lawrence Abbott of his intentions in early September 1907. He "knew," as he told Abbott, "that the best way to get American public opinion to support his policies for a strong navy was to arrest the attention and arouse the enthusiasm of the country in a dramatic fashion," and he did just that by sending the fleet into Pacific waters at a time of crisis in Japanese-American relations.[45]

The president's concern for public opinion was apparent in the manner he chose to announce the cruise, which consisted of a series of statements, leaks, and trial balloons designed to minimize its potentially sensational impact. On 1 July Roosevelt leaked news of the Pacific maneuvers to a number of reporters, who promptly wrote about it for their newspapers. On 2 July both Assistant Secretary of the Navy Truman H. Newberry and Secretary William Loeb denied the story, even though the usual reliability of the correspondents reporting it made its accuracy evident. Two days later, Loeb further muddied the waters by issuing a statement promising a long naval cruise, "possibly . . . to the Pacific" and "possibly . . . next Winter." Clearly something important was in the offing, something that Roosevelt wanted the public to get used to a little at a time, and he probably intended to announce the cruise's far eastern itinerary only after the excitement over the proposed long voyage had dissipated.[46]

This strategy was cut short, however, by an announcement on 4 July by Secretary of the Navy Victor Metcalf that a fleet of battleships would visit San Francisco during a winter practice cruise. After this untimely statement, caused by faulty communications within the administration, there remained little reason to withhold official confirmation of the fleet's movement, and Metcalf was authorized to make an additional announcement on 9 July. Still Roosevelt resisted stirring the nervous—or the jingoistic—with word of a cruise to the Far East, announcing as late as 23 August that the fleet's return route from San Francisco remained undecided.[47]

Realizing that, as he put it, "it would be an advantage to have the fleet written up," Roosevelt began in August to make plans for allowing correspondents to accompany the cruise. On 10 August, he informed Assistant Secretary of the Navy Newberry of the reasons for his decision: "The cruise around the world will be a striking thing," he wrote. "The people I hope will be interested in it, and in no way can their interest be better stimulated, with better result to the navy, than by properly writing it up." What the president desired were stories, filled with action and the taste of salt, that would allow the public to share—and identify with—the adventure of navy life. To do this would naturally require the efforts of the most skilled reporters, and Roosevelt wanted Newberry to consider who they might be. "But," the president went on, "it is absolutely essential to have men whom we can entirely trust on such a trip, and of course every article they send must be submitted to the Admiral." Aware that the news services would clamor to cover the cruise for their own purposes, TR advised Newberry to consult them on the matter but reiterated that "we will take no one of whom we do not approve."[48]

Newberry soon discovered that naval officers did not relish the idea of cluttering their ships with reporters; he thus suggested to Roosevelt that it might be best to have one "first-class man" represent all newspapers on the voyage. On first reflection the president thought this an excellent idea, probably because it would greatly facilitate the problem of controlling the content of eventual articles, and he nominated James B. Connolly, "the writer of the sea stories," for the job. Whatever its advantage, however, such a plan failed to take into account jealousies within the journalistic profession. None of the press associations was willing to see any of its competitors steal the limelight by covering the trip individually, and Roosevelt found it necessary to give up the idea of a single representative and accredit several correspondents to the battleships.[49]

The result of all this planning proved a steady flow of articles from the fleet, articles that filled newspapers and generated intense public interest in the cruise. Perhaps the most widely read of these were filed by Franklin Matthews, correspondent for the *New York Sun* wire service, who was one of few reporters to make the entire voyage. His colorful stories, carefully checked by naval officers, came close to supplying the kind of official saga of the journey that Roosevelt had envisioned, and they were published as a book in 1909. Most important to Roosevelt, of course, was a sudden swell in the navy's popularity. Writing to William Taft, he remembered the heavy criticism his plan for a Pacific cruise had engendered, commenting that public opinion was now "nearly a unit in favor of what I did." This did not surprise him. "I had the same experience in other matters," he told Henry Stoddard. "Once I acted instead of sitting around talking and pleading, I found all the support I needed." In the meantime, public awareness—and appreciation—of the navy had increased many times, due mainly to his usual combination of brash action with carefully planned publicity.[50]

As in the case of his efforts for the navy, Roosevelt generally believed in the success of his publicity campaigns. One reason for this was his care in choosing his projects; he was well aware that not even he could alter public attitudes on every question, at least in the short run. Failure to win public support would have posed a serious problem for the progressive Roosevelt, and he gave considerable thought to the constraints placed upon his freedom of action by threatened popular intransigence. In dealing with some issues, such as anti-Japanese sentiment in California, he found that the convictions of many people were "unalterable." But if public opinion might make the implementation of policy more difficult, it did not require its complete reformulation. Some instances only required a different statement of the issues; in others, more complicated public relations remained necessary. And even in the most extreme cases, where the public seemed obdurate in opposition, Roosevelt thought it possible to push an unpopular policy through without sustaining damage politically. This, then, was the heart of the progressive president's view of the relationship between public opinion and foreign policy: the people could be a help or a hindrance, depending upon the quality of the administration's public relations, but reelection never hinged on following their sentiments. Surely the electorate held no terrors for one who could write, as Roosevelt did, that "the people are always entirely capable of giving their hearty approval to two opposite policies or to men who represent diametrically opposite policies. So Maine stood heartily behind President McKinley as regards the Spanish war and the treaty of peace, and at the same time stood with equal heartiness behind Senator Hale, who was against the Spanish war and against the treaty of peace. So it is now." Holding such an attitude, and mastering available techniques for directing public sentiment, Roosevelt always remained in command of the relationship between the president and public.[51]

Chapter 4
Taft's Fate

 Inauguration Day 1909 dawned cold and stormy —a poor day to be a correspondent assigned to cover festivities in Washington. As they watched the seemingly endless line of military and political contingents pass the reviewing stand, reporters must have looked forward to the return of their usual White House duties, to the warm cordiality of gathering news from meetings with garrulous secretaries and in give-and-take with the president. So anxious were they, in fact, to hasten the return of their normal routine that a number of correspondents went directly from the parade to the executive mansion, only to discover an atmosphere there just as chilly as the blustery March winds outside. When they offered to pay their respects to the new president, the reporters learned from his secretary that Taft was not available and that they should be advised of the president's intention not to see them as often as had formerly been the rule. They could rest assured, moreover, that when and if the president wished to see them they would be summoned. To the somewhat startled newsmen, this represented a distinct, apparently intentional, lack of tact, and it indicated that their relations would be something less than ideal with the White House of William Howard Taft.[1]

Journalists had reason to expect better treatment from Taft. His past relations with the press, although marred by a desultoriness that occasionally bordered upon negligence, had always been conducted with a certain amount of cordiality. While secretary of war, he had met daily with several correspondents, providing them with half-hour conversations about the department and establishing himself as one of the more congenial members of Roosevelt's official family. Sometimes, to be sure, his efforts had betrayed a lack of understanding of the ways of reporters, as when it was necessary for an Associated Press representative to remind him to swear correspondents to secrecy before discussing a particularly sensitive subject, but nothing before in his behavior had indicated his ignorance of their normal—and all too human—sensitivities. Taft had also enjoyed a bounty of good publicity during his campaign for the presidency. As Charles Hilles later said, "he had the best press agent ever a man had" in Roosevelt, and reporters assumed he would endeavor while in office to maintain such useful contact with the press. Nevertheless, they found themselves rebuffed at the door of the presidential offices; they would have to get used to an unwilling subject in the White House.[2]

If reporters hoped that Inauguration Day confusion explained Taft's attitude, they soon learned that the problem ran much deeper. Their relations with the new president grew increasingly strained in the next few weeks. Within a month, newspapermen began to complain that Taft was purposely withholding information from them, and they warned members of the White House staff that "the press was getting very angry" with the new president. Besides advising correspondents that "the press would have to readjust itself to the new conditions,"[3] Taft's assistants seemed powerless to improve the situation. They could not convince the president that the answer to poor press relations did not lie in maintaining an even greater distance between himself and reporters. Thus, Taft compounded his problems by withdrawing even further from the limelight, until by November he could write that "I see very few newspapermen." The press responded by stepping up its criticism of what it perceived as a policy of secrecy, with the result that its relations with the White House became reciprocally worse.[4]

Even so, the situation might have been more or less tolerable had not the White House chief of staff adopted a similar attitude. With Taft determined to stay out of sight, it fell to his secretary to supply correspondents with news of his administration, and an adroit manager of the press—ex-secretary Cortelyou, for example—might have succeeded in salvaging the president's public relations. But Fred W. Carpenter, Taft's choice as secretary to the president, lacked both the tact and the appreciation of correspondents' need for news required by the job. In selecting Carpenter, Taft simply promoted his private secretary. This reflected Taft's misunderstanding of the secretary's White House duties, which had grown far more extensive than those Carpenter was prepared to perform. Reporters accordingly discovered news of the administration no more forthcoming through normal secretarial channels than directly from the president, and they soon began to look elsewhere for the information their editors required.[5]

"Elsewhere" included, for one place, the camp of Taft's enemies, and antiadministration news soon occupied a more prominent position in the newspapers. With the White House refusing to provide advance information of its plans and policies, the press frequently heard executive news first from Taft's detractors, re-creating the

kind of situation the presidential press release had been designed
to remedy in the first place. At the same time, news leaks began
to emerge from the White House. Although many of these unauthorized sources doubtless believed themselves to be assisting a
president needlessly alienating the press, others had personal—
sometimes vindictive—motives for confiding in reporters; in either
case, their information usually did the administration more harm
than good. Nevertheless, responsibility for such leaks must ultimately lodge with the president, whose nonchalance in press matters had resulted in lowered standards of confidentiality for White
House personnel and whose unwillingness to provide journalists
with information had sent them searching for less official sources.
All in all, Taft's treatment of the press caused him to lose his grasp
of the process of distributing White House news, placing control
over the president's public relations in outside hands for the first
time in a decade.[6]

The specter of his White House predecessor must have haunted
Taft's relations with the press, something pointed out by a number
of the new president's contemporaries. Taft was indeed unfortunate
to follow the president with the greatest talent of his time—perhaps
of all time—for giving reporters a good story. There can be little
doubt that Roosevelt's successor, no matter how hard he might have
tried to placate correspondents, remained destined to experience
difficulty measuring up to his predecessor's performance in the
"bully pulpit" of the White House. To the extent, at least, that no
one could have satisfied reporters, Taft received unfair treatment
from the press; yet his efforts fell so far short of the mark that he
was certain, Roosevelt or no, to draw some fire from the journalistic
profession. In choosing to limit White House contact with correspondents, Taft attempted to reverse a trend in executive press
relations antedating even the Roosevelt administration and failed
to fulfill journalistic expectations running considerably deeper than
the lively copy furnished by the White House's most recent occu-
pant. The reporters had grown, under the tutelage of McKinley and
Roosevelt in particular, to view the executive office as the chief
source of administration news, and they were understandably confused to find it suddenly a dry well. Small wonder, then, that journalistic critics accused the president of intentionally withholding
information from the press and public. They now saw the release of
White House news as automatic and could conceive of its denial as
nothing less than intentional obstruction of their efforts.[7]

Taft's difficulties with the press were also exacerbated by his disrespect for correspondents and their profession. Although even Taft was too astute politically to express openly his lack of esteem for the business of journalism, he did a poor job of hiding his feelings from White House reporters, who felt deeply the sting of presidential contempt. Arthur W. Dunn remembered one of his visits to the chief executive, when gathered newsmen, waiting for an interview with Taft, heard him snarl to Secretary Carpenter: "Must I see those men again! Didn't I see them just the other day!" By the time Carpenter ushered reporters into the president's presence, Taft was all courtesy and smiles, but for them at least the damage was already done. The cost of such behavior for Taft's press relations was best expressed by Dunn's own action. He had come to the president's summer home to gather information for an article on Taft's accomplishments during six months in office, but he decided, after his experience there, to write nothing at all.[8]

A number of other factors also contributed to Taft's failure to make better use of the press. For one thing, he seemed incapable of expressing himself interestingly, couching his public utterances in what one correspondent described as "a stodgy and soggy style" and betraying in nearly every statement severe difficulties with the written and spoken word. Taft's infelicity with language cost him the interest of reporters, who were naturally drawn to the makers of apt phrases; it also convinced him of the futility of trying to use the press as a national sounding board for his ideas. "I have not," he wrote Roosevelt on 21 March 1909, "the facility for educating the public as you had through talks with the correspondents," and he could see nothing, he said, to be gained from trying to do so.[9]

Another factor was Taft's reticent personality, which left him temperamentally unsuited for dealing with correspondents. As he informed William Allen White at the outset of his administration, "I am not constituted as Mr. Roosevelt is in being able to keep the country advised every few days of the continuance of the state of mind. . . . It is a difference in temperament." He could not keep the press and public informed, moreover, because he had no clear understanding of what constituted a good story. Lacking what reporters call a nose for news, the president was incapable of supplying White House newsgatherers with any quantity of usable material. This weakness appeared early in 1909 to Archie Butt, who noted that "neither the President nor his secretary gives out anything of real interest, nor do they understand the art of giving out news." This was not necessarily permanent: a more gregarious president might have learned the needs of reporters—he would certainly have established more contact with them—but Taft's taciturnity prevented any significant improvement in his personal understanding of the press.[10]

Taft's press relations were also crippled by his indolence, by what he described as his "indisposition to labor as hard as I might; a disposition to procrastinate." Slow-moving, weighed down by his 300 pounds, Taft seemed always to be behind in his work, causing Archie Butt to conclude that the president was likely to "be about three years behind when the fourth of March, 1913, rolls around" and Taft himself to comment to his aide that "it seems to me I will never catch up with my work, . . . there is so much to be done and so little time to do it in that I feel discouraged." Still, the burdens of office piled up daily. Taft could find few moments to spare for correspondents, and he instructed his secretary to limit his time in their company to a minimum.[11]

Most important, however, in shaping Taft's press relations was his interpretation of the office he held—what a recent historian has termed his "Conservative's Conception of the Presidency." Responding in part to requirements posed by an expanded foreign policy, McKinley and Roosevelt had greatly enhanced the power of the chief executive, including his ability to influence press and public. But Taft, although sharing his predecessors' interest in expansion, disapproved of their increasing presidential authority; he expressed this conservatism, among other ways, in his relations with White House correspondents. Here, as elsewhere, Taft's essentially pre-progressive notions of presidential conduct hampered his attempts to implement his policies and added to the woes of his already beleaguered administration.[12]

Although contending that "no one has a higher admiration than I" for Roosevelt's use of "his power to influence public opinion," Taft found his own limited conception of the presidency precluded his use of similar authority. In *Our Chief Magistrate and His Powers*, a series of lectures (later published) that caught the spirit of his presidency, Taft argued for a strict construction of presidential power, emphasizing its limitations rather than the opportunities it offered. Proclaiming "unsafe" the doctrine of an "undefined residuum" of presidential authority, he offered a definition of the presidency resembling Grover Cleveland's. This doubtless had an effect upon the president's willingness to influence press and public opinion. For Taft, there was always something unsavory, perhaps undemocratic, about the utilization of strenuous efforts to control the public; no wonder he developed a public relations approach that can only be described as laissez-faire.[13]

At the heart of the traditional conception of public opinion lay the notion that it would somehow take care of itself. As Taft wrote William Allen White early in his administration, "I have confidence in the second judgment of the people based on what is done rather than what is proclaimed or what is suspected from appearances." Public relations, for Taft, did not require the controlling influence of the executive to insure approval of wise policies, because, as he put it, "I have a profound faith in the people. Their final judgment will be right." Although it goes without saying that Taft was not the first—or last—president to declare his faith in the ultimate wisdom of the people, for such is one of the verities of democratic politics, Taft was unusual in behaving as if he actually believed it to be true.[14]

Taft thus chose to let his accomplishments speak for themselves. Even if, as seemed likely, such a policy resulted in poor publicity for his administration, Taft remained determined to eschew "any forced or manufactured sentiment in my favor" and "to wait for time and the result of my labors to vindicate me naturally."[15] As a president whose views of the office antedated the progressive reconstruction of its powers, Taft perceived an unnatural quality in the kind of press relations that facilitated management of public opinion; he had, as Archie Butt put it, "no conception of the press as an adjunct of his office."[16] When his few journalist friends commented, predictably, that his disregard for public relations was damaging his administration, Taft responded acidly, writing J. W. Pierce of the *Weekly Clintonian* (Iowa) that "I am anxious to point to things done, not to exploit with egotistic trumpet what I propose to do," and R. L. O'Brien of the *Boston Evening Transcript* that "I have an abiding faith that if I could get things done the credit would take care of itself ultimately."[17] He steadfastly rejected any suggestion "to set myself right before the people in any different way from that which is involved in the ordinary publication of what is done." For Taft, only this represented a legitimate use of presidential power over press and public opinion; he could, in good conscience, do nothing more.[18]

The result of Taft's fastidiousness was to return White House newsgathering to the ways of the nineteenth century. As usual, the perceptive Archie Butt took measure of the situation, writing that now "the papers print news as they hear it," rather than "in accord with the wishes of the President or his secretary." By setting aside established techniques for controlling White House correspondents, Taft surrendered much of his ability to influence press and public and made it nearly impossible to win support for his policies. There were, as he soon discovered, many disadvantages to the conduct of public relations in accordance with the principles of laissez-faire, but most important, and probably most galling for Taft, was the obvious fact that both press and public opinion now expected to be led.[19]

Faced with increasing criticism of his administrative style and, perhaps more important, with heavy Republican losses in the elections of 1910, Taft at last began to reassess his position on relations with the press and the electorate. He thus permitted the publication of two long magazine interviews, which he hoped would supply his policies with the kind of favorable publicity they so badly needed. Also, in order to focus more public attention on White House legislative proposals, he started in late 1911 to write "one-subject" messages to Congress, supplementing his long and dull annual messages with what Butt termed the "homeopathic" (small-dose) method of public relations. At the same time, Taft began reading his messages aloud to the cabinet and asking for contributions to lend vitality to his prose. "They are looking for political slogans, so the President told me yesterday," wrote Butt, "epigrams, so to speak, that the country can take hold of and repeat." What the president needed, according to Secretary of War Henry Stimson, who had learned the secrets of publicity from Roosevelt, were "catch phrases," a fact Taft seemed finally to have grasped.[20]

During 1912, Taft also showed an increased appreciation of the newspapers' role in influencing public attitudes. In March, he urged his brother Charles to go ahead with plans to buy a part interest in the *Washington Post*, explaining that he could "conceive that the paper properly managed would be a tremendous instrument for the formulation of public opinion the country over." Six months later, he ordered the executive departments to finish preparing their daily news items by noon, insuring their publication in the evening papers and making easier the duties of Washington correspondents. Still, Taft remained personally unable to warm up to the White House news corps, with the result that his efforts produced only a minor thaw in presidential press relations.[21]

In another attempt to mollify reporters, Taft decided to replace Fred W. Carpenter, his much criticized presidential secretary, with a man more skilled in handling the press. He chose Assistant Secretary of the Treasury Charles D. Norton for the White House job of rejuvenating the administration's press relations. Before accepting Taft's offer, Norton contacted several reporters "to get," as he told one of them, "a newspaperman's ideas as to what the secretaryship to the President should be" and learned that the best secretaries had occupied a place similar to that of "assistant to the President." Not only, he discovered, did such a position allow the secretary to carry out his traditional duties more expeditiously; it also supplied him with the authority needed for dealing effectively with White House correspondents. Determined to avoid the traps that had ensnared Carpenter, Norton took the White House post understanding he would have the kind of status Cortelyou and Loeb had found necessary to do the job properly.[22]

This change bore fruit quickly. With Norton in Taft's anteroom, "there was," according to Oscar Davis, "an immediate and distinct improvement in the relations between the President and the newspaper men." It soon became apparent, however, that Norton lacked his successful predecessors' knack for handling diverse personalities, with the result that his activities—and intrigues—as "assistant president" came to appear increasingly heavy-handed to other administration officials. For Taft, the cabinet disruptions triggered by Norton's accumulation of power were not worth an improvement in White House press relations, and after warning his secretary that he was swimming in deep waters, Taft asked him to resign in September 1911. As Norton would doubtless have testified, the office of secretary to the president had become an extremely difficult one, requiring both great authority and the discretion to use it judiciously.[23]

Disappointed with the outcome of Norton's tenure as secretary, Taft looked for a replacement who would return the office to its former tranquillity. He found him in Charles D. Hilles, another Treasury assistant. Because Hilles did not share the unfortunate Norton's ambitions, he managed to avoid running afoul of the president's other advisers, only to learn that his diminished stature weakened his influence with White House reporters. To his dismay, Hilles found himself hung on the other horn of Norton's dilemma, without the authority to perform his tasks properly. Nevertheless, many White House correspondents believed him to be a good presidential secretary, probably because he displayed a genuine desire to assist them in gathering news, and were sorry to see him resign after serving one year. To fill the office for the few months remaining in his administration, Taft appointed Carmi Thompson, who did generally better than any of his predecessors. Although in four years Taft employed four secretaries, he failed, for all his searching, to find the one man capable of supplying his policies with just the right kind of publicity, a fact that reflected, above all else, his own insufficient understanding of the job.[24]

If Taft's conception of the secretary's office remained basically anachronistic, it did not prevent him from at least considering a significant—and forward-looking—change in its composition. Beginning in September 1910, Secretary Norton conducted a widespread search for a public relations expert. He sought someone familiar with the ways of the press and with current techniques for influencing public attitudes; he wanted him to take over White House publicity duties as a kind of presidential press secretary. Responding to Norton's inquiry, Lafayette Young of the *Des Moines Capital* explained the problem as he understood it: "President Taft has done a tremendous work for good and . . . the public has not been informed about it. President Taft has no taste for blowing his own bugle. He could not call the newspaper men in and give them a breezy account of his own doings." The administration must therefore work behind the scenes to win publicity, "to get into print on all proper occasions," as Young put it, by giving out information that "ought to be prepared by some one and then should properly pass through your hands to the press." This task could be accomplished, Young went on, by hiring a press or publicity agent to serve on the White House staff, but there would remain the danger that "he might get his foot in it." A good choice, he concluded, would be a newspaperman; the best would be a country journalist, because such men knew more about the people than their urban counterparts.[25]

What stands out most strikingly in replies made by Young and others to Norton's inquiry is their sophistication: to implement their proposals would have required nothing less than the complete modernization of White House press relations. Young, for example, used modern terminology in pointing out that "Taft ought to be built up as a separate personality apart from his predecessor," as did Lucius E. Wilson in arguing that "the President, himself, must frequently *create* news." "It should be somebody's business," Wilson added, "to seek out the unusual features in the President's daily work and put them in shape for 'feature stories.' Even unfriendly newspapers would have to print this material because competition would compel it." In presenting his policies, the president must take pains to have his views repeated, because, as Wilson put it, "in other words, public opinion is shaped by constant hammering."[26]

An anonymous adviser even suggested the creation of a publicity bureau, which he saw concentrating on the dissemination of news stories. "The day of the editorial as an influence has passed," he argued in Rooseveltian terms. "Newspaper readers digest the news columns and 'think for themselves.' Effective publicity work must be done through the news columns." Discussing the organization of such a bureau, he commented that newspapers should be divided by geographical area, by type, and by time of publication and that the staff should know which papers would take anything and which only a certain amount of "stuff." By opening the door to suggestions of this type, Norton put the White House in contact with the most advanced public relations theories of the time, theories that, not surprisingly, found little acceptance in the administration of William Howard Taft.[27]

As it happened, in fact, the journalists' most innovative proposals fell victim to White House veto even before they reached the president, killed by a staff memorandum on the subject of publicity by "W.L.S." Although the writer (whoever he was) agreed with Young on the need for better executive press relations, he disagreed on the techniques that could most profitably be employed for their improvement. News stories should not, he contended, be supplied directly by the White House; this came off as merely condescending. Reporters should not be sent for but ought to come to the White House looking for stories on their own initiative. What was needed, he concluded, was to treat the press with a little more cordiality, as if correspondents were welcomed guests in the presidential offices. Their requests for information should be answered courteously and promptly, because it must not be forgotten that "the element of time is much to a journalist," and they should be given whatever useful material the White House can supply. These tasks could be performed most advantageously, he added, by the president's secretary; it would be unwise to hire a "theatrical" press agent, who might serve only to alienate reporters. In so arguing, the writer took what had become a conservative position on the question of publicity, calling basically for Taft to establish the kind of press relations characteristic of the two previous administrations. Predictably, Taft concurred in this decision and forfeited his best opportunity for adding potency to his halting relations with press and public.[28]

While the White House was ruling out novel techniques, things were changing somewhat more rapidly at the State Department. For State, Taft's first years in office were a time of exhilarating— and sometimes bewildering—innovation, as a long-overdue program of reorganization got underway. Based partly on the British model, the new system allowed increased specialization within the department by creating several new divisions and enhanced its efficiency in dealing with, among other things, press and public opinion. The need for improving departmental public relations was best expressed by Francis M. Huntington Wilson, the reorganization's chief exponent and architect. In an article for the 3 March 1906 edition of the *Outlook*, he labeled the lack of "constituted channels of communication for keeping Congress and the foreign office in sympathetic touch" one of the glaring deficiencies of the American system. As remedy, Huntington Wilson included improved procedures for influencing the press and public in the reform plan he submitted later in the year, and they became an integral part of the department's reorganization during the Taft administration.[29]

Huntington Wilson won the opportunity to implement his ideas when Taft's secretary of state, Philander Knox, appointed him to the second-ranking post in the department. Although a shortage of funds forestalled immediate action, the new first assistant secretary managed to carry through his program in the fall. At that time, he organized the Division of Information, designed to supply the department with what he termed "channels of communication" running in a number of directions. To this end, the division published a series of pamphlets known as the Information Series, which distributed dispatches, treaties, and other pertinent information to the department's embassies and legations throughout the world. In addition, it wrote digests of current foreign and domestic publications of interest to diplomats, drew up summaries of the latest views of political or economic importance, and supervised preparation of annual *Foreign Relations* volumes.[30]

Officially, the division's most important function remained dissemination of information within the department, suggesting to one historian that Huntington Wilson equated information with intelligence in its conception. In practice, however, "information" appears to have been taken in a somewhat broader context, as the division concerned itself with more general questions of departmental public relations. For one thing, documents published in the *Foreign Relations* series, although not meant for mass consumption, were intended for an audience considerably larger than the department itself. For another, the Information Series included, besides confidential pamphlets detailing departmental business, a sequence of booklets that constituted a public record of official pronouncements on foreign affairs. And finally, Huntington Wilson and Knox selected a public relations man as chief of the division. This was Philip H. Patchin, a well-known newspaperman who had served for a number of years as Washington correspondent of the *New York Sun* and who was highly skilled in the art of disseminating information. He soon served the entire department as unofficial adviser on matters pertaining to relations with press and public. Outside as well as inside regular channels, then, the Division of Information's primary objective remained fostering increased awareness of programs and activities of the State Department, an objective that reflected Huntington Wilson's personal concern for improved public relations.[31]

Another sign of this concern was Huntington Wilson's creation of the department's new Political Committee, which met at least weekly to discuss the political impact of foreign affairs, to approve the *Foreign Relations* volumes, and "to determine the attitude towards the press on important matters." Through this agency, Huntington Wilson hoped to alert the department's top officials to the importance of public relations and to enlist their help in handling the press and public.[32]

Huntington Wilson also played an important personal role in the department's ongoing relations with the press. As first assistant secretary, he composed and distributed the department's press releases; he also met the correspondents on a regular basis. Twice daily, at 10:30 A.M. and 3:30 P.M., he ushered Washington reporters into his office, where, as he wrote Henry Brown of the *New York Herald*, he was "always prepared to receive any special and individual inquiry immediately after the general meeting with the representatives of the press." In this way, he greatly increased the department's official contact with the press and enhanced its influence over what was published, producing changes that, as he was certainly aware, brought State into line with improved techniques developed earlier in the office of secretary to the president.[33]

Like almost everyone else, however, Huntington Wilson noticed that public relations were not the particular forte of the Taft White House, and he took it upon himself to send the president a memorandum about handling public opinion in foreign affairs. There had been, he noted in early 1910, an increase in the public's interest in diplomacy, which he attributed to expanded American international activity. Because this development had occurred "somewhat suddenly," it presented "a task new to a large section of our press"; he believed this was responsible for editorial unwillingness to cooperate. The European press, he added, had been long aware that what they wrote affected their nation's endeavors; American failures in this realm were largely the result of what he called "the newness of the task." The problem, as Huntington Wilson saw it, was that, although "the Department of State is always prepared to give to editors and journalists who desire to write thoughtfully and conscientiously all the information necessary to make intelligible the broad lines of the foreign policy of this Government," too few newsmen took advantage of the opportunity. A majority of newspapers—"the moulders of public opinion"—consequently based editorial interpretation on considerations other than the facts. One of these was partisanship, the effect of which was, he thought, "almost negligible because its animus is universally recognized"; another was the "systematic propaganda" of business interests slighted by administration policy. In either case, the administration had no recourse beyond continuing its current campaign of public education, combined with efforts to increase journalists' awareness of their responsibility for "moulding" public opinion in foreign affairs.[34]

For all his perspicacity, Huntington Wilson never did foster good relations with the press, partly because of what his colleagues at the department noted as superciliousness in his character. In responding to correspondents' complaints of mistreatment, for example, he blamed the journalists themselves for pursuing their efforts with insufficient ardor, "for it has been my aim," he advised one of them, "to arrange the giving out of such news as we have in the manner most convenient to all concerned." Predictably, reporters found his all-too-common flights of umbrage intolerable, and many chafed at his frequently sarcastic responses to their serious questions.[35]

Also preventing good departmental press relations was the secretary of state's own lack of understanding of correspondents. Reticent in the extreme, Knox never seemed to warm up to reporters; he thus enjoyed little success in turning their efforts to the department's advantage. And when this produced—predictably—criticism of State and its policies, the secretary could only respond with vitriol: "the reason the newspapers attack our foreign policies so frequently and violently," he noted, "is because they make it a point to attack whatever they don't understand." To make things worse, Knox intensified this conflict by his usual technique for handling reporters' questions. As a rule, he refused to comment on information the press received elsewhere until after it was published, whereupon he denied it acidly. Such behavior seemed destined to provoke misunderstanding, and Knox demonstrated little desire to alleviate its ill effect on the department's burgeoning relations with the press.[36]

Knox's neglect appeared most evident in early 1912, when he failed to include correspondents in his plans for an official visit to Central America. In a collective letter to the secretary of state dated 3 March 1912, a number of reporters requested what they considered routine advance information about Knox's itinerary, as well as advance copies of the secretary's proposed speeches and background information on special problems and objectives for each stop. Also, in order to avoid taking too much of the secretary's time, the journalists offered to meet him as a group to cover the important points of his journey. The correspondents closed on a didactic note, informing Knox that their only purpose was to give his work the "utmost publicity," a goal they could not hope to achieve without his assistance and cooperation. As the reporters' comments illuminated, releasing this type of information had been standard procedure for presidential trips since the time of McKinley, and the Department of State, despite the efforts of Huntington Wilson, continued to lag well behind the White House in this area.[37]

Although this gap closed somewhat during the Taft years, it did not signify an immediate improvement in the administration's handling of public opinion. On the contrary, because the White House had traditionally carried most of the burden in these matters, Taft's failure to establish good press relations resulted in a serious deterioration of the executive's ability to influence the electorate. This corrosion was evident in the treatment of a number of foreign policy issues, including "dollar diplomacy," arbitration treaties, and troubled relations with Mexico; it soon posed a difficult problem for both State Department and White House officials.

Dollar diplomacy, as practiced in China and Latin America, represented Taft's most innovative foreign policy. It attempted, through the offices of the State Department, to replace military might with commercial strength—America's long suit—as the arbiter of international questions and to enhance the position of the United States in world affairs. As such, and because its linking of official and business interests was certain to draw considerable fire, it deserved the administration's best publicity efforts. Yet this proved hardly to be the case.[38]

So feebly, in fact, did the administration attempt to influence public opinion on the question of dollar diplomacy that it even allowed its opponents to supply the policy's name, thus committing a public relations error of an enormity unthinkable in either the McKinley or Roosevelt administrations. Much of Taft's difficulty over dollar diplomacy was attributable to the derogatory connotations of the term, which, as Huntington Wilson put it, was first "applied as an epithet by a hostile newspaper man." As president, Taft was in a position to supply his policy with a positive name and interpretation; a more skillful practitioner of the art of public relations would certainly have done so, repeating, for quotation, his own descriptive phrases and finessing the connection between capital and foreign policy that his endeavors entailed. But nothing of this sort could be expected from Taft. He was aware, as he announced, that to "call a particular piece of statecraft 'dollar diplomacy' is to invoke the condemnation of muckraking journals, whose chief capital is in the use of phrases of a lurid character," but he made no effort to suppress use of the term. By early 1911, moreover, the

White House's inability to control the State Department had made the situation worse; both Knox and Huntington Wilson began to employ the phrase in their own remarks. On 4 May, for example, the assistant secretary described dollar diplomacy to the Third National Peace Conference as a way of pursuing peace in the world. "It means," he concluded, "the substitution of dollars for bullets." During the following eighteen months the phrase appeared often in State Department explanations, until by December 1912 Taft himself surrendered to the epithet and used the term in his last annual message to Congress.[39]

It is of interest to speculate why State Department officials accepted so readily this controversial term. In the case of Knox, this acceptance may be set down to innocence of public relations techniques, but the case of Huntington Wilson is somewhat more complicated. Perhaps he fell prey to his own arrogance, believing that he could prove his sharpness by turning the correspondents' phrase to the department's advantage. Or perhaps, as he later claimed, the phrase simply "gained such currency that it was more or less adopted." Either way, Huntington Wilson should have known better; no amount of cleverness or "currency" could counteract the negative impression given by the words "dollar diplomacy"—only another term could do that. By failing to develop another phrase, and by finally accepting "dollar diplomacy" to describe its efforts, the Taft administration allowed public attention to focus upon the most vulnerable element of its policy—its connection with Wall Street.[40]

A similar public relations failure accompanied Taft's efforts on behalf of the English and French arbitration treaties, the fruits of another of his administration's most advanced foreign policies. By including in the new agreements the arbitration of such formerly nonjusticiable issues as those concerning national honor, the president enhanced the utility of the earlier Root treaties—and incurred the inevitable rancor of a Senate jealous to protect its own foreign relations prerogatives. As a result, Taft could be certain of a stiff Senate battle over ratification, and he needed all the public support he could command for approval. He began, uncharacteristically enough, in good fashion, delivering in March 1910 a stunning speech to the American Arbitration and Peace League in New York, in which he declared that he did not "see any more reason why matters of national honor should not be referred to a court of arbitration anymore than matters of property or national proprietorship." To Taft's surprise, he saw his words praised by both press and public groups; he remarked later that "never in my experience was there such a unanimous expression of earnest interest in carrying out the proposal, and such fervent hope for a successful issue in the matter." But as soon became apparent, Taft did not know how to expand upon the interest thus generated; he spent the next year seemingly content to watch his public support dwindle and disappear.[41]

Taft's handling of the treaties illustrated his usual approach to problems of public relations. In April 1911 he informed Archie Butt of his reasons for failing to follow up his initial success. "I am not hunting this bird with a brass band," he told his aide. "I would rather the country should get aroused for it without my leadership, if this can be done." As the president should have known, however, his leadership was exactly what the public required to "get aroused" for the treaties; his unwillingness to supply it accounted for the public's flagging interest in arbitration. By adopting what might be termed a noninterventionist attitude toward public opinion, an attitude in eclipse since the days of Cleveland, Taft insured public obscurity and eventual defeat for more than one administration objective.[42]

The techniques Taft approved also reveal much about his ineptitude in the conduct of public relations. In late summer 1911, just after the treaties had been signed, Butt noted that Taft went to hear Dr. Randolph McKim preach on the subject of their propriety, adding that "of course the President is anxious to encourage this sort of thing." Such encouragement might have been useful, certainly, but in the absence of Taft's own efforts to win public support for the treaties, it represented an approach that was hopelessly naive and old-fashioned. Even when modern techniques were implemented, moreover, desultory application sacrificed much of their utility. Describing the 3 August 1911 signing of the treaty with England, for example, Butt commented that "there were a lot of correspondents turned into the room at the last minute with a view of giving as much publicity to the signing as possible." Butt's phrase "at the last minute" reflects both a lack of advanced planning and the president's unwillingness to allow correspondents to see the actual signing of the documents. By inviting them only for the handshaking aftermath, Taft failed to take full advantage of newspaper coverage and probably piqued as many reporters as he pacified.[43]

With the treaties about to come up for Senate consideration, Taft decided to make them the object of a speaking tour across the country. Determined, as he later wrote William Jennings Bryan, not to see the treaties defeated "without a whimper" on his part, the president arranged to deliver a number of major addresses in hopes of bringing public pressure to bear upon recalcitrant senators. Going to the people was not Taft's usual style, of course, but he recognized—

too late, as it turned out—that the treaties were doomed unless he took strong action. Traveling as far west as California, he sang the praises of arbitration as surety against unnecessary wars and assailed the argument that the treaties would dispossess the Senate of its constitutional powers in foreign relations. Taft's meager rhetorical skills proved insufficient to the task, however; his efforts seemed to meet with nothing so much as public indifference. Had he managed a more consistent campaign for public support, Taft's last-ditch speaking tour might have made some impact, but, as it was, the arbitration treaties, which Taft once described as "the great jewel of my administration," were clearly headed for defeat.[44]

Taft's failure to mobilize the public on this occasion was all the more remarkable for his realization that, as he wrote Theodore Marburg of the American Society for the Judicial Settlement of International Disputes, the movement to end war could only be made effective through the creation of an "aroused" public. Such reasoning was not original with Taft, of course; it had appeared variously in the platforms of all major peace societies and in the writings of such prominent figures as Andrew Carnegie. But the president's acceptance of this logic should have informed him of the need for leading public opinion. Any such connection was apparently missed by Taft, however, and the arbitration treaties received no more sustained publicity than his administration's other foreign policies.[45]

That these efforts were insufficient became all too obvious in early 1911, when the Taft administration tottered on the brink of intervention in the Mexican Civil War. This delicate situation presented Taft with what was probably his most difficult hour in the White House and brought home to him the fruits of two years' neglect of the press.

Intervention became an issue when the president ordered the army to mobilize 20,000 men on the Mexican border. Fearing for the lives and property of Americans, Taft acted hastily, failing even to consult the State Department. He also neglected to take the White House press corps into his confidence. Something had to be said about the movement of so many troops, however, and the president decided to dissemble, instructing his secretary to release a statement implying that the army had moved to the border solely to conduct spring maneuvers. Any connection between their location and the current unrest in Mexico, he suggested, was nothing more than coincidental.[46]

It is unlikely that the press would have accepted such an explanation from any president, but coming from Taft it produced immediate editorial disbelief. A more astute handler of newsmen—Roosevelt, for example—might have briefed them confidentially on the reasons for mobilization and explained the need for secrecy; he would certainly have offered them a story about the troop movement that reporters could have repeated without demeaning themselves. For failing to do either, Taft met a chorus of newspaper criticism, scoring him, among other things, for an invasion of Mexico that he had no intention of conducting. Only when details about the troops and their equipment were published did Taft recognize his error, and he announced—more convincingly, if still short of the truth— that their real purpose was to prevent filibustering and smuggling of contraband across the border.[47]

Even this account did not silence newspaper talk of intervention, however, and Taft soon found it necessary to embellish his explanation. On 12 March, six days after ordering mobilization, he dispatched a letter to General Leonard Wood designed to supply background information to leaders of public opinion. Circulated— for information, not publication—among a number of prominent newspaper editors, the letter represented an attempt to calm fears of aggressive presidential action. After describing the "assumption by the press that I contemplate intervention on Mexican soil" as "gratuitous," Taft assured all readers that he doubted "whether I have such authority under any circumstances, and if I had I would not exercise it without express congressional approval." Thus, he concluded, he had only mobilized troops so that, "if Congress shall direct that they enter Mexico to save American lives and property, an effective movement may be promptly made." This was largely eyewash. Taft had not been so fastidious about congressonal consent in authorizing a number of other interventions in Latin America; nor did the argument appear in explanations designed strictly for private consumption. But it provided the president with an explanation that convinced the editors of his honorable intentions.[48]

So successful did Taft find this technique, in fact, that he then wrote background letters to individual editors. In a note to Talcott Williams of the *Philadelphia Ledger*, he attempted, as he put it, "to possess you of the facts by giving you some light to enable you to take such editorial course as you think wise." Admitting use of a ruse to cover the recent mobilization, he argued that his real motives, were they made public, might have been misunderstood by the Mexicans. He also took a turn at guiding editorial opinion, telling Williams what he perceived as the military usefulness of the troops: to frighten the Mexicans into regarding American rights and citizens seriously. In letters of this type Taft was doing his utmost for his Mexican policy. But although his efforts showed some results, they could not overcome the almost total disorganization of his administration's long-run relations with the press.[49]

The extent of this disorganization was evident in a letter from Huntington Wilson to Knox dated 10 March 1911. On that date, four days after mobilization, the assistant secretary of state "asked the President whether there was any particular point of view he wished encouraged on the part of the press in regard to the maneuvers, etc." only to discover there was not, "except that the theory of maneuvers, as one element, was to be insisted upon." By this time, Taft was already backing away from the maneuvers explanation, yet when asked—and it is important that he had to be asked—he instructed the State Department to continue placing that construction upon mobilization. Huntington Wilson noticed that the president was floundering. He noted that "simply from the point of view of the President's own interests, I have personally felt some anxiety lest the press should fail promptly to shake down into a logical attitude toward the maneuvers and their bearings," concluding that "I, myself, believe it would have been better to make no bones of it." Taft was considering just this, of course, but his administration's handling of press and public opinion was in such disarray that the question had not even been discussed with the State Department.[50]

Taft had discovered a useful argument, however, in deferring to Congress's war-making power on the question of Mexican intervention. Not only did it reassure editors fearing precipitous action on his part; it also restrained those pressing for intervention in the civil strife that wracked Mexico during the next two years. This pressure grew intense after April 1911, when disorders resulted in the deaths of two Americans in Douglas, Arizona, just north of the border. In response to subsequent interventionist demands, Taft issued a moderate statement, describing the situation with Mexico as one that required the restraint of all American citizens and reiterating his intention to take no action without prior congressional approval. In coming months, he would return often to this argument, fending off interventionist pressure from Democratic critics as well as Republican advisers worried about former president Roosevelt's interest in the issue. It proved to be his most valuable contribution to the molding of public opinion on Mexico.[51]

When the autumn of 1911 brought relative tranquillity, Taft attempted to defuse the Mexican issue by directing Secretary of War Stimson to withdraw most of the troops. Peace turned out to be short-lived, however; a new outbreak of violence in February 1912 caused

Taft to instruct Stimson once again to "increase the guard along the border, as quietly as possible, to such strength as will amply insure the protection of American citizens and their interests." Realizing that even a troop movement accomplished, as he put it, "as quietly as possible" would not pass unnoticed, Taft ordered his secretary to prepare a public explanation. This statement, issued orally by Secretary Hilles on 24 February, informed reporters that the soldiers had been transferred "in order to readjust and redistribute the troops along the border." Hilles's announcement, no matter how disingenuous, seemed at least plausible and suggested that Taft was finally beginning to understand something about public relations.[52]

Still, the president did not receive the kind of cooperation his new sensibilities should have provoked, probably because he had failed for too long to cultivate newspaper support. He also continued to be plagued by his administration's characteristic lack of coordination, which resulted in much teeth gnashing among his top advisers. As early as 1910, the State Department's Hugh Gibson had submitted a memorandum complaining of unauthorized dissemination of news by officials in the Navy and War departments. Citing several examples in which State had been embarrassed by this "leakage of information," Gibson charged that no absolute control existed over statements released by the service departments. He argued strongly for tighter centralization of administration press relations. Now, fifteen months later, Huntington Wilson contended that this same problem was partly responsible for Taft's Mexican difficulty, citing at least one bellicose army colonel who had granted an inflammatory newspaper interview. The solution, as the assistant secretary saw it, was to exercise closer control over administration statements. This was a solution that Taft seemed powerless to supply.[53]

Unable to police his own administration, Taft remained surprisingly intolerant of remarks by private citizens who, he believed, were adding to American difficulties in Mexico. He hoped to halt incendiary statements appearing in some newspapers and queried Attorney General George Wickersham about the possibility of taking legal action against offenders. No matter how much he wished to help, Wickersham replied, there were no statutes against this type of activity. "The mere use of intemperate language is not dealt with in Federal law," he continued. Nothing came of this idea, although Taft had introduced an issue that would loom much larger during Woodrow Wilson's years in the White House.[54]

That Taft never understood the need to coordinate his administration's public relations became apparent in February 1913, when unsettled conditions brought about by the Huerta coup in Mexico once again caused him to reinforce units patrolling the border. As if forgetting the price he had paid for it before, the now lame-duck president repeated his previous error of neglecting to consult, or even to inform, the State Department, leaving its spokesmen again unable to respond to correspondents' questions. Huntington Wilson, who learned first of Taft's decision through unofficial channels, felt compelled to petition the president for "authority to inform [the] press today that [the] movement of troops from Omaha to Galveston" represented no policy change. Taft granted this permission but ordered his own secretary to preempt the State Department by issuing, on the same day, a statement describing the movement as simply part of a long-term plan to strengthen the Galveston garrison. Huntington Wilson knew nothing of this explanation, and when, as probably happened, he heard it first from a reporter, he had little reason to wonder at the administration's low credibility.[55]

No matter how bad his handling of the press might have been, however, Taft managed to resist its pressure for intervention in Mexican affairs. His failure to cultivate better relations with White House correspondents made this resistance more difficult, but it did not make it impossible, at least not by 1913. Relying on the kind of obtrusive public relations techniques put out of fashion by McKinley's administration, he demonstrated them to be, on selected issues anyway, still capable of winning support. This seemed to be sufficient for Taft, who displayed even less anxiety over public opinion than his predecessors. As he told Archie Butt early in the Mexican imbroglio, he "would make no explanation of his act until compelled to do so" and would wait until "the people got good and ready for an explanation" before giving it to them. Such remarks betrayed more than reticence about action; they also reflected his belief that the public did not need to be informed. Thus, conservatism in the White House seemed to cut both ways: it aroused Taft's scruples against certain aspects of progressive management but prevented him from taking the public's wishes any more seriously.[56]

Chapter 5
Wilson Meets the Press

With Woodrow Wilson, progressivism returned to the White House, bringing renewed interest in presidential management of press and public opinion. Like Theodore Roosevelt, Wilson believed that democratic government required a strong chief executive, an opinion he had, indeed, formed while watching his progressive predecessor in action; and he too perceived directing public opinion as the hallmark of presidential leadership. The president, Wilson wrote in 1908, is "the political leader of the nation, or has it in his choice to be. The nation as a whole has chosen him, and is conscious that it has no other political spokesman. He is the only national voice in affairs." This assigned the president a great responsibility: only he could create a united public. But it also provided him with immense opportunity. "Let him once," Wilson continued, "win the admiration and confidence of the country, and no other single force can withstand him, no combination of forces will easily overpower him." He also noted that this was Taft's failure. "The American people are disappointed because he has not led them," he wrote in 1910; they "long for someone to put the pressure of the opinion of all the people of the United States upon Congress." Holding such views, the new president seemed destined to seek techniques for enlarging his influence with the press and public; no wonder that his administration produced revolutionary changes in executive handling of public relations.[1]

By the time of his election, Wilson already displayed an understanding of the executive's influence over public opinion; he also showed a willingness to turn it to his own advantage. First while president of Princeton University and later while governor of New Jersey, he had appealed controversial issues directly to the people, calling for a popular mandate to insure his policies' success. He had also demonstrated an appreciation for less direct public relations techniques, maintaining an open door to statehouse correspondents who publicized his proposals. These two—public appeals and press relations—remained the chief weapons in the president's publicity arsenal, and Wilson came to Washington determined to employ them both.[2]

To help him do so, Wilson appointed Joseph P. Tumulty secretary to the president, the White House position most intimately concerned with public relations. Tumulty proved a good choice for the job. He was not only experienced in dealing with the press but also had a thorough understanding of what he must do in the president's anteroom. At Trenton, he had served as Wilson's private secretary and had learned to combine the skills that made him, according to Wilson, "one of the ablest young Democratic politicians of the State" with a concern for the needs of statehouse reporters; he would find both useful in Washington. Tumulty expressed his understanding of his new position in an article in 1921 for the *New York Times*, in which he described the White House secretary as the "connecting link between the President and the outside world." Because, he went on, the president could not possibly answer personally the many questions posed by newsmen, "it devolves upon the Secretary to do the best he can to supply them with such information as it may be thought wise and prudent to give out"; this made him "publicity director" for the White House.[3]

On 4 March 1913—Wilson's Inauguration Day—Tumulty called a conference with reporters, informing them that "you boys are great personages in public affairs, and in Washington I will look after the publicity of this administration myself." Turning on his warmest Irish charm, Tumulty told the newspapermen that information would be more readily accessible in the Wilson administration and that his office would remain open to them at any time. The "boys" were understandably skeptical. They had heard it all— including the blarney—several times before and knew that whatever became of Tumulty's good intentions must depend primarily upon the president himself. Tumulty realized this too, of course, and turned his immediate attention to the problem of persuading Wilson to cultivate good press relations.[4]

This did not appear a difficult task, considering both Wilson's record at Trenton and his preinaugural remarks about subjecting the government to what he termed "pitiless publicity." In fact, Wilson had made himself the butt of much sarcasm by Washington sophisticates by announcing an "open door" policy for the White House and by asserting—in his best progressive rhetoric—that all public business must be conducted in public. Revelations of this sort made even the most captious correspondent happy, and Tumulty might have expected help from Wilson in wooing the favor of the press. But the secretary soon learned that the president's behavior did not always mirror his theories; the personal pursuit of publicity was not Wilson's strong point. Still—as official Washington was also to discover—Tumulty could be as stubborn as his boss, and the secretary spent much of the next eight years importuning the president for improved public relations.[5]

At the top of Tumulty's list was the innovation of regular presidential press conferences, which he believed would enhance the chief executive's personal influence with White House reporters. Wilson expressed interest in the idea, and when Tumulty lined up support from several other administration advisers, he agreed to give it a try. The secretary moved quickly to make necessary arrangements, and on 15 March—eleven days after his inauguration—the new president opened his first White House press conference. In so doing, he broke considerable new ground. Taft had conducted occasional question-and-answer sessions with correspondents, but he had shown no inclination to establish them on a regular basis; Wilson now pledged to meet the press at least once—and sometimes twice—weekly. The new president also made conferences a normal part of White House routine, scheduling them during regular business hours and treating them as any other official appointment. This meant a great deal to Washington reporters, who had grown accustomed to maintaining what was at best a hit-and-miss relationship with the president but who could now count on the opportunity to question him at predictable intervals.[6]

If correspondents believed Wilson might take them to a kind of journalistic promised land, however, they would ultimately be disappointed. As reporter Edward Lowry remembered the first conference, "there was a pause, a cool silence, and some one ventured a tentative question. It was answered crisply, politely, and in the fewest possible words. A pleasant time was not had by all." Indeed, to judge by the comments of those present, a pleasant time was not had by any, and perhaps the most interesting aspect of these first conferences was the vitriol with which journalists remembered them in their memoirs. David Barry, for example, thought the innovation a poor substitute for the personal meetings with correspondents dating from McKinley. Wilson's gatherings, Barry concluded, "were not in fact conferences at all. The newspaper men would, when they screwed up courage enough to do so, ask questions bearing upon various phases of the news of the day, and the President would answer or sidestep them as he chose."[7]

But these were the recollections of the 1920s, when Wilson's stock as a public leader had reached its nadir. In 1913, reporters took a different view. Charles Willis Thompson, for instance, whose own memoirs criticized the conferences, wrote glowingly of the president's performance for the *New York Times*: "As he went on talk-

ing, the big hit he was making with the crowd became evident.
There was something so unaffected and honest about his way of
talking," Thompson concluded, "that it won everybody, despite the
fact that many of the men there had come prejudiced against him."
Two months later, journalist Richard V. Oulahan agreed. "Things
at the White House are working out first rate," he wrote Thompson. "The semi weekly talks with the President are now on a good
working basis."[8]

This contemporary interpretation appears to be the correct one.
Despite the fact that Wilson was surprised to find over a hundred
reporters at his first conference—he "did not know what he was
up against," according to Thompson—he managed to handle them
with tact and aplomb. The difficulty was not a small one. As journalist Oliver P. Newman wrote to Ray Stannard Baker, the president "could not be as frank as he could have been with one; and he
was plainly embarrassed." Too many reporters made an air of confidentiality impossible and faced Tumulty with a serious dilemma.
Limiting the size of the audience might have improved the president's performance, but it would also have destroyed much of the
conferences' value. Only by meeting all interested correspondents
could Wilson put an end to newspaper complaints about a "privileged press" under Roosevelt and Taft, and only in this way could he
expand his personal influence to include all major newspapers. He
would simply have to get used to being interviewed by a crowd.[9]

And get used to it he did. Over the next two years, Wilson grew
skillful at fielding the questions of assembled reporters, developing
a style that in many ways resembled that of the second Roosevelt.
But this could only be a long-run solution to his problem; Wilson's
immediate need was for the establishment of some kind of rapport
with the working press. He thus moved the second conference to the
East Room of the White House, probably because he thought the
atmosphere there seemed more relaxed, and opened it by remarking
that he had found their first meeting excessively formal. This might
be remedied, Wilson continued, if he could be certain his exact statements would be held in confidence; he thus asked correspondents to
avoid direct quotation. Also in his opening remarks, which were
distributed—"not to be published"—to reporters, Wilson took time
for a few kind words about the profession of journalism. Displaying
Tumulty's obvious influence, the president informed those in attendance that a large part of the success of public affairs depended on
newspapermen, and especially on reporters, "because the news is
the atmosphere of public affairs." "Unless," he went on, "you get the
right setting to affairs—dispense the right impression—things go

wrong." Sweetening his remarks with that bit of cajolery, he renewed his request for a "partnership" with reporters, asking their
help in "lubricating" change.[10]

Even if newsmen remained willing to help, however, some could
not resist the temptation to use an occasional presidential quotation. In July 1913 this practice finally placed the conferences in
jeopardy, as Wilson, angered by the publication "in certain evening
newspapers" of his comments on relations with Mexico, threatened
to discontinue the meetings altogether. Reporters responded quickly,
demonstrating clearly that they still held out hope for their sessions
with the president. The *New York Sun*'s E. A. Fowler wrote Tumulty
to apologize for the story in his paper violating the president's confidence. And Richard V. Oulahan represented all correspondents in
requesting that conferences be continued. Acting as chairman of the
Standing Committee of Correspondents—an organization formed
by the White House press corps for just such an emergency—Oulahan recommended tightening press conference regulations. From
now on, he suggested, each reporter should enter meetings "with the
distinct understanding . . . that there shall be no further quotation
of the President direct or indirect without his express consent or
the consent of his official representative." Oulahan also proposed
that the White House staff should exercise "closer supervision . . .
over those who may be admitted to such conferences," reminding
Tumulty that it was only a few members of the press who violated
the ethics of the profession. What was needed, according to the
standing committee, was not the termination of the conferences but
White House enforcement of the kind of rules correspondents were
powerless to impose upon themselves. Wilson agreed, adopting the
proposed regulations and allowing the twice-weekly meetings to
continue.[11]

With conference rules providing a firm footing, Wilson could concentrate on answering reporters' questions. Years later, journalists
would remember that the president's answers often seemed devious
and sometimes intentionally misleading, giving Richard Oulahan
"the impression that he was matching his wits against ours." There
was, to be sure, some truth in this assessment; some questions
simply could not be answered, and the conferences occasionally
degenerated into verbal tugs of war between the president and
press. Such was the case with the reporters' first question on 2
February 1915:

> *Question*: Mr. President, can you say anything about the
> shipping bill?

> *The President*: That needn't bother you.
> *Question*: It does.
> *The President*: Well, you must not let it.
> *Question*: It doesn't bother us, Mr. President, we just want to
> know about it.
> *The President*: It is going through all right.

The most striking things here are the skill—and good nature—with which Wilson evaded the question and the fact that he appeared in the end to make an answer without surrendering anything of value. As the president soon discovered, evasion was a necessary art for anyone meeting regularly with reporters.[12]

But it was not the most important art. The conferences' ultimate value would come from answering questions, not evading them, and Wilson worked hard at supplying as much newsworthy information as possible. In part, he hoped to achieve success through preparation; as he later told George Creel, he studied for the conferences as diligently as a professor did for a lecture. This paid off in the president's obvious grasp of complex and varied issues, a grasp that generally allowed him to make the press conferences a valuable news source for reporters.[13]

Still, Wilson knew that the real art of answering questions was not in preparation; it was in giving out information in a way that would catch the reporters' interest. This had been the key to Theodore Roosevelt's success with the press, and there were some correspondents who frankly doubted the new president's ability to duplicate TR's performance. The Roughrider himself had once described his Democratic opponent as "too academic" and had mimicked his professorial demeanor for an audience of approving reporters. But if this was ever so, it was not true of Wilson's performance in his press conferences. There he displayed a genuine talent for talking to the "boys" in a language they could understand, for trading his academic—or presidential—phrasing for the language of the newsroom.[14]

For Wilson, this meant colorful language, and the president's well-known facility with words did not fail him during his press conferences. On 22 December 1914, for example, he was asked if he knew anything about a report that the ship purchase bill was "ready to be put on the track and slipped through when the proper moment comes." This was the kind of question the president could appreciate: a subject phrased in its own terms. He could not resist answering in kind, remarking that "perhaps it would be more appropriate to say 'put on the ways.'" Wilson then attempted to respond to the question, saying that he did not know, "speaking seriously, just what are the details of the plan of handling the bill in the House" but that he was "glad"—adding yet another pun—"to hear that it is ready to be launched." This sort of thing made good copy, even if it could not be directly quoted and attributed to the president, and it went a long way toward enhancing Wilson's relations with reporters.[15]

Another characteristic of Wilson's press conferences was humor. For the most part, historians have made too little of this side of Wilson's personality; their image of an austere Presbyterian minister's son could not have been formed by attending the president's regular meetings with the press. At one of his first conferences, for example, Wilson was asked: "What about the recognition of Mexico?" "Well, I don't know," he replied. "We don't decide that— that is decided between brawls! *(Laughter)*" A few months later, the president was asked if he had heard that "bankers seem to be worrying as to what would happen if this dictatorship [in Mexico] would collapse." "Why I should think they would," was his reply. A month later, the question of Mexico was raised again, with reporters wanting to know if it was true that Wilson's emissary had attended a reception given by President Huerta.

> *Question*: The afternoon paper said Mr. O'Shaughnessy was there, they played the Star Spangled Banner, and Mr. Huerta embraced Mr. O'Shaughnessy.
> *The President*: I wish he had embraced his opinions.

In general, Wilson's humor took on this sharp and incisive tone, perhaps in emulation of what Arthur S. Link has termed his father's "caustic wit."[16]

On other occasions Wilson's humor took the form of answering questions with anecdotes. On 24 November 1914, for example, he was asked how he liked certain courses of action suggested for him by the newspapers. "I am like the Scotch caddie," the president replied. "You remember the old caddie. He was taking a person for a very poor player; at least he was playing very badly that day. And he ended in defeat, and he said, 'I dare say you have seen a worse player on this course?' The old fellow didn't say anything, so he thought and said, 'I dare say you have seen a worse player on this course?' The old caddie said, 'I heard you the first time. I was thinking!'"[17]

Wilson also used humor to define his relationship with reporters. This often surfaced as good-natured sparring about what he and the newsmen expected of each other, as in the case of this opening for the 22 May 1913 press conference:

> *Question*: Well, what's the news? The President knows it.
> *The President*: I wish I did. I don't know half as many things as you fellows do.

On another occasion Wilson was asked if he had read the Sunday papers. "I merely saw the headlines yesterday," he retorted. "I wanted to be in a good humor on Sunday and I didn't read them." Of course, this sort of thing contained an element of risk, because it often implied criticism that some reporters might take to heart. But there can be no doubt that Wilson's decision to express his criticism humorously softened the blow. Then, too, Wilson often employed humor to demonstrate his sympathy with the problems of the working press. "I know how some editors have to be watched," he informed the newsmen after one of his complaints about a misrepresentation of his remarks. Overall, Wilson's humor clearly enlivened his press conferences, making them both more useful and more enjoyable for reporters.[18]

Wilson's conferences also benefited from a relaxed atmosphere. The person most responsible for this was, of course, Wilson himself; it was inevitably his place to set the conferences' tone, and he attempted to keep the meetings as casual as possible. This was best achieved by opening the conferences on an informal note. On 11 June 1914, for example, the president began by remarking, "Well, I haven't anything to say. Have you?" On another occasion, he opened a meeting by stressing his role as a public servant: "What's your pleasure, gentlemen?" he asked. At times, Wilson's insouciance seemed almost to get the better of him, as when he responded to a question about his attitude toward Congress with the remark, "I ain't got none." Whatever its grammatical merit, such a remark reflected the president's growing rapport with the press.[19]

It also reflected his appreciation of the conferences' usefulness. As Wilson learned to feel comfortable in the presence of reporters, he grasped the many uses to which his meetings might be put. These proved essentially the same as those developed by McKinley and Roosevelt for the press release; indeed, Wilson's conferences represented a kind of verbal extension of the press release idea. As such, their most important purpose remained the presentation of information, and Wilson often used his new forum to make statements to reporters. This often took the form of an opening remark detailing an important policy or event. On other occasions Wilson waited to be asked, then treated reporters to an obviously well-prepared statement. This technique was somewhat risky, however, because the journalists might neglect to ask the proper questions. Wilson found the solution to this problem in his 15 May 1913 conference, when he told reporters: "There is one question which, if I am properly informed, I would ask me, if I were you." Clearly, the president had a point he wanted to make, and he was determined to make it whether the newsmen were interested or not.[20]

One advantage to the press conference was that presidential statements could be made off the record. Such background information was of great value to newsmen, but it seemed difficult—and dangerous—to release in written form. In his press conferences, Wilson felt protected by the stricture against quoting the president directly; he could also go off the record whenever he wished to avoid even indirect reference to his views. This allowed him to give reporters material otherwise unavailable to them, material that enabled newsmen to make a more accurate assessment of administration policy. A good example of this occurred during his 13 July 1913 press conference, when he claimed his right of confidentiality three, times. Asked about his Central American policy, Wilson replied: "I am now speaking to you gentlemen for your information, not for the newspapers," then explained the delicacy of trying to help countries in that area without appearing predatory. After further discussion, a reporter asked if European nations could object to Wilson's policy. "Well," the president responded, "speaking freely to you in confidence, they would have a right to object but—(*Laughter.*)" Later, Wilson's questioners turned to the subject of Mexico, asking what the president's latest information was. "Well, just among ourselves," he answered, "it is to the effect that the Huerta government can't last."[21]

Another benefit of the press conference was its usefulness for dispelling rumors. On 5 June 1913, for example, Wilson cautioned reporters against believing unconfirmed reports, warning that they should not publish anything until they heard it from "authoritative sources." Compliance with this proved generally unobtainable, of course, and the president often had to satisfy himself with denying the truth of stories after they appeared in the press. An example of this occurred on 24 August 1914, when Wilson opened his conference thus: "I see by the papers, gentlemen, that an impression has gotten abroad that we are going to drop the suggestion of the government's buying ships. I learned that for the first time from the newspapers. It is an entirely wrong impression, absolutely wrong impression." Another rumor prompted the following exchange at Wilson's 5 January 1915 conference:

> *Question*: Mr. President, I notice in the *Post* this morning a dispatch from London, probably Associated Press, indicating that the United States Government might send a representative to the Vatican to cooperate there, with a view to helping the efforts of the Pope to bring about peace.
>
> *The President*: I took that as one of the many ways in which the *Post* amuses itself, sir. Of course it is ridiculous.
>
> *Question*: Mr. President, that is an Associated Press dispatch.
>
> *The President*: I don't know where these things are invented. I think not very far away from Washington.[22]

Wilson knew that many rumors were invented "not very far away from Washington"; indeed, some came from within the White House itself. On 12 January 1915 he told reporters that "I saw an article headed 'Note Unsatisfactory to Wilson,' or something like that. I thought of writing to the editor and asking him how he found out. He didn't ask me, and nobody asked me, and I have not expressed an opinion, because I haven't studied the note yet. It is merely preliminary, anyway." In fact, this story, had been leaked from the president's own executive offices, but it was the kind of report that he could not afford to acknowledge officially. Thus, Wilson found his press conferences useful for disputing the authenticity of rumors—even when he had started them himself.[23]

For all their usefulness, however, the conferences were not without problems. One difficulty was the reporters' habit of asking the wrong kind of questions, such as when they attempted to pin Wilson down with a speculative query. On other occasions, the newsmen failed to address themselves to the president's special knowledge. An example of this occurred during the 21 April 1913 conference, when a reporter asked a question about Congress. "You have been here much longer than I have," Wilson retorted, "and you can make a better guess than I can." This sort of thing—and the president's response to it—reflected the most fundamental difficulty of the conferences: the different goals he and reporters held for the meetings. From Wilson's perspective, little might be gained from answering journalists' all-too-pointed questions about issues of interest to them; he wanted instead to guide their thinking on topics he considered ready for public education. He thus invited the newsmen to join him in a partnership "to help," as he put it, "the public understand the issues at hand" and naively hoped they would accept his judgment on questions to be discussed. Of course they would not. Reporters had their own criteria for determining topics of interest, and their unwillingness to cooperate made the press conferences something of a disappointment for Wilson.[24]

Still, he kept them on his calendar until 1915, moving them from Thursday afternoons to 10:00 A.M. on Tuesdays, a time designed to allow reporters to make their deadlines for the afternoon edition. Then in July he canceled the sessions abruptly, citing increased pressure of foreign affairs for his action, and refused to set a date for their renewal. Of course this announcement did not exactly please newsmen, one of whom charged that the president had "abandoned his press conferences as soon as he could find a suitable pretext" for doing so. It did not please Tumulty either. But the secretary's pleas had no more effect than those of reporters, and he was forced to take upon himself the entire burden of handling relations with the press.[25]

There the burden remained for the rest of Wilson's first term in office, despite Tumulty's periodic remonstrances against continued presidential silence. Following Wilson's reelection, however, the secretary thought the time right for pressing the issue of renewed meetings with reporters, and he wrote himself a memorandum to "take up with the President the question of resuming newspaper conferences after the convening of Congress." Tumulty found the opportunity to do so on 6 December when he asked Wilson if he would not fix a time for a new round of meetings. Wilson replied positively, informing his secretary that "I *can* make them a fixture for Mondays and Thursdays at 12:30, but I would very much prefer 2:30 in the afternoon as the hour." This was good news for Tumulty, who quickly canvassed correspondents and found that they considered one meeting a week sufficient. Reporters also disliked the idea of midafternoon meetings; they still had deadlines to worry about. Tumulty suggested to Wilson that he set the conferences for 12:30 P.M. on Mondays. Wilson affixed his characteristic "okeh," and press conferences went back on his calendar.[26]

They proved short-lived, however, as heightened pressures in foreign affairs during December persuaded Wilson to discontinue them again. Their eclipse was made permanent four months later, when American entry into the World War presented new problems of security. Responding to a call for renewed conferences a year later, Wilson explained that when meeting with newspapermen "I am dependent . . . upon the discretion and good will of the least discreet and friendly member of the conference." It is "very difficult," he continued, "for me to talk as frankly as I should like to talk with the general body of correspondents down here, but it is not a matter which I have finally closed my mind about by any means." With this last remark, Wilson was something less than candid; he had firmly decided to rule out future press conferences. But he was truthful about his reasons for their cancelation. If he had found it difficult to be open with newsmen in peacetime, he found it impossible to do so in time of war, and he held no regular conferences after the end of 1916.[27]

The ultimate failure of Wilson's news conferences did not isolate the administration from the press. Tumulty proved more than capable of taking up the slack. From his first days in office, the secretary met every morning with White House reporters, a task he described as "delightful interludes in a busy day." He made public the routine comings and goings of White House business and presented news of the president's decisions on policies and appointments in a way that rarely failed to capture reporters' interest. He had a talent, according to David Lawrence, for "revealing, bit by bit, and with an air of mystery, things which appeared to be great secrets, data which Tumulty, with all the arts known to the practiced publicity expert, divulged with an idea to headlines and conspicuous display." He also seemed to know what newsmen were after—and whether or not he ought to give it to them—and could be as coquettish or as straightforward as the situation required. For their part, Washington journalists were quickly taken by his easy humor, and Tumulty became one of the most popular presidential secretaries.[28]

As Tumulty was well aware, however, his own popularity remained unimportant compared to the president's. He thus kept his eyes open for opportunities to demonstrate presidential goodwill, frequently prompting Wilson to write letters to newspapermen expressing gratitude for their efforts on his behalf. At one time or another Tumulty convinced Wilson to send friendly letters of appreciation to Frank Noyes and Melville Stone of the Associated Press, Henry Watterson of the *Louisville Courier-Journal*, J. Frederick Essary of the *Baltimore Sun*, and Arthur Brisbane of the *Washington Times*. He thus courted the friendship of editors and correspondents, enhancing Wilson's popularity and winning vital cooperation from the press.[29]

If he could be generous with the carrot, however, Tumulty could also wield the stick. He had to do so, in particular, to solve the recurrent problem of premature release of presidential statements and addresses, a breach of confidence that endangered the administration's ability to control the timing of its own publicity. Shortly after Wilson's inauguration, Tumulty complained to R. A. Farrelly of the International News Service that one of its subscribers—the *Atlanta Georgian*—had violated the release rule by publishing the inaugural address in an edition that reached the street nearly an hour before the indicated time. Calling for an investigation of the matter, Tumulty made it clear that the wire service remained responsible for indiscretions by its member newspapers; he also implied the possibility of White House retribution. Later in the year, he wrote the president of the American Press Association about his organization's practice of sending presidential messages to subscribers on postal cards before release. "It seems to me," he warned, "that this is somewhat dangerous, and I write to request that, if this is your practice, you discontinue it and rely upon telegraphic release from Washington." In his reply, the APA's Courtland Smith informed Tumulty that his association had always relied upon telegraphic transmittal but that the recent Fourth of July speech was an exception caused by holiday communications problems. He vigorously defended the wire service's past behavior, expressing his fear of losing the privilege of advance releases in the future. As both Smith and Tumulty knew, prior copies of presidential pronouncements were essential to the success of any press association. The threat of their denial was a potent weapon in the hands of the White House.[30]

Tumulty also improved existing arrangements for releasing confidential material. Piqued by a State Department press release marked "for publication in regular afternoon editions, not noon editions," that had caused considerable confusion, the secretary adopted the practice of fixing an exact release hour for executive information. The problem arose from imprecise definition. Many newspapermen claimed that their regular afternoon editions went to press early and were not properly noon editions despite their midday appearance at newsstands. Others complained of being scooped by this practice. There often existed, in fact, differences of several hours between the release times observed by various newspapers—a matter of some importance to journalists involved—and sensitive material was occasionally published prior to official release. Tumulty's exact release times put an end to long-standing press conjecture about the meaning of such terms as "regular morning" and "afternoon" editions and moved a step closer to preventing the premature appearance of confidential material.[31]

Tumulty was not always cast in the role of disciplinarian, however; sometimes he defended reporters against the wrath of an angry president. In 1915, for example, he interceded on behalf of a *New York Herald* correspondent who had written an erroneous story about a break between Wilson and Colonel Edward M. House over relations with Mexico. The piece so infuriated the president that he not only ordered the reporter barred from White House offices but also demanded his dismissal by the *Herald*. The severity of this punishment shocked the remainder of the White House press corps. Friendly correspondents sought the assistance of Tumulty, who understood that Wilson's popularity with the press was more important than disciplining the mistake of one overzealous reporter. He accordingly persuaded the president to withdraw his request for the newsman's discharge and quietly readmitted him to his morning press conferences.[32]

Although Wilson's public relations were usually handled by his White House factotum, the president did have some ideas of his own on the subject of publicity. One of these was the personal presentation of messages to Congress—a practice in eclipse since the days of John Adams—that Wilson revived to focus wider public attention on his proposals and policies. This idea developed from Wilson's view of the president as simultaneous leader of Congress and public opinion; it also expressed his willingness to employ presidential publicity to win support for his legislative program. If, as chief executive, he could be assured of newspaper space by merely sending his thoughts to Congress, he could certainly command headlines by presenting them in person. This was exactly what Wilson had in mind.[33]

Headlines did not require public pronouncements, however; they could also be won by talking with reporters privately behind the scenes. This took the form of news leaks, which Wilson used effectively to place important pieces of information before the public. On 28 January 1914, for instance, the *New York Times* carried a detailed report of what the president called "a Foreign Clearing House Committee meeting" at the White House. According to the *Times*'s correspondent, Wilson had informed the gathering, which included members of the Senate Foreign Relations Committee, that at a "critical moment" in the Mexican imbroglio the United States was estranged from virtually every important nation in the two hemispheres. This was, the president said, a dangerous situation, and could result in war with one or more of the world's leading powers. Wilson set forth a "threefold remedy" for extracting the United States from "this maze of foreign difficulties," including repeal of the Panama tolls discrimination, confirmation of a treaty making a cash settlement with Colombia, and lifting of the embargo on arms to Mexico. As the reporter put it, this story had been "pieced together" "little by little" during the twenty-four hours following the meeting; in fact, it had been leaked to the *Times* by Wilson himself, probably through Washington correspondent Charles Willis Thompson.[34]

This episode provides a nearly ideal illustration of the value of presidential news leaks in dealing with questions of foreign affairs. The threat of war at a time of crisis in Mexico supplied the president with tremendous leverage in presenting his foreign program to Congress. But the danger was such that Wilson did not want to discuss it openly, and it was for this reason that he turned to the device of leaking the information to a trusted reporter. Whatever happened, the president could not be accused of intentionally alarming the American people, and if necessary for diplomatic reasons he could always deny the accuracy of the story. He thus enjoyed the best of both publicity worlds: his information made headlines without requiring the risk of personal accountability.[35]

On other occasions, Wilson publicized his ideas by granting interviews to individual reporters. This practice offered obvious advantages over either press conferences or news leaks by allowing the president to discuss important questions in depth and with candor. But it was also a movement away from Wilson's more generalized treatment of the press and threatened, as such, to revive the complaints of favoritism that had plagued Theodore Roosevelt. Interviews also seemed likely to make excessive demands upon the president's time, as the granting of even occasional exclusives might provoke all reporters to request equal treatment. For Wilson, this seemed the greatest difficulty, and he remained always cautious about granting journalistic requests for private meetings. In June 1914, for instance, he accepted an interview with John Reed thus: "Okeh, if you [Tumulty] think other newspapermen will not follow his example in too great numbers." Two years later, Wilson employed similar reasoning to deny an interview request from the editor of the *New York Times.* The problem, as the president explained it, was that he could not do such a thing for one newspaperman without doing it for all; this should be obvious to "even a newspaper editor." Wilson did not, he concluded, want to begin "this policy of interviews" because "it would inevitably be only a beginning." The result was that this technique found only occasional use in the Wilson administration.[36]

One area where it was used to advantage was the president's relations with Mexico. In late 1913, Wilson consented to an interview with correspondent Edward G. Lowry; the outcome was a sympathetic article, "What the President Is Trying to Do for Mexico," in the January 1914 *World's Work*. By paraphrasing Wilson's comments and quoting directly from his published remarks, Lowry presented the president's Mexican policy in a lucid and straightforward manner. This was necessary, according to Lowry, because even though "President Wilson has tried twice and in the most public way imaginable to make clear" his "basic assumptions," certain elements of the public have refused to understand. Lowry thus reduced these assumptions to a simple ethical formulation: Huerta had to go because he represented the corrupting influence of foreign interests and concessionaires responsible for most of Mexico's problems. The writer also drew a logical connection between the struggle in Mexico and the struggle at home: "President Wilson's policy is to fight for the Mexicans the fight we have been and are fighting for ourselves, to divorce Big Business from governmental affairs." This was powerful publicity, indeed, representing something close to the maximum that might be achieved through the interview technique.[37]

Wilson also used press interviews to improve his public image. In December 1914 he granted an "exclusive" of this type to Samuel G. Blythe, who had earlier in the year written a favorable article—also based on an interview—dealing with the president's Mexican policy. The more personal later article, which appeared as "A Talk with the President" in the 9 January 1915 edition of the *Saturday Evening Post*, presented Wilson in distinctly human terms and attempted to dispel the popular stereotype of the president as a cold man of intellect who lacked feelings. Wilson turned again to this device during the campaign of 1916, granting interviews to two trustworthy journalists, Ida Tarbell and Ray Stannard Baker. Both Baker's article, which appeared in *Collier's* for 7 October and Tarbell's, which was published in the same magazine three weeks later, showed Wilson as a "fine, humorous, cultivated American gentleman." The president, Tarbell continued, was "open as a book"; she had never met a man who was "more just and more gentle in his estimate of people, less bitter, emotional, prejudiced, and yet never for an instant fooled." Clearly, Tarbell's Wilson was not the stiffly formal president of popular conception. Nor was he the distant-minded professor. "The common things of life *interest* him," she wrote; "here at last we have a president whose real interest in life centers around the common man." This last was, of course, the real issue—Wilson needed badly to be seen more as a "man of the people"—and it explained his willingness in this instance to employ the interview device.[38]

Another of Wilson's personal projects was the creation of a federal "publicity bureau" to enhance administration control over the press. Troubled by his treatment after one year in office, Wilson discussed this possibility in a letter to Charles W. Eliot. "We have several times," he informed the Harvard president, "considered the possibility of having a publicity bureau which would handle the real facts, so far as the government was aware of them, for all the departments." This might have centralized the machinery for disseminating administration news—a long-term presidential objective—and prevented unintentional release of damaging information. But its most important purpose was to strengthen the executive's position with White House correspondents and their editors. The "real trouble" was not that reporters were getting too little or inaccurate information; it was that, as Wilson put it, "the newspapers get the real facts but do not find them to their taste and do not use them as given them, and in some of the newspaper offices news is invented." By proposing a publicity bureau, Wilson hoped to put an end to misunderstandings about the nature of the "real facts" and to see to it that newspapers had no excuse for failing to print news as they received it. This idea represented a significant step toward increasing executive control over Washington news, but it resulted, for the time being at least, in little more than venting presidential anger at the press. Cooler White House heads prevailed—marshaled, no doubt, by Tumulty—and Wilson's centralization scheme lay dormant until American entry into the World War.[39]

Wilson's vision of a publicity bureau developed primarily from his concern over public misinformation about foreign affairs, an area about which, he remarked to Eliot, he had wondered "since I came here . . . how it ever happened that the public got a right impression." A similar question presented itself to Secretary of State William Jennings Bryan, who commenced his own search for better publicity methods during his first weeks in office. Bryan reinstituted the practice, allowed to lapse by Knox, of regular meetings with the press and attempted to supply reporters with large quantities of background information. This quickly proved troublesome, however. Correspondents refused to be guided in their questioning by the administration's publicity needs, and Bryan found it necessary after only four months in office to reevaluate his policy of openness with the press.[40]

The problem, as Bryan informed the president, was that "I am asked a great many questions by the newspaper men which seem to me improper for the reason that I cannot answer them without sacrificing public interests" or refuse to answer them without giving

reporters "an opportunity to misconstrue the reason for the refusal
and guess at the answer." It was not, he went on, only that correspondents might guess wildly about administration intentions; it
could be just as bad to have them guess the truth. He could not, as
he saw it, "announce that we are about to do a thing, for when the
announcement is made the thing is practically done; and yet a
failure to answer these questions cannot but indicate what the
answer would be if I answered them." An example of this unacceptable type of question had come up, he continued, at a recent conference on Mexico, when correspondents wanted to know if Ambassador Henry Lane Wilson intended to resign. No answer seemed
satisfactory, and Bryan concluded that this sort of "cross-examination" could do the administration no good. He still believed in giving
newspapers everything proper, but as he told Wilson, it now "seems
to me that international questions differ from local ones to such an
extent that a different rule must be applied."[41]

Such a "different rule" had already been drafted by the secretary
of state. He now proposed it to Wilson for adoption in all the department's dealings with the press. Designed, not surprisingly, to
preclude the kind of questions described by Bryan, the new rule informed State Department officials that "the policy of this government on international questions, insofar as announcement is made
from the Department, will be announced when the President thinks
that the public interests will be promoted thereby. Until these announcements are made, questions concerning such policies will not
be answered." Bryan thought strict adherence to this regulation
"would not allow the enquirer to determine the time of the announcement" but would return complete control over release of
publicity to the administration. It also granted the State Department an almost total right to secrecy and left reporters free to do
little more than collect announcements from administration spokesmen. Questions could still be asked, of course; they simply would not
be answered until the president decided it was the proper time to do
so.[42]

Apparently unaware of his new rule's potential effect on the
department's press relations, Bryan also proposed that "it would be
well to have an understanding with the newspaper men" about the
nature of their inquiries. As Bryan saw it, the reporters should
agree "that their questions will be confined to matters of fact and
not include efforts to search out the unannounced policies of the government by cross-examination." This might make unnecessary the
application of Bryan's secrecy rule, but as the secretary soon discovered, it was just the sort of thing to which correspondents would

never agree. It seemed designed to deprive them of the right to ask the kind of questions they—and their editors—found most pertinent and reduced even further the value of the department's faltering press conferences. Predictably, journalists persisted in cross-examining the secretary; Bryan could only refuse to answer. The Department of State thus proved, ironically, no greater fount of information under the tutelage of the Great Commoner than under those of his more conservative predecessors.[43]

It is interesting to note that on this question Wilson apparently shared his secretary of state's naiveté. The president responded on 31 July, assuring Bryan that "I think your judgment in the matter is quite right and that a rule such as you formulate would not only be wise but would, if fully explained to the newspaper men, satisfy them." Of course it would not. Wilson should have known better, and his uncritical acceptance of Bryan's proposal probably reflected his own concern over difficulties in meetings with the press. It also betrayed his own desire to employ White House correspondents in the manner suggested by the secretary. Wilson's chief complaint about his press conferences, it will be recalled, was that reporters seemed determined to ask questions he did not yet choose to answer, stealing all initiative for the meetings. This was what Wilson—and Bryan—hoped to change. They desired a much more docile kind of press, willing to receive and publish announcements without attempting to wrest additional information from administration spokesmen. They did not find such a press in the capital city, however, and their efforts to transform Washington reporting only damaged their relations with the newsmen.[44]

Bryan's press relations reached their nadir in February 1915 when he informed Wilson that it might be necessary to exclude reporters altogether from the State Department. Not only had Bryan failed to domesticate Washington correspondents, leaving them free to question him on any subject they pleased; he now found them guilty of affronting his dignity as well. Bristling over this latest offense, the secretary suggested that national security might best be served by refusing all admittance to newspapermen, and he asked the president's opinion on the prudence of such a step. Inasmuch as Bryan's proposal conflicted with Wilson's well-known principle of "pitiless publicity," it might seem surprising that the president did not reject it outright; that he did not reflected his own mistrust of the press. As usual, Tumulty saved the day for journalists—if not, indeed, for the administration—by convincing Wilson that although the secretary of state's anger might be justified he would be unwise to close the department's doors to reporters.[45]

If Wilson and Bryan shared a mistrust of correspondents, they also shared a powerful weapon for influencing public opinion on their own: both were moving and articulate speakers. In the traditional conduct of public relations, no skill had been more important than the ability to make stirring speeches before crowds; its usefulness, although perhaps now surpassed by the more indirect methods practiced by Tumulty and others, had by no means disappeared by the time of Wilson's administration. No matter how deficient the president's understanding of other aspects of public relations, he clearly demonstrated a great awareness of the value of forceful speechmaking. For Wilson, this represented the epitome of executive leadership, the one undoubtedly legitimate and dignified manner in which a president could win public support, and he took great pains while in the White House to perfect the style of his public pronouncements. Here, too, he relied heavily on Tumulty's sensitivity to nuance, taking the time, as he told writer Ida Tarbell, to "try" his speeches on the secretary, "who has a very extraordinary appreciation of how a thing will 'get over the footlights.'" As a result, Wilson's public appearances proved extremely effective, wielding considerable influence not only with the public but with newspapermen who attended as well.[46]

Shortly after Wilson's inauguration, however, it became apparent that rhetorical skills were beneficial only if employed with great care. On 18 March the president issued a graceful statement to the press outlining his reasons for withdrawing American support from the Six-Power Consortium in China, only to discover that his publicity had provoked a greater controversy than the decision itself. The problem was that Wilson had neglected to notify the State Department of his impending action, an oversight that placed officials involved in the China loan in a very difficult position and that resulted in the resignation of Assistant Secretary of State Francis M. Huntington Wilson. As the department's officer charged with meeting the press, Huntington Wilson had suffered many similar oversights during the Taft administration, and it is difficult to understand why he chose to resign at the first such incident under the new president. Perhaps he simply found Woodrow Wilson's gaffe just one embarrassment too many—the assistant secretary's behavior could be erratic when he felt slighted. At any rate, this new controversy drew attention away from the president's statement and neutralized the effect of his skillful phrasemaking, a fact Wilson acknowledged at the next cabinet meeting by vowing to withhold future press releases until after communicating them through channels.[47]

Wilson also faced difficulties at the start of his administration with the Huerta regime in Mexico. By late summer, the president and secretary of state were showing concern over the public appeal of their Mexican policy—even though they were by no means certain just what that policy would be. To meet any eventuality, Bryan sent the president a memorandum proposing an intervention plan "which," as he put it, "I believe we can defend before the public." Discussing the possibility of sending troops to Mexico, Bryan cautioned that "any intervention should be accomplished by a public statement that our purpose is not one of aggression, but that we are acting in the discharge of a duty to humanity and civilization." He thus rehearsed the kind of argument that the administration might be expected to employ if intervention became necessary and insured that the administration would not lack a public relations strategy.[48]

The president and secretary of state also displayed heightened interest in the activities of Washington correspondents, as they now attempted to bring publicity tightly under their own control. On 2 August, for example, Bryan found it necessary to chasten reporters for the construction placed by some of them—especially the representative of the *Washington Post*—on the administration's request for increased military appropriations. Pointing out that their reports had "deliberately misconstrued" the request to be the last step before intervention, he informed the correspondents that he "did not know of any theory consistent in an interest in the public on which such a misrepresentation could be explained" and lectured them on their responsibility to keep the public correctly informed. Later, the secretary would admit to Wilson that he had probably been too vigorous with his criticism, but he still contended that something must be done to prevent journalists from using "scareheads" to arouse public opinion at inappropriate times.[49]

By the first week in August, however, all Washington insiders— including newsmen—became aware of a strengthening of the administration's Mexican policy. Bryan's "intervention or recognition" proposal of 20 July had been leaked by the State Department, and reporters now began to press for an explanation of its meaning. From the administration's standpoint, this called for tightened security and a reconsideration of usual techniques for releasing policy information to the press. On 9 August Bryan was asked, as he remembered later, "by one of the newspaper men (I think he is the one who was barred from the White House) whether a statement of your Mexican policy would be given in advance with a release date." This procedure, it will be recalled, had been employed regularly since McKinley to insure the widest possible publicity and had been utilized to advantage by Wilson on a number of previous occasions. Nevertheless, Bryan informed reporters that he had not yet consulted the president on the matter and advised Wilson that he was opposed to its use in this instance. To issue an advance statement, he warned, would compel the administration to "risk the use that would be made of it." "You would be powerless," Bryan continued, "adequately to punish anyone who misused the confidence, and such a thing goes through so many hands that it would be impossible to locate the leak, if one occurred." This decision would do nothing for the administration's relations with reporters, of course, and the secretary of state proposed to offer them a disingenuous explanation. Because no definite time had been established for the announcement, he argued, no time could be fixed for its release. It did not, therefore, fall under "the rules prescribed for ordinary documents which are to be published at a certain date."[50]

Wilson responded two days later, agreeing with Bryan that because, as he put it, "there are some quarters in which we could not trust the recipients of such confidence" it would be "most unwise" to give reporters an advance statement. Wilson had already informed newspapermen of the release procedure his administration intended to follow in this instance. There would not be, he said, any overall statement of policy; instead, the administration would release each step of its program as it developed and would keep correspondents informed of any change in its Mexican relations. In this way, Wilson gave the appearance of conducting diplomacy in what he had earlier termed "the glare of publicity" without having to release his entire policy in advance and allowed his progressive rhetoric on the value of openness to serve his real desire for secrecy. The drawback to this practice, as both Wilson and Bryan were surely aware, was the limitation it placed upon publicity received by the administration's ultimate policy statement, a consideration apparently secondary to confidentiality in the thinking of the president and the secretary of state. Still, Wilson remained anxious for good relations with the press, and he made it a point to caution Bryan—who seemed to be growing a little edgy—that to insure the support of correspondents "we shall have to be patient dealing with them and making them content with that program."[51]

Wilson also developed another idea for publicizing his Mexican policy, one that would bring some of the benefits of prior release without incurring any of the risks. On 10 August Bryan suggested that inasmuch as the president's earlier congressional addresses had been so successful he might employ the same technique for publicizing his Mexican policy. Wilson quickly perceived merit in this proposal—he had probably been thinking along similar lines without informing the secretary of state—and made plans for a 27 August appearance on Capitol Hill. His message made public the details of recent American proposals to Mexico, through which Wilson hoped to "mediate" the civil war by promising recognition of a new government selected under what he termed democratic conditions. Because these included both an armistice with revolutionaries and Huerta's pledge not to run in the upcoming elections, they had little chance of acceptance by the Mexican government. But Wilson's effective use of publicity won considerable support for his policy of "watchful waiting." In this case, as in many others, the president's talent as a phrasemaker flattered his policies, and the term "watchful waiting" gave apparent substance to Wilson's drift and inactivity after the inevitable failure of his mediation scheme.[52]

"Watchful waiting" ended on 1 February 1914, when Wilson announced the termination of a United States embargo on the shipment of arms to Mexico. This intensified the conflict waged within sight of American territory and increased the threat of violence to American lives and property. Wilson thus ordered two additional regiments to patrol the border. As the president realized, however, this seemed likely to increase the alarm of editors concerned over the possibility of war with Mexico, and he approved Secretary of War Lindley M. Garrison's suggestion "to forestall any guesses or alarming statements in the press concerning this matter" by releasing a calming statement to reporters. On 11 March Garrison assured the press that there was no cause for alarm, that soldiers had been sent only "to allay as far as possible the fears of the people on the border."[53]

Although this interpretation did "allay the fears" of most administration critics, it did not go far enough to satisfy some of the cabinet. On 6 April Secretary of the Interior Franklin Lane called attention to an article in the *New York Times* defending the president's Mexican policy and suggested that Wilson order it printed in pamphlet form for general distribution. Lane contended that the article, which was already pasted in Tumulty's "yellow journal" of clippings, could have a great impact on the public—if properly presented. "It should be set up in large type," he wrote the president, "double spaced, with plenty of sub-heads so that it will be attractive reading. The American people are pretty largely governed by head lines today." Wilson agreed with Lane's assessment of the article's value and informed the interior secretary that he had already arranged for its insertion in the *Congressional Record*. He said nothing further about Lane's pamphlet proposal, however; this sort of thing had to await American participation in the World War.[54]

The climax of Wilson's personal feud with Huerta began on 9 April 1914 over a petty incident—the arrest and temporary detention of several American sailors—in the Mexican port of Tampico. At that time the president was out of Washington vacationing with his family, and his absence from the capital left administration press relations in confusion and disarray. Bryan, in charge over at the State Department, not only failed to issue an official release on the incident—indeed, the first reports were wired from Mexico City rather than Washington—but later uttered statements to correspondents that directly contradicted the tone Wilson intended to take. Returning to Washington, Wilson wasted no time correcting the impression given by his secretary of state, informing reporters who met his train that the United States would pursue the matter vigorously and that "the salute [to the American flag] will be fired." He further developed this stern attitude in a 15 April press release, in which he castigated the Huerta regime and stressed that the Tampico incident, inconsequential by itself, "must not be thought of alone." Huerta's behavior, Wilson continued, amounted to nothing less than "studied contempt" of American honor and resulted in "flouting" "the rights of American citizens" and "the dignity of the government of the United States." At last Wilson had discovered a suitable pretext for pressing his attack on Huerta; he would now make it the basis for an emotional appeal to the American people.[55]

Five days later, Wilson addressed Congress on the subject of his Mexican policy. Once again, he accused "the representatives of General Huerta" of being "willing to go out of their way to show disregard for the dignity and rights of this government" and rehearsed the inflammatory events of the past few days. Because, he continued, it now seemed necessary to convince Huerta that "no further occasion for explanation and professed regrets should arise," he asked for the support of Congress "to enforce respect for our government." This meant the use of force; the president had already decided to seize the port of Veracruz and—he hoped—bring about the downfall of Huerta. For his efforts, Wilson received a standing ovation from Congress and, as he clearly intended, the emotional backing of both editors and letter writers.[56]

Despite the brilliance of Wilson's prose, however, the public relations of this episode were—like the episode itself—marred deeply by bungling and unprofessionalism. While planning the seizure of Veracruz, neither president nor secretary of state suspected resistance to the point of bloodshed, a delusion that seemingly reflected less their ignorance of the Mexican people than their desire to believe in their own beneficence. The White House thus failed to prepare any advance explanations for the fighting that broke out in Mexico, and Tumulty arrived on the morning of 22 April to find, as he remembered, "the newspaper correspondents attached to the Executive offices uninformed of what had happened in the early morning." Characteristically, the secretary took charge, notifying newspapermen of the action and sending them jumping, "as one man, to the door, to flash this significant news to the country." For the rest of the day, Tumulty remained largely on his own; he certainly could not count on much help from the president, who was badly shaken by the unexpected Mexican resistance and who appeared "pale" and "parchmenty" when he finally did agree to receive reporters. That Wilson's ill-conceived policy did not result in a public relations—or military—disaster depended largely on the skill and caution of the president's subordinates. They apparently lacked his ability for self-deception and thus managed to make the most of what might have been a very difficult situation.[57]

There seemed no evidence of poor planning, however, in the public relations for a later, even more difficult, operation—the March 1916 punitive expedition into Mexico. Angered by the death of Americans in Pancho Villa's frequent border raids, Wilson decided to send General John J. Pershing in pursuit of the revolution leader. At the same time, he issued a press release designed to guide newspaper comment. Appealing to reporters' patriotism, Wilson asked them to "be good enough to assist the administration in presenting this [the administration's] view of the expedition to the American people." He requested this favor, Wilson continued, because both Americans and Mexicans must understand that Pershing's mission called only for the capture of bandits raiding along the border and because dangerous war pressure might result if the public perceived administration intentions as bellicose.[58]

What Wilson feared was that public opinion might support a war he had no intention of fighting. He thus called upon newsmen "to avoid such erroneous impression" by agreeing "not to interpret news stories regarding the expedition as in any sense meaning war, to withhold stories of troop movements and preparations that might be given that interpretation, and to refrain from publishing rumors of unrest in Mexico." Even for Wilson, this was asking a great deal of journalists. His requests foreshadowed the strictures he would place upon them during the World War, and it is perhaps surprising that he received so much genuine cooperation.[59]

That he did so was due at least in part to his administration's careful coordination of its public relations. By the time of Wilson's statement, both the State and War departments had issued calming press releases that defined the expedition in terms similar to the president's. There was, according to Secretary of War Newton D. Baker, "no intention of entering Mexico in force"; the troops would be "withdrawn" as soon as the de facto Mexican government could "take control of the situation." It remained for Secretary of State Robert Lansing to define the legalities of the affair. In a 13 March press release actually written by the president, Lansing contended that the expedition did not constitute "intervention of any kind in the affairs of our sister Republic." "On the contrary," he argued, "what is now being done is deliberately intended to preclude the possibility of intervention."[60]

The greatest danger of a break in this united front was presented by the army, where an overzealous officer might set off a public powder keg by making too much of the troop movement into Mexico. To prevent this, Baker made certain that General Frederick Funston understood the strictly limited nature of the expedition. "It is of the highest importance," he wrote, "that no color of any other possibility or intention be given." No word or action from the army should "afford the slightest ground of suspicion of any other or larger object." Strengthened by such tight coordination, publicity for the Pershing expedition was handled with remarkable smoothness.[61]

Even this threatened to be insufficient three months later, when American and Mexican troops clashed at the village of Carrizal. There was now, according to Lansing, an increasing "probability" of war with Mexico, requiring the president to prepare a new explanation of American behavior. No matter what happened, Lansing thought, the Wilson administration should avoid use of the word "intervention" and should deny that any invasion of Mexico was for that purpose. This was necessary because intervention implied interference, which the administration had consistently disavowed. Wilson agreed with this—he had, he wrote, thought of saying the same thing to Lansing—and nonintervention remained the basis of the administration's public relations for its increasingly difficult Mexican policy.[62]

Ultimately, Wilson did not have to use this careful planning because he succeeded in avoiding war with Mexico. One reason for this was his willingness to use his personal influence with the press. On 30 June, in the wake of the Carrizal incident, he addressed the New York Press Club with a ringing statement of his desire for peace. "Do you think," he asked, "that the glory of America would be enhanced by a war of conquest in Mexico?" Surely there was no honor for the strong in defeating the weak. Moreover, he argued, "force will not accomplish anything that is permanent"; only patience might do that. Finally, Wilson told the journalists about his many letters from the people asking for peace. He was, he said, the servant of the "rank and file" of the common people who "constitute the United States."[63]

Also favoring a peaceful Mexican settlement was the increased likelihood of American involvement in the World War, which had remained Wilson's primary foreign problem since the summer of 1914. As such, it received the administration's most thorough and original public relations campaign, stretching over almost three years of American neutrality and culminating in the creation of the innovative Committee on Public Information.

Chapter 6
Wilson Faces the Nation

 When the European war broke out in August 1914, Wilson wasted little time soliciting the aid of White House reporters for his policy of neutrality. In a press conference on 3 August, he urged them to guard against fueling the fire of public opinion, requesting them to strive for complete neutrality; he also lectured them, in characteristic fashion, on their great responsibility in times of crisis. "Of course, the European world is in a highly excited state of mind," Wilson told the correspondents, "but the excitement ought not to spread to the United States. So far as we are concerned, there is no cause for excitement." The president also thought it was the reporters' duty to help keep the public calm. "If I might make a suggestion to you gentlemen, therefore," he said, "I would urge you not to give currency to any unverified rumor or to anything that would tend to create or add to excitement."[1]

Wilson expressed similar sentiments three days later when he instructed the navy and war secretaries to forbid public comment by service officers on "the military and political situation in Europe," an order he hoped might prevent the military from taking sides—at least publicly—in the conflict. Taking sides was what Wilson desired most to avoid. He feared not only the complications that a breakdown in public neutrality might pose for his policy of nonintervention but also the divisiveness that it might produce among the American people, and he based his initial campaign on the need for complete impartiality.[2]

The keynote of this campaign was the president's 18 August appeal to "my fellow countrymen," in which he argued that a mere observance of the form of neutrality would not be sufficient, as he put it, to "safeguard the nation against distress and disaster." What was needed, Wilson believed, was a more comprehensive kind of neutrality, one based on public willingness to suspend judgment about the war. Only this would allow the American people to avoid the "divisions amongst us" that the president most feared. "The United States," Wilson continued, "must be neutral in fact as well as in name during these days that are to try men's souls. We must be impartial in thought as well as in action." Such impartiality was not easy to achieve, however—not even for the president himself—and although Wilson's appeal won almost unanimous approval in the press, there remained reason to doubt its long-term effectiveness with the American people.[3]

To increase this effectiveness, Wilson proposed that the federal government make use of its own facilities for distributing his proclamation. On 3 September he asked Tumulty to investigate the feasibility of this idea, requesting the secretary's opinion about "whether there is any fund from which he [the president] can have his letter on neutrality printed and posted, for example, in the city post offices." Such action might increase his appeal's publicity in two ways: by insuring the widest possible distribution and by allowing his statement to remain in the public gaze for an extended period of time. Wilson was thus attempting to overcome weaknesses he recognized in reliance on newspaper publicity, a technique that he and other presidents had always found adequate in the past but that would seem increasingly inadequate as war approached the United States. What Wilson's proposal represented, then, was the first step in a new direction, the novelty of which appeared in the fact that neither the president nor his secretary knew where to find funds for printing the proclamation.[4]

Nevertheless, Tumulty forwarded the suggestion to the Post Office Department, requesting that agency to take whatever action possible on the matter. One day later, Assistant Postmaster General Daniel C. Roper replied that although it would be both "feasible and desirable" to gain "greater publicity" by displaying the neutrality statement in post offices his department had no funds for printing the document. He thought such funds might be available in the State Department, however, and assured the president that his office would take care of distribution. As it turned out, State did have money for this type of publication; within two weeks 60,000 copies of the president's remarks—translated into four languages— were printed and displayed in post offices nationwide. The result was to transform the nation's post offices into a kind of national bulletin board, an idea that would later play an important role in the Creel committee's publication of the wartime *Official Bulletin*.[5]

Besides anticipating the CPI's efforts to improve publicity, the first Wilson administration also foreshadowed the committee's interest in a new medium of communication—motion pictures. During the next few years, Wilson's concern would often focus on the films themselves, but in September 1914 his interest remained limited to the audiences they attracted into movie houses across the country.

The possibility of addressing these audiences first appealed to Secretary of State Bryan, who was an early fan of the medium. In late August, Bryan attended a movie theater where the management, in keeping with the president's neutrality plea, requested that no sentiment be shown during newsreels depicting war scenes. The effect impressed the secretary of state, and although he admitted the impossibility of preventing all demonstrations, he believed that a similar request from the president himself might cool viewers' ardor. This was not the only benefit to be gained from a presidential statement, however; it would also, according to Bryan, "at the same time give greater publicity to your appeal for neutrality." What the secretary of state had in mind was a presidential statement—in Wilson's own handwriting—copied on film for projection at the start of each theater's program. It must explain the need for neutrality and appeal for cooperation from those in attendance. Wilson, who saw readily the value of publicity in movie houses, agreed with Bryan's proposal and forwarded a neutrality message to the secretary. With this action, Wilson first took advantage of the large and ready-made audience of moviegoers. It would become the target, three years later, of one of the Creel committee's most innovative publicity campaigns.[6]

War in Europe also heightened the administration's concern over security of official information. This was especially true in the State Department. On 1 October Wilson informed Counselor Robert Lansing that he was "deeply disturbed" about the *Chicago Herald*'s disclosure of recent British orders-in-council and called for a "very searching investigation" into the source of their information. "We are certainly," the president explained, "going to be drawn into very difficult situations if we cannot stop the apparent leaks in the State Department." To do so, Wilson suggested that Lansing find out who the guilty correspondent "consorts with" in the department—"you know that he was once connected with the Department," Wilson added—and put a stop to the flow of information between them. Lansing failed to do much to improve security, however, at least before the spring of 1917, and leaks of official information continued to plague the administration throughout the period of neutrality.[7]

Not surprisingly, correspondents proved less than happy about this tightening of security, expressing their displeasure over new regulations in the autumn of 1914. One protest was prompted on 28 October by Secretary of the Treasury William G. McAdoo, who responded to Wilson's concern over newspaper publication of shipping manifests and statistics by ordering all information on outgoing cargoes withheld for thirty days after sailing. As McAdoo predicted, the newspapers did complain—"howl," as he put it—about the order, but their protests only bounced off a president who considered it their duty to cooperate in time of national emergency. This remained Wilson's attitude throughout the war, and it placed considerable strain on his relations with White House reporters.[8]

Always important, newspaper cooperation became essential as the war drew nearer the United States. This became apparent in early May 1915 when a shocked America learned of the *Lusitania's* sinking by German submarines. As he described it to Tumulty, Wilson's latest difficulty was this: "I am keenly aware that the feeling of the country is now at fever-heat and that it is ready to move with me in any direction I shall suggest, but I am bound to weigh carefully the effect of radical action now based on the present emotionalism of the people. I am not sure whether the present emotionalism of the country would last long enough to sustain any action I would suggest to Congress." It was thus necessary to consider "in the most careful and conscious way" the course of action he must follow and "to calculate the effect upon the country of every incautious and unwise move."[9]

While he mulled over this dilemma, Wilson instructed Tumulty to make a calming statement to the press: "Of course the President feels the distress and gravity of the situation to the utmost," it read, "and is considering very earnestly, but very calmly, the right course of action to pursue. He knows that the people of the country wish and expect him to act with deliberation as well as with firmness." Two days later, Wilson took advantage of a speaking engagement in Philadelphia to voice another plea for public restraint in the current crisis. The result was his famous "too proud to fight" speech, in which he told his cheering audience that "there is such a thing as a man being too proud to fight. There is such a thing as a nation being so right that it does not need to convince others by force that it is right." This was another example of Wilson's well-known ability to construct a striking phrase, but it served in this instance only to augment his difficulties. As Tumulty predicted, the phrase "too proud to fight" gave comfort to Wilson's detractors, who perceived in it a form of stubborn cowardice that they focused on in renewed attacks against the president. Wilson responded at his next press conference, answering a reporter's question about his Philadelphia speech by saying that "I was expressing a personal attitude, that was all. I did not really have in mind any specific thing. I did not regard that as a proper occasion to give any intimation of policy on any special matter." The president thus did everything but retract his offending statement. Clearly, the ability to hone a sharp phrase cut in two directions; in this case Wilson himself suffered for the keenness of his prose.[10]

If these results seemed discouraging to the president, they appeared less so to the secretary of state. Bryan thus proposed a similar attempt three days later, at the time that Wilson's note to Germany about the *Lusitania* appeared in the press. In two letters to Wilson dated 12 May, Bryan contended that, although "it is well to act without delay in order to give direction to public opinion," the president should do something to moderate the impact of his words. He should, according to the secretary, issue a statement explaining that "strict accountability" did not necessarily mean immediate accountability and promising that the principle of Bryan's beloved "cooling-off" treaties would be extended to Germany. Wilson saw merit in this suggestion but thought it unwise to give out a direct statement. "The same purpose," he informed Bryan, "would be served by such a 'tip' as the enclosed, accompanying the publication of the note." It also seemed prudent, the president continued, "that this tip should be given out from the Executive Office, while the note was given out by the Department of State." In this way, Wilson reasoned, the moderating statement could be made to appear less than official without diluting its effectiveness.[11]

The purpose of Wilson's "tip"—its official title was "Proposed Notice for Publication"—was to inform the press that "there is a good deal of confidence in administration circles that Germany will respond to this note in a spirit of accommodation." Furthermore, the draft continued, "while Germany is not one of the many nations which have recently signed treaties of deliberation and inquiry with the United States . . . she has assented to the principle of such a treaty; and it is believed that she will act in this instance in the spirit of that assent." This statement was just what the secretary of state had in mind, but it was never to have any effect on public opinion. Its release was killed by other members of the administration, including Tumulty and Lansing, who convinced the president that the tip would lay him open to a charge of "double-dealing" with the Germans. As it turned out, the publication of Wilson's *Lusitania* note did not have the bellicose effect on public opinion that Bryan feared; it seemed, at least temporarily, to provide the kind of public guidance desired by the president.[12]

This proved small consolation for Bryan, who grew more convinced that Wilson was steering a collision course with Germany. By 31 May, when the German government's unyielding reply arrived in Washington, the secretary feared that war was imminent and determined to do whatever he could to prevent further worsening of relations. He was thus deeply alarmed by the president's proposed response, which—for all its somber eloquence—threatened to raise the level of controversy beyond the danger point. In a frenetic burst of activity, Bryan spent the early days of June exploring possibilities for blunting the force of Wilson's rejoinder, only to discover that the president had now grown implacable on the issue of submarine warfare. Bryan could not soften Wilson's ominous return note; his only recourse was to refuse to sign it. He did so by tendering his resignation on 8 June.[13]

Bryan's resignation did not mean that he was withdrawing from the public debate on relations with Germany. On the contrary, Bryan believed he could participate more effectively as a private citizen, and he intended, following his resignation, to use his well-known rhetorical skill to convince the public of the need for temperate negotiations. On 5 June, still inside the administration, Bryan warned the president that "the sober judgment of the people will not sustain any word or act that provokes war." He hoped later to demonstrate this truth by bringing, as he put it, "the real sentiments of the people to the surface." He apprised Wilson of this intention three days later, in his letter of resignation: "It falls to your lot to speak officially for the nation; I consider it to be none the less my duty to endeavor as a private citizen to promote the end which you have in view by means which you do not feel at liberty to use."[14]

With this polite throwing down of the gauntlet, Bryan entered what may have been the most difficult of his many public crusades. As he realized, it would be no simple matter to combat what he called "the Prestige and Power" of the presidency, and he quickly found himself vilified by pro-Wilson editors. Still he seemed to have some effectiveness with his massive audiences—even unfriendly newspapers concurred in this evaluation—and it was in their direction that his campaign was clearly aimed. From Wilson's standpoint, Bryan did appear a threat worthy of consideration, despite the fact that presidential mail, like newspapers, overwhelmingly supported the administration. In the end, of course, Bryan's defeat seemed inevitable. He found arrayed against him not only the power of the presidency but the force of events as well; he soon discovered himself as powerless to slow the drift toward war from outside as from inside the administration.[15]

Potentially more troublesome than Bryan's fulminations were the attacks of those espousing an expanded national preparedness. This position, too, found expression in Wilson's cabinet—Secretary of War Lindley M. Garrison served as one of its foremost spokesmen.

When the *Lusitania* crisis convinced Wilson that the state of national defense remained inadequate, he decided to launch his own preparedness campaign in the summer of 1915. As he saw it, this would provide him—and his diplomacy—with the kind of military force that even European nations would feel required to respect. Even more important was Wilson's awareness of presidential responsibility for leading public opinion, which he saw he must exercise to prepare the way for the kind of militarism required by American intervention. This did not mean, of course, that Wilson wished to lead the country into the war. On the contrary, one of his reasons for adopting the issue was his fear that others might use it to do just that; he hoped to achieve a "reasonable" preparedness, "very self-restrained and judicial," to replace the bellicose position of its early advocates.[16]

But the movement's erstwhile leaders did not surrender easily. The battle joined on 12 August when Garrison submitted his "Outline of Military Policy" to the president. In an enclosed letter the secretary of war pressed for strong administration publicity. Because, Garrison argued, "whatever of value is to be accomplished will be in response to public opinion," a determined effort should be made to line up support for preparedness. "The public knows this matter is being studied for the purpose of formulating and submitting a policy for consideration and adoption," Garrison continued, and to maintain silence might produce undue speculation about administration intentions. And finally, the secretary contended, publicity for his own plan might provide a kind of "trial balloon" on preparedness and allow the president to determine public attitudes about national defense. "Before final decision you should be advised of the trend of public opinion," Garrison argued. Widespread publicity "will result in the fixing of public attention upon the subject matter, giving it something to discuss and consider, and thus will elicit public opinion. In this way you will be enabled to gather what that opinion is and to act accordingly."[17]

Wilson remained unconvinced by these arguments, however. On 16 August he informed the secretary of war that "my judgment does not coincide with yours as to the publicity test." The danger here, according to the president, was that if later changes needed to be made in Garrison's proposal there might appear a difference of opinion between the two of them. Troubled times made unity important, Wilson continued, and "my judgment is, therefore, that it is best to keep the matter for the present for private consideration." It seems highly likely, moreover, that Wilson suspected the secretary's motives, that he perceived in Garrison's desire for publicity an attempt to win public approval for his own aggressive brand of preparedness. He saw this indicated in the secretary's "superficial paper," which, as he wrote Edith Galt, "was evidently prepared with a view to publication." This indicated that Garrison was fishing for the president's permission to continue—now with administration authority—his own previous campaign. This permission a wary Wilson had no intention of granting.[18]

Wilson also doubted Garrison's sincerity in proposing a trial balloon on the subject of national defense. According to Secretary Tumulty, this technique was employed rarely by the Wilson administration, despite reports to the contrary by numerous observers. "I have often heard it said," Tumulty wrote in 1921, "that 'feelers' are put out in the press by the White House to 'take soundings' on public opinion of the country on this or that projected policy, but like the death of Mark Twain such reports are 'greatly exaggerated.'" Press releases of new policies—and this was the kind of statement Garrison was proposing—described decisions already made and policies already determined, for the purpose of preparing rather than assessing public opinion. To Wilson, Garrison's proposal must have seemed doubly disingenuous: not only might he convince the public by presenting his plan ostensibly for approval, but he intended to ensnare the president as well.[19]

Also shying Wilson away from publicity was his fear of locking himself into a plan that might prove undesirable in the future. "The desires of the nation, I think, are quite clear on this matter," he wrote Garrison, but "I think the detail of the policy the country is generously willing to leave to us. It must, necessarily, be a matter of official information and expert opinion." As Wilson seemed keenly aware, early publication of Garrison's proposal, and especially of its details, might bind him to the plan by making its later rejection an embarrassment to the administration. This was just the sort of thing Wilson wished to avoid, and he wasted no time informing the secretary that he did not approve immediate publicity.[20]

Garrison did not give up easily. He soon renewed his appeal for publicity, repeating his earlier arguments about the importance of following public opinion. He also developed a new approach. Because, Garrison contended, leaks concerning the program seemed inevitable anyway, it might be best to bring the entire plan into the open as quickly as possible. What the secretary did not tell the president, however—and it was certainly relevant under the circumstances—was that he had already published his plan in the *Independent*. Unaware of this, Wilson continued his objection to immediate publicity and called upon the secretary to concentrate his efforts on perfecting the details of his proposal. Wilson had now found time, he wrote Garrison on 18 August, to read "with studious attention" his "Outline of Military Policy" and was "sorry to say that it does not contain what I hoped it would. In view of what you wrote me in your letter, it is evident that you were thinking chiefly while preparing it of making the test of public opinion to which you referred. The paper is, therefore, lacking in the detail which is necessary." With this mild chastisement, Wilson reminded the secretary of war that it remained their duty to make policy; too much concern with public opinion could only impede their efforts.[21]

The president wrote Garrison again one day later, renewing his criticism of immediate release. He could not, as he put it, agree that publicity would serve any useful purpose: "I think the method of preparedness is something which the country is not prepared to discuss. The demand for reasonable preparedness is clear enough and our own judgments go with it. We are not being driven, but are going of our own accord." Nor could he accept the secretary's contention that leaks might make disclosure necessary: "It seems to me a very serious matter that there should be leakages of any kind in the War Department with regard to official information, but if that is inevitable, we must endure it and act upon our best judgment notwithstanding." Wilson's best judgment harked back to his remarks about the primacy of policy making; he informed Garrison that "it is not the best way to go about our difficult job to try our suggestions out before public opinion on their practical and professional side." With this letter Wilson closed debate on the question of publicity. He and Garrison continued to disagree over the more fundamental issue of preparedness, however, until the secretary of war resigned from the cabinet in early 1916.[22]

In the meantime, Wilson continued his own, less specific, campaign on behalf of preparedness. Spurred by Tumulty, he took advantage of speaking opportunities in the autumn of 1915 to deliver, as the secretary requested, "something to the country, *in a general way*, with reference to national defense." Wilson did not commit himself to any particular proposal. Nor did he excite unduly the passions of the American people. He simply attempted to center national attention on the general question of preparedness, readying public opinion for the more difficult battle he knew lay ahead.[23]

He opened this battle on 4 November with an address before the Manhattan Club at the Biltmore Hotel in New York City. Taking great pains to avoid any semblance of militarism, the president revealed the program he planned to submit for congressional approval—a program that embodied, at least in part, the Continental army concept developed by Secretary Garrison. Wilson realized that this idea might appear a radical, and perhaps dangerous, departure from American traditions, and he carefully pointed out that his objective remained only the creation of a suitable defense. This objective, he told his audience, represented more than just the requirement of "a Nation too big and generous to be exacting yet courageous enough to defend its rights and the liberties of its people wherever assailed or invaded"; it also represented his "solemn obligation" as president. It was thus, he concluded, his duty to "ask for the hearty support of the country, of the rank and file of America, of men of all shades of political opinion," in fulfilling his program of national defense.[24]

But Wilson received less "hearty support" than public criticism, which emanated, to his surprise, largely from circles that usually backed his domestic efforts. The president had made a serious miscalculation: he had seen in the press, and especially in his mailbags, a dramatic reversal favoring preparedness after he espoused it in the summer. But he had overlooked the considerable number of important opinion leaders his efforts had failed to convert. Wilson's critics did not, perhaps, represent a large proportion of national sentiment, but they were articulate as well as influential with congressmen of the president's own party. The Continental army seemed in serious trouble. Wilson nevertheless went ahead with his plan of presenting the program in his annual message to Congress, but the length, organization, and delivery of his 6 December address betrayed his anxiety. Congressional response proved less than favorable; by January 1916 Wilson knew he could not count on support even from Democratic members of the House Military Affairs Committee, and he gave up all hope for the Continental army plan.[25]

What most troubled Wilson in January 1916 was not the demise of this particular program—he could produce similar results by expanding the National Guard anyway—but the public's apparent failure to rally around the idea of national preparedness. On 17 January, Tumulty proposed that the president do something about this situation, writing that "I cannot impress upon you too forcibly the importance of an appeal to the country at this time on the question of preparedness." The problem, as Tumulty saw it, was that, "because of the apparent inability of the country to grasp the importance of this question," national opinion had remained "indifferent" to it. This indifference had been nurtured by pacifists and by the average citizen's fear of excessive militarism. It remained for the president to provide leadership toward the middle course of sensible defense. "The great bulk of the people are looking for leadership," Tumulty continued, and would be happy to follow the president instead of Bryan or Roosevelt. Wilson must not forget, the secretary concluded, that "the American people are a sentimental people and even on a question as deep and as vital as national defense they ask for 'entertainment and guidance.'" As Tumulty's quotation marks suggest he knew, "entertainment and guidance" seemed an odd combination of services for a president to provide, yet he had convinced himself that only by supplying them could Wilson create interest in the all-important issue of preparedness.[26]

The president apparently agreed. On 18 January, he wrote Carter Glass that "I feel it is my duty to explain this matter to the country and summon its support." On the same day, he discussed the matter with his cabinet and instructed Tumulty to alert reporters to an impending presidential "swing around the circle" for the purpose of wresting initiative from those opposed to reasonable preparedness. It was this initiative that Wilson had allowed to slip away in the weeks following his speech to the Manhattan Club; he now determined to regain it.[27]

Beginning on 27 January, Wilson took his message to cities and towns from New York to Kansas, appearing before crowds estimated at a million persons. The president began boldly enough. He now recognized that his earlier remarks had been too placid, and he issued a series of stark warnings to the American people. At Cleveland, Ohio, he informed his auditors that "the world is on fire. Sparks are likely to drop anywhere. If all could see the dispatches I read every hour, they would know how difficult it has been to maintain peace." He quickly diluted these warnings, however, and spoke at Pittsburgh, Milwaukee, and Chicago in tones considerably less strident. He even paused in Des Moines to belittle those who favored American intervention. But this did not remain the president's final position. He seemed to sense that once again caution was restricting his effectiveness and resurrected his former hard-hitting style in a speech at Topeka, Kansas. He soon grew still more forceful, admonishing his audience in Kansas City that "there is not a day to be lost, not because of any new critical matter, but because I cannot tell what may happen in twenty-four hours," and closing the meeting with a chorus of "America." By the time of his final speech at Saint Louis, Wilson's style resembled a patriotic rodomontade, and he overstepped his own definition of propriety by declaring that the United States Navy "ought, in my judgment, to be incomparably the greatest Navy in the world."[28]

For all his peregrinations, Wilson evidently succeeded in focusing public attention on preparedness. His mail, which had largely supported him for several months anyway, picked up markedly in February; it also grew even more favorable to the creation of an expanded national defense. Wilson did not overlook this change in sentiment, writing on 23 February that the country seemed to be "swinging steadily and heavily towards the side of preparation" for adequate defense. Nor did journalists writing about national affairs. Allan L. Benson, for example, commented that the country's newspapers now insisted on an expansive military policy. "This public opinion," Benson concluded, "was formulated by the President, as the spokesman of the people." Even more percipient was Herbert Croly's *New Republic*, which described Wilson's effort as "a wonderful example of that opportunity for aggressive leadership which the Presidency of the United States places in the hands of the bold political strategist and the effective platform speaker." Here was the very heart of the progressive conception of the presidency, a conception that Croly had frequently advertised—and that Wilson had now clearly demonstrated.[29]

Within a month, however, Wilson faced his first administration's stiffest challenge to presidential leadership in foreign affairs. This was the threatened congressional adoption of the Gore and McLemore resolutions, which proposed a warning to all Americans against traveling on armed merchant vessels. At the time, Wilson remained deeply involved in negotiations over the right of neutrals to do exactly that—it was indeed Lansing's exposition of America's position in these negotiations that had renewed congressional interest—and he could hardly countenance a resolution limiting the impact of his own arguments. He thus decided to take the earliest opportunity to rally the public behind his position, hoping in this way to dissuade Congress from rash action.[30]

This opportunity presented itself on 24 February, when Senator William J. Stone sent the president a letter explaining his own concern over travel by Americans on armed merchant ships. Wilson's response, written with Tumulty's assistance, made a bold statement—clearly designed for public consumption—of his reasons for opposing the Gore and McLemore resolutions. It remained Wilson's intention, as he reminded the senator, to keep the United States out of war, and he expected to be able in the future, as in the past, to do so. Nevertheless, Wilson continued, his duty in this crisis seemed clear. "No nation, no group of nations, has the right while war is in progress to alter or disregard the principles which all nations have agreed upon in mitigation of the horrors and sufferings of war," and he could not, for his own part, "consent to the abridgment of the rights of American citizens in any respect. The honor and self-respect of the nation is involved." This represented Wilson's strongest rhetorical style, strengthened by his debater's sense of hyperbole and melodramatic appeal, and its use here demonstrated the significance he attached to the threat of the resolutions.[31]

It was characteristic of Wilson to answer this threat publicly, and he distributed mimeographed copies of his letter to White House reporters. As Wilson certainly intended, it received wide publication in the next morning's newspapers, and their impact upon congressional, if not public, opinion seemed immediately apparent. Within hours, the number of senators and congressmen favoring the resolutions fell to only a handful, and the president remained assured of a free hand in dealing with the armed-ship controversy. As in the case of preparedness, Wilson overcame this serious challenge to presidential authority by exerting his capacity for public leadership.[32]

Wilson's leadership stemmed from more than rhetorical ability, however; he also showed himself to be a skillful administrator in questions of public opinion. His handling, for example, of his December 1916 request to the belligerents for acceptable terms of peace displayed both an appreciation of the value of secrecy and a willingness to exercise ultimate authority over executive departments. When dispatched to the European powers, Wilson's note had been seen only by Lansing, State Department Counselor Frank Polk, and a few confidential clerks, and Wilson took pains for the next forty-eight hours to keep it secret from all other members of his administration. He did not even brief the omnipresent Tumulty, apparently because he feared that the secretary—who had recently fallen in Wilson's estimation—might inadvertently tip White House correspondents. And although some more prescient newspapermen were able to guess that an appeal was in the offing, Wilson appears to have succeeded in avoiding any official revelation about the note.[33]

Wilson saw the usefulness of publishing his request, however, and only wished to maintain secrecy until the time was right for its appearance. The right time, Wilson decided, was the morning of 21 December, and he asked Lansing to release the note to reporters on the preceding afternoon. Lansing thus alerted correspondents attending his morning conference on the twentieth that he would have an important announcement that afternoon—and warned them of the need for secrecy, even of his intention, in the meantime. Still following Wilson's instructions, Lansing distributed the note to newspapermen a few hours later, then proceeded to overstep his authority by issuing a statement interpreting the president's endeavor. According to Lansing, the note meant that "the United States was drawing nearer to the verge of war," and it indicated "the possibility of our being forced into the war." This far transcended the interpretation Wilson had in mind; he quickly summoned his secretary of state to the White House and ordered retraction of the offending remarks. Lansing complied immediately, issuing a second statement in which he said that "I did not mean to intimate that the government was considering any change in its policy of neutrality." Whichever of Lansing's statements was in fact true—and there is reason to suppose his first more accurate—Wilson had clearly demonstrated his intention to retain the control of publicity firmly in his own hands.[34]

This control grew even more important in early 1917 when Germany's resumption of unrestricted submarine warfare drew the United States to the brink of war. Wilson learned of this new policy on the afternoon of 31 January, and he relized immediately, according to Tumulty, that "this means war. The break that we have tried so hard to prevent now seems inevitable." He remained nevertheless unprepared—despite the urgings of both his secretary and Lansing —to call upon the American people to ready themselves for war. On 3 February he informed Congress of his decision to sever relations with the German government but spoke in terms both restrained and carefully measured. "We do not desire any hostile conflict with the Imperial German Government," he asserted. "We shall not believe that they are hostile to us unless and until we are obliged to believe it."[35]

Wilson hoped to avoid being thus obliged, but he found it increasingly difficult to do so. On 25 February, while being pressured by his cabinet for stronger action, Wilson received a message from Ambassador Walter Hines Page in London that canceled all of his doubts about Germany's intentions. This was a copy of the famous Zimmermann note, in which the German foreign secretary proposed an alliance combining his country and Mexico—and ultimately Japan —against the United States. On the next day, Wilson appeared before Congress to ask for the arming of merchant ships, as well as for the employment of "any other instrumentalities or methods that may be necessary and adequate to protect our ships and our people in their legitimate and peaceful pursuits on the seas." Still Wilson refused to abandon all hope for peace. He phrased his message in unwarlike terms and avoided any mention of the Zimmermann note, but there was no mistaking the fact that he was moving the United States closer to war.[36]

Although arming merchant ships seemed to meet broad public and congressional approval, there remained considerable dissension over empowering the president to employ "other instrumentalities or methods." It seemed apparent, in fact, that unless something was done to convince the country of the need for such broad authority the president's request faced certain rejection by Congress. Wilson could not tolerate this result, because he feared that it would leave him incapable of dealing with German threats to American shipping. He thus decided that it was necessary to take a strong step—he would release the Zimmermann note to the press. This possibility had first been raised on 27 February, when Lansing had gone to the White House to discuss the note and, as he remembered, "the way to use it, with the President." Among those urging its publication at that time were Tumulty and Colonel House, who argued that it would make, as House put it, a "profound impression" on both Congress and the country, but Wilson believed its contents too inflammatory to serve his still peaceful purposes. By the next day, however, Wilson's concern over the arming bill had overcome his fear of the note's dangers, and he called in the secretary of state for additional consultations on its use.[37]

Wilson and Lansing discussed methods for releasing the note, which was so sensational—and of such dubious origin—as to make its authenticity questionable. Lansing thought it unwise for the department "to give out the telegram officially at this time," because "it would be charged that it was done to influence opinion on the bill for arming merchant vessels"—which of course it was. The solution to all these problems, as the secretary of state saw it, was to release the note in an indirect manner, such as through a representative of the Associated Press. This technique would not only eliminate speculation about the president's motives; it would also put the administration in a position where, when reporters asked about the note, "we could say that we knew of it and knew that it was authentic." Thus, Lansing argued, the president could put himself in the enviable position of confirming his own rumor, a method that would at any rate "attract more attention" to the note than issuing it officially. Wilson saw merit in this ingenious proposal, and Lansing put it into effect a few hours later.[38]

The result went much as Lansing had predicted: a public sensation, followed by overwhelming House approval of the arming bill. Incredulity about the telegram's genuineness also afforded the president the opportunity to substantiate its authenticity—and to expand its impact upon public opinion. With that, Wilson would probably have been happy to see the matter closed, but a Senate filibuster against the armed-ships measure forced him to strike a note in the public debate certainly more strident than he wished. This was his famous remark, uttered when the Senate adjourned without action on the arming bill, that "a little group of willful men, representing no opinion but their own, have rendered the great Government of the United States helpless and contemptible." Provoked by Senate noninterventionists, Wilson exaggerated the situation of the United States—it was neither helpless nor contemptible —and fell prey to his own rhetorical ability by adding unwittingly to public alarm.[39]

Even more alarming than Wilson's stridency was the U-boat sinking, two weeks later, of three American merchant ships. If, as Lansing believed, the Zimmermann telegram had "resulted in unifying public sentiment throughout the United States against Germany," the destruction of these three vessels left little doubt about America's chances of remaining outside the war. Wilson soon indicated that his own war decision had been made, calling Congress into special session on 2 April—"to receive a communication concerning grave matters of national policy"—and initiating a series of diplomatic and military moves that could mean nothing else. To rising popular uncertainty, Wilson prepared his war message for Congress, a message he hoped would unite public opinion for the difficult times ahead.[40]

He delivered it on 2 April, reviewing before a joint session of Congress the reasons for American intervention, and explaining, in some detail, the objectives for which the United States must fight. Most important was his belief that "the world must be made safe for democracy. Its peace must be planted upon the firm foundations of political liberty." "We shall fight," he proclaimed, "for the things which we have always carried nearest our hearts,—for democracy, for the right of those who submit to authority to have a voice in their own Governments, for the rights and liberties of small nations, for a universal dominion of right by such a concert of free peoples as shall bring peace and safety to all nations and make the world itself at last free." It was one of Wilson's most brilliant addresses, at once emotional and restrained, and its conclusion seemed an almost irresistible call to war. "To such a task we can dedicate our lives and our fortunes, everything that we are and everything that we have, with the pride of those who know that the day has come when America is privileged to spend her blood and her might for the principles that gave her birth and happiness and the peace that she has treasured. God helping her, she can do no other."[41]

The response was quick and decisive. Congress showed enthusiasm with a thunderous cheer—then passed the war resolution within four days. A similar response came from the nation's news organizations, which promptly offered their services for publicizing the president's ideas. Wilson learned, for example, from the American Press Association's Courtland Smith that "on behalf of the country press and serving twelve thousand of those papers we consider it our duty and our privilege to give your proclamation the widest possible publicity through every department of our service." Like cooperation could also be expected from the public, which felt the same patriotic impulse as Congress and the press and which flooded the White House mail room with statements of its support. To no one's surprise, Wilson's call for war succeeded in rallying virtually all segments of society; he could count, for the time being at least, on almost total national cooperation.[42]

The president would need this cooperation to prosecute the war. To an even greater extent, however, he would require public support for his postwar program, which included continued American involvement in European affairs. This meant an end to the tradition of "isolation" and required a major shift in public attitudes about America's role in the world. To bring about such a change, Wilson engaged in a speaking campaign that spanned more than two years and that produced some of his most brilliant addresses. It was to be sure, the kind of task that only a leader of Wilson's stature could undertake; certainly no other president in this period tried so hard to alter such a major principle of the public's faith.

Wilson began his campaign in May 1916, almost a year before the United States entered the war. At that time, the president was involved in efforts to bring about a negotiated settlement in Europe, and he took advantage of an invitation from the League to Enforce Peace to outline his vision of the postwar world. Wilson took great pains in composing this address, "because I realize," he wrote House, "that it may be the most important I shall ever be called upon to make." He decided early on to avoid proposing a specific plan; it was more important first, he realized, to gain general agreement on American membership in some sort of postwar organization. This was the goal of the speech he delivered on the evening of 27 May at Washington's New Willard Hotel.[43]

The president began his address by disclaiming any interest in the outcome of the war in Europe; "with its causes and its objects," he said, "we are not concerned." Still, the prosecution of the war had "profoundly affected" the lives of the American people, and "we are not mere disconnected lookers-on." This connection meant that the United States had a deep interest in the permanence of the peace to come and that Americans must take an active part in the postwar world it could create. "We are participants, whether we like it or not," he said, "in the life of the world. The interests of all nations are our own also."[44]

With the need for internationalism established, Wilson proceeded to discuss what he called the fundamental beliefs of Americans: the right of every people to determine its own government; the equal rights of all nations, large and small; and the right of all to be free from aggression. "So sincerely do we believe in these things," he said, "that I am sure that I speak the mind and wish of the people of America when I say that the United States is willing to become a partner in any feasible association of nations formed in order to realize these objects and make them secure against violation." With these words, Wilson proclaimed the end of American isolation and made his public commitment to a postwar league of nations. This speech marked the beginning of his long and arduous campaign for American acceptance of that commitment.[45]

Wilson built on this foundation three days later in his Memorial Day address at Arlington National Cemetery. In this speech, he reiterated his contention that the United States was ready to cooperate in world affairs, that the American people "were ready to become partners in any alliance of nations that would guarantee public right above selfish aggression." He also took this opportunity to answer criticism of his earlier address, remarking that "some of the public prints" had reminded him of Washington's injunction against "entangling alliances." But, he responded, entanglement was not what he intended. "I shall never myself consent to an entangling alliance, but I would gladly assent to a disentangling alliance." The league that he proposed, Wilson continued, was of the disentangling sort—it would free the world's people from selfish combinations and unite them "to preserve the peace of the world upon a basis of common right and justice."[46]

Of course, 1916 was an election year, and Wilson utilized some of his many speaking engagements to remind the public of its duty in the postwar world. On 2 September, he accepted the Democratic nomination by calling upon the American people to "contribute" its "full force" to the "organization of . . . peace upon world-wide foundations that cannot easily be shaken." This was necessary because "no nation can any longer remain neutral." Thus, the United States must surrender any lingering notions of "Little Americanism"; involvement in world affairs was now unavoidable.[47]

Wilson returned to this theme a month later. Speaking on 5 October at Omaha, Nebraska, he started by acknowledging the isolationist sentiments of the Midwest, then warned that "the world no longer consists of neighborhoods. The world is linked together in a common life and interest such as humanity never saw before." This made American separatism impossible and required that the United States lend its "full force" to a "league of nations." He repeated this call a week later at Indianapolis: "I have said, and shall say again, that when the great present war is over it will be the duty of Americans to join with the other nations of the world in some kind of league for the maintenance of the peace." And two weeks later, speaking at Cincinnati, he declared that "the business of neutrality is over"; the time had come when "we must have a society of nations."[48]

The president closed his reelection campaign with a final call for expanded American involvement in the world. "The United States," he said, "was once in enjoyment of what we used to call splendid isolation." But that day had passed. "The world will never be again what it has been. The United States will never be again what it has been." The country could no longer behave as it had done when it was "provincial and isolated"; it would have to find a new relationship with the world. There could no longer be any doubt, he concluded, that "the day of isolation is gone."[49]

Victorious in November, Wilson returned to his antiisolationist theme early in 1917. On 22 January he delivered his famous "peace without victory" address to the Senate, combining a call for a negotiated settlement of the war with a restatement of his views on American involvement in the world. Once again, he discussed the need for a "definite concert of power" that would make future wars impossible, then remarked that "it is inconceivable that the people of the United States should play no part in the great enterprise." To provide such a service would be an "honor" for the American people; there would be no doubt that "they do not wish to withhold it." This was especially important because the principles of lasting peace coincided with those held by most Americans. These were "peace without victory," the equal rights of nations, the freedom of all peoples to determine their own government, freedom of the seas, and a limitation of armaments. Wilson was certain, he went on, that "the people and Government of the United States will join the other civilized nations of the world in guaranteeing" a peace on such terms; he could speak with "boldness and confidence" because to do so would be a "fulfillment" of America's heritage. He was proposing nothing more than "American principles" and "American policies."[50]

By the time of Wilson's second inauguration on 5 March, the United States had drawn very near to involvement in the European war. Thus, the president used his address to make one final peacetime statement of his ideas on the postwar world. Most important, of course, was the need for continued American participation in international affairs; this was, indeed, a matter about which the United States had no choice. "We are provincials no longer," Wilson said; the events of the war had made Americans "citizens of the world." There could be "no turning back. Our own fortunes as a nation are involved, whether we would have it so or not." Speaking with unsurpassed eloquence, the president asked for public support in the difficult days ahead. "United alike in the conception of our duty and in the high resolve to perform it in the face of all men, let us dedicate ourselves to the great task to which we must now set our hand." America's period of uninvolvement had clearly passed.[51]

One month later, the United States entered the war. True to his earlier efforts, Wilson used his 2 April war message to link the need for military action with his plans for the postwar world. He wanted to make clear, he said, "what our motives and our objects are." His own had not changed; he had "exactly the same things in mind now" as in his earlier messages to Congress. "Our object now, as then, is to vindicate the principles of peace and justice" and to set up "such a concert of purpose and of action as will henceforth insure the observance of those principles." This would require, in the future, a "partnership of democratic nations," in which the United States would continue to play an important role.[52]

Entrance into the war only strengthened Wilson's view of the necessity for American cooperation in the postwar world. This was made clear in the president's famous Fourteen Points speech, delivered to Congress on 8 January 1918. In outlining his program for a settlement, Wilson drew the connection between America's involvement in the war and its continued involvement in the peace. "We entered this war," he said, "because violations of right had occurred" against which the world must be secured "once for all." This would be in the interest of all nations; indeed, "all the peoples of the world are in effect partners in this interest." There could be no doubt, then, that "the program of the world's peace, therefore, is our program." For Wilson, the most important part of this program was the fourteenth point, "a general association of nations" to afford "mutual guarantees of political independence and territorial integrity to great and small states alike." It was in such an organization —and for such a purpose—that the United States must continue to play an active role in the postwar world.[53]

Wilson reiterated this view in his 11 February address to Congress on the German and Austrian replies to his statement of war aims. "Covenants must be entered into," he said, for the insurance of peace and justice, and "those covenants must be backed by the united force of all the nations that love justice and are willing to maintain it at any cost." This was, to be sure, a heavy commitment, but Wilson regarded it as an essential one. His goal was nothing less than the creation of a "new international order," without which "the world will be without peace and human life will lack tolerable conditions of existence and development." With so much at stake, Wilson made it clear that the United States could not "turn back."[54]

The president chose Independence Day for his next public pronouncement on his postwar program. Speaking at Mount Vernon on 4 July, Wilson drew a connection between the task faced by Washington in 1789 and that facing the present leaders of America. The goals of 1918 were, he said, "only the fruitage" of what the Founding Fathers had "planted," except that this generation "shall make not only the liberties of America secure but the liberties of every other people as well." As Wilson saw it, this could be done through a peace established in accordance with four principles, including the creation of an "organization of peace" to "make it certain that the combined power of free nations will check every invasion of right." This was, Wilson concluded, a fitting subject to discuss at Mount Vernon, because he fancied that "the air of this place carries the accents of such principles with a peculiar kindness." They were, after all, Washingtonian in nature.[55]

Wilson presented his most detailed discussion of a postwar league of nations on 27 September 1918. The occasion was the opening of the Fourth Liberty Loan campaign, which the president employed to call for continued public sacrifice both during and after the war. To make this sacrifice worthwhile, Wilson argued, the war must be followed by a "secure and lasting peace." But this could only be accomplished if the world's peoples were willing "to pay the price, the only price, that will procure it" and to create "in some virile fashion" an instrumentality to protect it. "That indispensable instrumentality," Wilson continued, "is a League of Nations." For his own part, the president was confident that the United States was "prepared to assume its full share of the responsibility" under the league. There was no reason to fear in this a violation of "Washington's immortal warning against 'entangling alliances,'" for "only special and limited alliances entangle." America now recognized the "duty of a new day" in which a "general alliance" might "avoid entanglements" and keep the peace.[56]

On 11 November 1918 Wilson went before Congress to announce the terms of the armistice ending the war. He also issued a final wartime reminder of the need for American involvement in the peace. This must be, the president argued, "a peace as will satisfy the longing of the whole world for disinterested justice." Wilson saw ample reason to suppose that this kind of peace was possible; it seemed manifest in the "humane temper" of the victors. But it should not be supposed that achieving such a peace would be easy. "We must be patient," he said, "and helpful and mindful above all else of the great hope and confidence that lie at the heart of what is taking place." In this way the United States could play a part in the important events to come.[57]

With these speeches Wilson attempted to deflect the public's faith in the principle of isolationism. This was, to be sure, an important objective, the success of which will be discussed later. But it represented only a small part of the president's wartime publicity. Indeed, the war ushered the United States into a new era of public relations, as men (and women), materiel, and ideas were mobilized on a scale previously unknown, resulting in the aggregation of increasing power in the hands of the executive. To deal with this power, Wilson created a number of new organizations. One of these—the Committee on Public Information—would soon revolutionize the process of executive publicity and alter irreversibly the president's relationship with public opinion.

Chapter 7

Dr. Wilson and

Mr. Creel

 Shortly before delivering his war message to Congress, Woodrow Wilson summoned *New York World* editor Frank I. Cobb to the White House. The president, it developed, was anxious over dangers he foresaw in war—dangers to threaten democracy's very existence—and wanted to share his fears with a sympathetic journalist. "Once lead this people into war," he told Cobb, "and they'll forget there ever was such a thing as tolerance. To fight you must be brutal and ruthless, and the spirit of ruthless brutality will enter into the very fibre of our national life, infecting Congress, the courts, the policeman on the beat, the man in the street." Wilson's words might suggest that he feared too much rather than too little support for the coming war; yet it is difficult to find any indication of this in his behavior. He had, on the contrary, already begun to formulate plans for the Committee on Public Information, an organization designed to centralize the control of all war information and destined, by the time of the armistice, to go far beyond previous executive excursions into public relations and propaganda.[1]

The idea for the CPI came from Josephus Daniels, an old progressive Democrat serving the Wilson administration as secretary of the navy. In his official capacity, Daniels was charged with preparing plans for some kind of wartime censorship; as a long-time journalist, he also recognized that something more than censorship was required for effective leadership of public opinion. As early as 7 March, the secretary invited George Creel to dinner for a discussion of what he termed the "paper fight" of propaganda certain to develop from America's involvement in the war. Ten days later, he conferred with representatives of the press associations about appointing a newspaperman as civilian censor. At the same time, Daniels worked out an agreement with reporters for voluntarily censoring information on ship departures, and he convinced himself that an arrangement of this type could provide necessary wartime censorship without sacrificing friendly relations with the press. He thus proposed the creation of a censorship committee organized to avoid the compulsion feared by journalists while providing the government with an agency for disseminating prowar publicity. This was the embryonic CPI. The president approved it, along with the appointment of Creel as chairman, on 9 April; during the next two years, it would expand almost beyond even the navy secretary's recognition.[2]

If Daniels's conception proved pale beside the later reality, Wilson's appeared even more so. As the president saw it, the committee's primary function was to censor potentially dangerous information, with publicity playing only a subsidiary role. It was on this basis that he agreed to proceed with the secretary's suggestion. What might seem a lack of presidential vision, however, was actually a reflection of Wilson's situation; there can be little doubt that censorship, not publicity, seemed most pressing in the days following his war declaration. Wilson's restraint also reflected his information. His advisers—Daniels, in particular—sold him on the CPI by stressing its least innovative features, expecting to expand its duties in the future.[3]

Wilson soon learned that the committee's responsibilities might far exceed censorship. On 13 April he received a letter from the secretaries of war, navy, and state officially proposing the CPI's creation and describing the functions they believed it could serve. The secretaries agreed that censorship seemed necessary to prevent, as they put it, "premature or ill-advised announcements of policies, plans, and specific activities." But, they argued, "America's great present needs are confidence, enthusiasm, and service"—needs that could be met only if "every citizen is given the feeling of partnership that comes with full, frank statements concerning the conduct of public business. It is our opinion," they continued, "that the two functions—censorship and publicity—can be joined in honesty and with profit" in a Committee on Public Information, which "can proceed to the framing of regulations and the creation of machinery that will safeguard all information of value to the enemy, and at the same time open every department of government to the inspection of the people as far as possible." Thus, Wilson learned that his advisers regarded publicity as the CPI's most valuable service, a knowledge he reflected in wording the executive order that established the committee. Any remaining presidential doubts about the CPI's scope were doubtless eliminated that same afternoon, when Wilson had the first of many meetings with the voluble Creel, who could hardly have refrained from outlining his most expansive plans for the new organization.[4]

Although Wilson expressed initial interest in censorship rather than publicity, he was not slow to grasp the possibilities envisioned by Daniels and Creel. As a progressive, the president had long appreciated the importance of public information, not least for its ability to win support for administration programs and policies. He now perceived the benefits of publicizing America's role in the World War and wasted little time throwing his complete support behind the committee and its controversial chairman, meeting frequently— sometimes daily—with Creel and taking an active part in several of the committee's campaigns. Wilson also defended the new organization's expanded conception and justified its release and control of war news with such impeccably progressive principles as the public's right to know as much as possible about government activities. Ironically, Wilson continued to pressure Congress for additional censorship authority, resulting in passage of the Espionage, Trading-with-the-Enemy, and Sedition Acts, but he still managed to convince the American people that the CPI expressed his primary desire to disseminate large quantities of information.[5]

In George Creel, Wilson appointed a chairman with credentials to enhance the organization's progressive image. While working on the editorial staffs of the *Denver Post* and the *Rocky Mountain News*, Creel had earned a reputation as a crusader for social—and often radical—reform. He consistently supported progressive candidates for offices held by the usual boss-run politicians and wrote in favor of such standard progressive devices as the initiative, referendum, and recall. Creel's activities became national after 1913, when he contributed articles supporting Wilson's New Freedom to such liberal magazines as *Everybody's* and *Pearson's* and when he co-authored, with Edwin Markham and Ben Lindsay, a scathing report on child labor in America. It was, no doubt, ample testimony to Creel's progressivism that, even as designated head of an organization many saw as dangerously repressive, he was attacked primarily for his radicalism.[6]

Although Creel's progressivism later played a vital part in the CPI's development, it was not his chief qualification for the post of committee chairman. More important, from Wilson's perspective, was his skill as a propagandist, which Creel clearly demonstrated while serving in several important capacities on the president's staff during the 1916 campaign. Not only did Creel write *Wilson and the Issues*, a campaign book serialized and later published in paperback; he also undertook what he called the "rehabilitation of Josephus Daniels." The secretary of the navy had been seriously maligned during Wilson's first administration; Creel did much to repair his image, and Daniels repaid him by suggesting his name to the president for the job of CPI chairman. Nor was writing the only talent Creel displayed during the presidential campaign; he also showed himself adept at organizing a publicity network. As Creel saw it, "my prize contribution to the campaign . . . was the organization of a committee of publicists and authors for the issuance of statements and pamphlets," a contribution that recommended him for the administrative duties he would encounter as head of the CPI. With such experience, it was no wonder that the energetic chairman discovered a wide range of innovative techniques for expanding his committee's effectiveness.[7]

Not even Creel could find time for innovation in the hectic spring of 1917, however; he was preoccupied with such concerns as locating an administrative staff and establishing makeshift—and woefully inadequate—offices in the murky shadows of the Navy Library. At that time, too, the chairman set out to define the role that the CPI would play in the already burgeoning war effort. Censorship was to be the least of it. Creel believed that establishing a European-style censor remained unnecessary, and he could not, at any rate, picture himself serving in that capacity. Nor did he see censorship as the solution to the government's chief information problem, writing at the war's close that "with the nation in arms, the need was not so much to keep the press from doing the hurtful things as to get it to do the helpful things." By the time of his appointment, Creel had already conferred with Navy Secretary Daniels in designing the CPI as more than a censorship organization, and they had doubtless agreed that the administration's ultimate problem must be a lack of public enthusiasm. From Creel's perspective, this seemed a serious problem indeed, one that had to be remedied before the war could be prosecuted effectively. What the situation required was a massive dose of prowar publicity—Creel liked to call it "expression" rather than "suppression"—to convince the public and to render censorship unnecessary by supplying the press with all the legitimate news it could handle. Not only did this conception of the CPI seem in keeping with the new chairman's progressive principles; it also allowed their use in justification of his efforts to win public support for the war.[8]

Still, censorship topped the committee's list of immediate objectives and would have to be established in some form before Creel could turn his attention to the larger problem of publicity. As the most expeditious solution, the chairman simply adopted the voluntary censorship worked out before the declaration by the various departments. But this quickly proved insufficient, and Creel decided there was need for a new, more authoritative set of regulations under the auspices of the CPI. He thus collaborated with the president to draw up the committee's "Preliminary Statement to the Press," which he delivered to Washington correspondents on 28 May and which included the CPI's guidelines for voluntary censorship of war information. Arguing that "public opinion is a factor in victory no less than ships and guns," the "Preliminary Statement" placed news of the war in three classifications: dangerous, should not be printed; doubtful, in need of approval by the CPI; and routine, does not affect conduct of the war. It also pointed out particular abuses, such as use of "special correspondents" who did not sign their copy, that the committee hoped "patriotic" newspapers would halt.[9]

Then, as later, Creel never seemed to tire of protesting that establishment of voluntary guidelines represented the extent of his censorship; he found no criticism of his role in the CPI more rankling than the claim that he served primarily as censor. The chairman was in fact much more of a censor than he was ever willing to admit, although he largely confined his personal efforts to wheedling cooperation from straying journalists. As member of the president's Censorship Board under the Trading-with-the-Enemy Act and as Postmaster General Albert S. Burleson's chief authority on subversive material, Creel was the linchpin of all the administration's censorship activities. This fact, surely, escaped the notice of few newspapermen, and it explained in large measure the chairman's nearly phenomenal success in winning their compliance. Still, Creel was correct to bristle at charges that he was nothing more than a glorified censor: he spent relatively little time in that endeavor, and had defined objectives for the CPI considerably more important—and innovative—than the mere administration of wartime censorship.[10]

If by the armistice the CPI was to become, as Creel described it, "a vast enterprise in salesmanship, the world's greatest adventure in advertising," its first few weeks remained dominated by the most pedestrian of its many branches—the Division of News. There was, indeed, little innovative about this first of the CPI's divisions; it represented the logical extension of presidential efforts over twenty years to centralize the release of information, and its greatest achievement came in fulfilling, as far as war news was concerned, this long-standing White House objective. Any success owed much to the perceptiveness of Creel, who understood that the gathering of war information could not be, as he put it, "left safely to the peacetime practice of the press with its uninterrupted daily swing of reporters through the various departments, the buttonholing of clerks, and the haphazard business of permitting minor officials to

make unchecked and unauthorized statements." Nor could adminis-
trators be trusted to issue just the right kind of information. They
not only failed to appreciate the value of publicity but demonstrated
an utter lack of what Creel called "news sense" as well, with the
result that valuable material often remained buried while triviali-
ties were released. What the situation required, according to Creel,
was "official machinery for the preparation and release of all news
bearing upon America's war effort." This became the responsibility
of the Division of News.[11]

Although the machinery created by this division seemed novel
only in scope, it nonetheless proved a highly effective instrument for
disseminating wartime news. For the first time in the executive's
history, there existed an individual agency charged with releasing
information from such disparate branches as the army and navy, the
White House, the Department of Justice, the Department of Labor,
the Council of National Defense, and the War Industries Board;
the result was a previously unimaginable continuity of tone and
purpose in administration news and publicity. To insure, moreover,
that content as well as timing remained under the division's control, Creel placed CPI personnel—mostly former journalists—in the
many agencies it served, with orders to oversee preparation of all
war-related press releases. Not surprisingly, all of this developed
into a task of terrific proportions, requiring the division to remain
open twenty-four hours a day and seven days a week and involving,
by war's end, the issuance of more than 6,000 news releases.[12]

The large number of newspapermen employed by the CPI raises
an interesting question: how difficult did reporters find the transi-
tion from gatherers to disseminators of news? As newsmen, the committee's new employees had bridled at the "canned news" quality of
administration press releases; as members of the CPI bureaucracy,
they now prepared such releases as part of their regular duties.
It might be supposed, accordingly, that they found their new role
an uncomfortable one; yet there is no evidence of this in the records
of the CPI. On the contrary, Creel—a former journalist himself—
believed that ex-newspapermen were happy in the CPI, and he
attributed much of the News Division's success to their energy and
enthusiasm.[13]

One result of the division's extensive activities was the White
House's temporary eclipse as the primary source of information. As
reporters rushed to set up shop in the new press room of the CPI—
now occupying larger quarters in a rented house on Jackson Place—
they found increasingly little time for chasing down stories of their
own. At the same time, they received scant information directly

from the White House, where Secretary Tumulty showed respect for Creel's prerogatives by terminating his daily news conferences and by channeling all White House press releases through the CPI. Tumulty continued to work behind the scenes to foster good administration press relations, but he virtually disappeared from news columns as a source of information. The Division of News thus supplanted the White House as the authoritative voice in executive affairs.[14]

In taking over the release of White House news, Creel faced a number of questions that had worried presidential secretaries for at least two decades. On 8 June, for instance, he wrote Wilson about the reporters' request for advance copies of an upcoming presidential message and expressed his doubts about the prudence of continuing such practice in time of war. Creel realized that prior releases had become what he termed "established custom" and understood that there had been as yet no serious breach of confidence. But he was now convinced that the advance copy system would have to be discontinued. As the chairman saw it, the threat of leakage caused by prior release had been made more serious by the war, requiring extraordinary steps to prevent it in the future. And, Creel concluded, because the problem had arisen from the announcement that a presidential statement was forthcoming, he suggested that no future announcements of this type be made until the moment of actual release.[15]

As Creel soon discovered, however, playing it safe in the matter of advance releases exacted a heavy price in diminished publicity, and he was eventually forced to reconsider his initial decision to eliminate them. Procedures for prior release had been worked out over several administrations, as we have seen, to insure maximum coverage and impact for presidential announcements; Creel soon found this purpose as important in time of war as it had been in time of peace. He accordingly decided that the advantages of prior release outweighed the risk of a breach in security and quickly reinstituted its use by the CPI's Division of News. Although this decision did nothing more than leave the procedure exactly where it had been when the war began, it eliminated any lingering doubts about the feasibility of advance releases in wartime and demonstrated Creel's clear preference for publicity over security.[16]

Although this preference remained evident in virtually all activities of the Division of News, it did not guarantee immunity against the disaffection of the press. Within days of its creation, the division came under fire from several Washington correspondents, in whom, according to Creel, "long training had developed the conviction that nothing in the world was as important as a 'story,'" so strongly that "not even the grim fact of war could remove the obsession." Part of the problem lay in Creel's objective of disseminating information as widely as possible; there now existed fewer possibilities for journalists to obtain the kind of scoops that they so highly valued. Correspondents also feared the loss of their personal independence, perceiving in what they saw as the press-agentry of the division an attempt to make them and their papers little more than promoters for the war effort. Considerable truth resided in this charge, despite Creel's many attempts to refute it; the division did see the press as its own instrument. But newspapermen soon lost desire to pursue the matter, as—with other sources of information drying up—they became acutely aware that the division seemed indispensable to their efforts. And when, eventually, the division's novelty began to fade, reporters recognized that its activities differed only in scale from those they accepted at the White House, and they established a fragile truce with the CPI's more efficient press bureau.[17]

Compounding the division's press difficulties was the fact that it also administered Creel's regulations for voluntary censorship. Correspondents understandably chafed at the idea of receiving news from the same organization that denied them the use of other—often more exciting—tidbits of war information. This was indeed a shortcoming in the general conception of the CPI, and it helped produce the committee's bitterest wartime dispute, the well-known "Fourth of July hoax" controversy, which reflected journalistic disapproval of the CPI's ability to command both censorship and publication.[18]

The dispute began on 27 June 1917 when a misunderstanding allowed the Associated Press to put out a story announcing the arrival of American soldiers in France. At that time, many troop transports still remained in the dangerous Atlantic U-boat zones, leaving Creel and other administration officials furious over this obvious breach of voluntary censorship. Immediately, the chairman confronted the press with its failure to keep the troops' landing in confidence. One week later, with hostility still permeating the Washington atmosphere, Creel received word—hastily relayed to correspondents—that the last American troopships had now arrived safely in Saint Nazaire. This was exciting news, but it was not all. Within a few hours there followed a thrilling story detailing the ships' repulsion of several enemy submarines, a story Creel himself prepared from messages cabled by the fleet's admiral. Direct and vibrant, this was exactly the kind of copy that reporters had been most lacking, and their editors splashed Creel's submarine story across the headlines of 4 July editions throughout the country.[19]

There soon developed some doubt about the story's truthfulness, however, especially in light of an AP dispatch from London denying the existence of any submarine attack at all. The press let out a terrific uproar. It understandably felt itself used in perpetrating a publicity hoax on the American people, and it now seemed willing to settle for nothing less than Creel's hide in retribution. To make matters worse, the CPI chairman soon admitted, in the course of reiterating—correctly—that there had indeed been a U-boat attack on American ships, that his story was perhaps an "elaboration" of a "cryptic" report from the fleet's admiral. This only supplied Creel's detractors with additional ammunition. Anti-Wilson forces in Congress also entered the fray, attacking the CPI's motives as purely political and threatening to make the CPI an embarrassment to the administration. Ultimately, the issue of the submarine attack proved unimportant, but it did have an effect on editorial willingness to trust the motives of CPI releases.[20]

There existed, to be sure, plenty of reason for the press to mistrust Creel's motives; the U-boat story was unquestionably an example of his desire to use the news for publicity purposes. In this instance, Creel's tone was set by Secretary of the Navy Daniels, who exclaimed on hearing of the troops' safe arrival that it would make a great "Fourth of July present for the people." Creel attempted to package the story as just such a present and was undoubtedly guilty of exaggerating the U-boat danger as well as of phrasing his report in patriotic bombast. Yet he did nothing more than perform the job of CPI chairman as he perceived it. For Creel, publicity remained the CPI's primary responsibility, and he could see no better way to achieve it than by dramatizing American accomplishments, even if this meant overstating the truth to supply good copy—and even if it meant occasionally incurring the wrath of reporters used by his endeavors.[21]

If the News Division had difficulties with correspondents, it also found it hard to get along with at least one member of Wilson's official family. This was Secretary of State Lansing, who believed that the activities of his department were, as he put it, of "much too important and too delicate a nature to be dealt with by men who were by no means expert in international affairs" and who dealt with the CPI's threatened intrusion of his domain by creating an expanded State Department information bureau. The problem was at least partly one of personalities: Lansing disliked Creel's flashy style of publicity about as much as Creel disdained the secretary of state's concern with protocol. And it certainly did not help that the two officials held widely divergent political views. As a result, Lansing not only rebuffed the division's plan to place a representative in his offices but also forced it to fight a continuing battle over its right of access to any State Department news.[22]

Not surprisingly, Wilson soon found himself drawn into this controversy, and he endeavored on several occasions to gain Lansing's support for the Creel committee. On 29 June, he wrote to ask the secretary's cooperation in seeing to it that "matters that are not merely matters of departmental information may be handled through Mr. Creel who is constantly acting under my suggestion and guidance." This apparently had little effect, because the president found it necessary—five months later—to answer Third Assistant Secretary of State Breckinridge Long's complaints about the press with yet another lecture on the need for cooperation with the CPI. The committee, Wilson reminded Long, had been created to handle just the kind of press problems now described by the assistant secretary, but its success had been hampered by the failure of the State Department "to act through Mr. Creel's committee in the matter of publicity." In addition, the president scolded, the lack of coordination and central management engendered by State Department stubbornness had created embarrassments for the administration that were "very serious indeed," and he suggested that Long take steps to effect closer cooperation with the CPI in the future.[23]

The State Department's decision to go its own way may have tangled the administration's conduct of publicity; it also produced a dramatic increase in the department's own awareness of the press. Perhaps predictably, this first manifested itself in concern over security, provisions for which had remained decidedly lax in the prewar State Department. Lansing tackled this problem personally, instituting a system of passes for access to the department. As the secretary described it, this change was designed to prevent the entry not only of enemy spies but also of "some American newspapermen, who, being too indiscreet or too indifferent to considerations other than 'news value' or to the chance to write a sensational story" might embarrass or damage the government by premature publication of information. No longer, under this system, might correspondents roam freely the corridors of the State Department; they were now supervised closely both to and from appointments. Nor might they continue their prewar habit of discussing affairs with various members of bureaus and divisions whenever they pleased. The department's staff was ordered, under pain of being "summarily dismissed," to avoid talking with reporters, "even on insignificant matters of fact or detail," and to leave all questions of publicity to the secretary of state and appropriate divisions.[24]

To improve publicity, Lansing also refurbished the department's ten-year-old Division of Information, renaming it the Division of Foreign Intelligence and adding to its public relations duties. He now charged the division with such responsibilities as preparing news releases, controlling departmental publicity, and filling requests for information from Congress, universities, and the public. Lansing also appointed Philip Patchin, a former journalist who had been the old Division of Information's first chairman, along with Hugh Gibson, a Class-1 foreign service officer, to head the new division and assigned them an administrative staff that would number fourteen by the end of the year. With the secretary's support, the division achieved almost total centralization of State Department news for the duration of the war; it ultimately ranked second only to the CPI in overall dissemination of wartime news and propaganda.[25]

All of this did not, of course, endear Lansing to reporters, who saw in his combination of security and publicity nothing less than intentional obstruction of their efforts. By sealing the department from the press, the secretary of state forced newsmen to accept the DFI's statements at face value, and interfered with the normal activities of the press far more alarmingly than the avalanche of information proffered by Creel. To seek redress, correspondents turned to their old friend Tumulty but found even him powerless to convince Wilson —who favored any measure to enhance security—of the need to interfere. Lansing, too, proved implacable, defending his new system as working "most satisfactorily" and claiming, somewhat disingenuously, that correspondents now received four times as much departmental news—he did not say of what value—than under the "unsystematic method previously employed." The real problem with reporters, according to the secretary of state, came from a few who had previously enjoyed special connections; there could be no solution until the press accepted the more democratic distribution afforded by the Division of Foreign Intelligence. This ultimately appeared to be the result. Correspondents realized that State was no longer an open source of information and turned their attention to gleaning whatever news they could from the DFI's smooth-running machinery.[26]

While Lansing reorganized State Department press procedures, Creel took steps of his own to enhance the effectiveness of the CPI's Division of News. In early summer, he established a news service for the rural press, which often could not afford to subscribe to news services or to hire correspondents of its own and which was therefore, according to Creel, "experiencing a sense of neglect" by the CPI. This new project took the form of a weekly *War News Digest*—

the papers it served were weeklies—prepared by a special section of the division supervised by a small-town editor. Ultimately, more than 12,000 rural newspapers, many of which had no other connection with official Washington, received the kind of information given daily to their larger counterparts in the press room of the CPI, adding their readers to those reached regularly by the division's accounts of the war.[27]

Even so, the commercial press proved unable to satisfy all of the CPI's needs for news dissemination, and the committee soon found it necessary to establish a gazette of its own. This was the *Official Bulletin*, the first official daily newspaper in American history. It filled an obvious void in commercial coverage by allowing the CPI to insure authoritative publication of such important news items as texts of orders, proclamations, and reports. Its idea was not original in 1917; a similar proposal had been made during Wilson's first administration. But the war gave the need for an official newspaper greater currency, and the president himself suggested the *Official Bulletin* to Creel during the first weeks of the CPI's existence. As Wilson saw it, a combination of political motives and circulation concerns prevented commercial papers from printing sufficient quantities of routine government news; they thus could not be counted on to inform the public or government branches of important administration activities. To remedy this situation, Wilson deemed it necessary to go beyond the mere issuance of press releases; the CPI must enter the newspapers' own field of publication.[28]

Creel balked immediately at this suggestion. He informed the president that the CPI's press problems were already bad enough without threatening newspapermen with government competition. As an ex-journalist himself, Creel could understand the profession's sensitivity to being supplanted by a government gazette, and he feared that an *Official Bulletin* might generate sufficient criticism of interference with private enterprise to destroy the official newspaper's—and perhaps the CPI's—usefulness to the administration. His objections registered little effect on Wilson, however, who insisted that the publication was too important to be halted by journalists' petty anxieties, and the nervous CPI chairman prepared the bulletin's first issue to appear in early May.[29]

Aware that public availability was essential to the *Official Bulletin*'s success, Creel attempted to guarantee it the widest possible circulation. He made arrangements with the War and Navy departments to display the bulletin on all military posts and naval stations and ordered it sent as a kind of glorified release sheet to every newspaper in the country. Most important was his agreement with the postmaster general to place the bulletin conspicuously in the nation's 54,000 post offices. There, especially in small communities, it provided many Americans with their only daily link to the CPI's war information. The *Official Bulletin* soon became a vital part of the committee's publicity efforts, publishing news otherwise unavailable and reaching through private subscription—which Creel, fearing interference with private enterprise, did not promote—a total circulation of over 118,000 copies daily.[30]

As it turned out, Creel proved correct to worry about the commercial press; it wasted little time launching a bitter attack against the new *Official Bulletin*. Nor did Creel find this criticism easily quieted, despite his many disclaimers that the publication "will not," as he put it, "interfere with the legitimate functions of the press in any manner, nor will official news be delayed or withheld in order to give the *Bulletin* any special news significance." To make matters worse, journalists managed to interest Congress—ever-vigilant of Creel—in the bulletin's threat to the freedom of the press, prompting a full-scale congressional investigation of the gazette. Creel responded sharply. He cut off the bulletin's circulation to newspapers and instructed his editor to inform inquiring journalists to "take it up" with their congressmen. This only increased the anger of his critics, and by autumn 1918 Congress made it clear that it did not intend to fund the *Official Bulletin* beyond the war's conclusion. Not even Wilson's continued support proved sufficient to save the gazette as an official publication. Still, several departments offered to take over the bulletin when the CPI disbanded, and the president decided to allow continued publication under private auspices, demonstrating the value his administration perceived in the CPI's *Official Bulletin*.[31]

CPI news dissemination no doubt increased executive control of wartime information, but it could not by itself produce the kind of prowar sentiment the president desired. To achieve this, Creel found it necessary to employ techniques more persuasive than informative, techniques destined to take the CPI deeply into the nascent field of official propaganda. Then, as now, the term *propaganda* bulged pregnant with connotation, and it is not surprising that Creel—who argued, somewhat simplistically, that the truth could not be propaganda—took every opportunity to deny its applicability to CPI activities. Nevertheless, if wartime propaganda is understood as an attempt to boost public morale by the presentation of one's own cause as the symbol of everything good and of the enemy's as evil personified, there can be no disputing the term's appositeness for describing Creel's efforts. Indeed, Creel himself often stated the committee's objectives with just such a textbook definition of propaganda, and his accuracy was revealed in many persuasive CPI programs.[32]

The first of these was a CPI pamphlet campaign. Conducted by the committee's Division of Civic and Educational Cooperation, it attempted to put into "convincing print" the administration's position on the war. The need for this sort of campaign had been felt immediately by both Wilson and Creel, who understood that only continuing persuasion might sustain public support. But they soon discovered that no one in the Wilson administration knew how to accomplish such a task. Creel accordingly followed European precedent and ordered preparation of a book of documents on America's prewar relations with Germany, only to find it lacking the punch and effectiveness he and the president desired. "Big books were not what we wanted," Creel wrote at the end of the war, "and long, tedious state papers were not what we needed." The persuasion of public opinion, as Creel understood it, required the articulation of arguments and ideas—not just the publication of documents—as well as a format interesting enough to elicit the public's interest, and the CPI chairman soon launched the civic division on a program of what he termed "popular pamphleteering."[33]

If Creel wished the division's activities to be popular, however, he also hoped to endow them with a reputation for scholarship. He accordingly appointed Guy Stanton Ford, professor of history and dean of the Graduate School at the University of Minnesota, to direct the new organization and suggested he recruit a cadre of scholars to write the division's publications. Ford proved a happy choice for the job; he combined knowledge of the pamphlets' subject matter with professional contacts in the American Historical Association—he would later be its president—and the National Board for Historical Service. He soon displayed a genuine talent for producing stirring pamphlets scholarly in appearance. Scholarship proved secondary, however. For all its footnotes and bibliographies, the work of the division remained essentially propaganda; its pamphlets were conceived and executed primarily to create strong public sentiment for the war. Highly effective, at least partly for the reputations of their writers, the pamphlets strike a melancholy note in the history of American scholarship. And although it seems appealing to depict Ford and his associates as innocent academics seduced into state service by worldly politicians, the evidence suggests they knew exactly what they were doing in the CPI.[34]

Chief among the division's immediate problems were complicated questions of publication and distribution. Creel first envisioned a rather narrow scope for his pamphlet program, planning an edition of only 20,000 copies—just enough to supply the nation's newspapers—for an annotated version of the president's war message. There existed, Creel believed, good reasons for operating on a small scale. Not only might it keep problems to a minimum; it might also allow the division to employ such available facilities as the Government Printing Office and the postal service. But, as the chairman soon discovered, newspaper publication generated considerable public interest, and the division received a flood of requests for individual copies. Creel's personal expansiveness quickly took hold, and he inflated his plans for the division. No longer were newspapers the primary recipients of Ford's pamphlets; Creel now hoped to inundate the public directly with propaganda material. And no longer did it prove possible to employ existing government agencies for publication and distribution; Creel now found it necessary to hire private publishing houses and to establish a mass circulation network that included labor unions, service clubs, and even the Boy Scouts.[35]

While adapting more traditional forms of propaganda to wartime needs, the CPI also pioneered in the executive's use of a promising new medium of communication—the movies. A curiosity since the turn of the century, film making came into its own during Wilson's first administration and soon found its way into the president's arsenal for influencing public opinion. Wilson had expressed interest in use of newsreels for presenting administration programs as early as 1913, but because he feared an invasion of the White House by cameramen he had decided to limit his personal involvement to cooperation in filming public events. This decision did not, of course, entirely satisfy film makers, who took every opportunity to remind the president, as one of them put it, "what a valuable educational and publicity agent the motion picture news reel, reaching millions of people every week, has become." Film makers also continued to press for admittance to White House events and ceremonies, but not even the support of Tumulty proved sufficient to win this for newsreel companies. For the time being, they had to remain satisfied with limited assistance from the camera-shy Wilson.[36]

The war finally convinced Wilson to deepen his involvement in moviemaking. The president had expressed awareness of this medium in his September 1914 request for public impartiality, but he did not put films to positive use until the preparedness controversy of early 1916. At that time, he heard again from Paramount Pictures' Edward L. Fox about the value of motion picture propaganda, and especially about the advantages to be gained by addressing a mentally "captive" audience. Fox's arguments clearly intrigued Wilson, and he not only instructed Tumulty to inform the producer that he would assist him "at the earliest possible moment" but stepped up his contact with other film makers as well. The White House soon enlarged its efforts to win increased newsreel exposure and took advantage of the new medium for publicizing Wilson's preparedness program.[37]

As Wilson soon discovered, however, his use of newsreels presented a number of serious new problems. One was the issue of favoritism, which had long troubled presidential relations with the press; it now threatened to place even more complicated obstacles in the way of executive dealings with newsreel companies. Wilson had avoided this issue while he limited his involvement to filming public events, but he warned Tumulty in April 1916 that their expanded cooperation with some studios might provoke the anger of jealous competitors. There could exist, Wilson realized, nothing like equal access to filming special presidential remarks—there were simply too many newsreel companies for that—and he could see no alternative to risking the anger of studios left out. Another new problem was Wilson's fear of appearing stiff and unnatural in speeches staged only for the camera. "I am willing to have these pictures made," he responded to a request from Fox for filming pronouncements on preparedness and Americanism, "but I think that much better than the sentences dictated in cold blood would be to cull what he needs out of my speeches on preparedness and my recent speeches where they refer to Americanism." A moving public speaker, Wilson had devoted a lifetime to cultivating his oratorical skills; it is not surprising that he preceded even his staff in grasping the limitations of performing only for the camera. Still, he could not avoid employing this technique in some instances, and he refused to allow his desire for effective presentation—or for the goodwill of rival film companies—to prevent his increased use of newsreels.[38]

Preparedness also prompted the executive's earliest cooperation in making feature films. Thomas Miranda, Tumulty's friend and general manager of the B. S. Moss Motion Picture Company, first suggested the use of features in February 1916. There remains no record of subsequent White House action on Miranda's proposal, but the president soon informed his secretary that he approved using feature films to spread foreign policy propaganda. Tumulty thus secured War Department approval for what its producer termed a "comprehensive moving picture of the United States Army," designed to help recruiting and promote preparedness. Both Tumulty and Wilson cooperated in the film's production, implementing the kind of part-nership between the executive and motion picture studios that later proved invaluable to the Creel committee.[39]

Wilson's appreciation for the effectiveness of movies also surfaced in his attempted censorship of films he found objectionable. Worst of these was *Patria*, a January 1917 serial release that depicted—in a manner described as "inflammatory" by several cabinet members—a ruthless Mexican-Japanese invasion of the United States. To com-bat the film's negative effects on public morale and on relations with Mexico and Japan, Wilson asked its distributor to withdraw it from the nation's movie houses. "The character of the story disturbs me very much," he wrote to Pathé's J. A. Berst. "It is extremely unfair to the Japanese and is calculated to stir up hostility in the coun-try which may be harmful." He thus called upon the film indus-try's patriotism to secure *Patria's* withdrawal—he had no legal basis to interfere—and hoped that Pathé would be more careful about distributing such films in the future.[40]

Berst did not give up so easily, however. He informed Wilson that his company was willing to cooperate with any reasonable request but hoped it might be possible to satisfy the president's complaints with changes in the movie's composition. Pathé would suffer, Berst argued, severe financial difficulties if the film, which cost three-quarters of a million dollars to make, had to be withdrawn alto-gether; he asked Wilson to reserve judgment until after viewing the revised print. Wilson agreed but soon discovered that Berst's editing changes fell far short of bringing *Patria* up to his own standards. Only more serious alterations might do that, and Wilson took it upon himself to inform Berst of their content. "It would seem desir-able," he advised, "to omit all those scenes in which anything Japa-nese appears, particularly those showing the Japanese and Mexican armies invading the United States, pillaging homes, kidnapping women and committing all sorts of other offenses." It was, as Wilson certainly understood, just such proscribed scenes that gave the film its interest; their omission would render the movie pointless if not plotless. Pathé determined nevertheless to try, composing a screen-play that seemed innocuous compared to the original. The resulting *Patria* contained no recognizable flags or insignia, presenting in-vasion scenes that, according to International's Grenville S. Mac-Farland, "carry no stamp of nationality." "I do not believe that you appreciate," MacFarland chided Wilson, "the expense, time and money, of making these changes," and he went on to explain that he had not understood them himself when he agreed, as he put it, "so cavalierly" to make the alterations the president requested. In the end, Wilson found little satisfaction in Berst's modifications, informing Tumulty that a number of objectionable items remained in the film. Still, Wilson realized they could not be removed without destroying the picture entirely and decided to rescind his objections to its continued public exhibition.[41]

Wilson's interest in the fledgling motion picture medium was likewise reflected in the CPI, which attempted with several programs to transform movie houses into propaganda centers. Creel understood that any effort of this type had to begin with the films themselves, and he endeavored shortly after his appointment to induce movie studios to cooperate in promoting the war effort. Not only did he make a personal plea for support before the National Association of the Motion Picture Industry; he also enlisted the prestige of the president in his campaign. "The film has come to rank," Wilson wrote to association president William A. Brady, "as a very high medium for the dissemination of public intelligence, and since it speaks a universal language it lends itself importantly to the presentation of America's plans and purposes." Wilson accordingly requested Brady's help in organizing the motion picture industry "so as," as he put it, "to establish direct and authoritative cooperation" with the CPI. This presidential appeal to moviemakers' patriotism produced a barrage of feature films designed as much for propaganda as for entertainment—a most effective combination. They included such titles as *To Hell with the Kaiser* and *The Kaiser, the Beast of Berlin* and starred such Hollywood luminaries as Charlie Chaplin and Mary Pickford. The CPI played no direct part in the production of these films, but its encouragement of movie industry participation in the war effort gave it some responsibility for their many excesses.[42]

Besides such general pleas for cooperation, Creel also interfered directly in the production and distribution of some individual screenplays. One was *The Curse of Iku*, a film that mirrored *Patria*'s anti-Japanese sentiments—and that met the same fate from Creel its predecessor had suffered from the president. Indeed, by the time Creel approved the alterations made by *Iku*'s producers, the film's length had been reduced from nine reels to five, and it had become, according to the chairman himself, so "poor and feeble" that no further demands seemed possible. A more serious example of Creel's willingness to censor movies occurred in the case of *The Spirit of '76*. This film was produced by Robert Goldstein, who had assisted in making D. W. Griffith's *Birth of a Nation*, and it attempted to do for the revolutionary war what Griffith had done for Reconstruction. It was, of course, sensational, presenting the British—now America's cobelligerents—in the kind of lurid terms the CPI reserved for the Germans. Because *The Spirit of '76*'s barbs stung actual, rather than putative, friends of the United States, Creel perceived it as a greater menace to morale than either *Iku* or *Patria*. The government's response was thus more severe. Federal officials seized the film under Title XI of the Espionage Act; Goldstein was sentenced to ten years in prison for its production. And although the severity of this case must be deemed exceptional, it demonstrated the compulsion behind other CPI requests for screenplay modification.[43]

Creel did not satisfy himself with overseeing commercial film production, however; he also involved the CPI in the actual process of making motion pictures. He began on a strictly limited basis, enlisting the Signal Corps to film such wartime activities as troop training and shipbuilding and selling the edited material to various commercial newsreel companies. He also compiled the best Signal Corps footage into short feature documentaries, which—for fear of competing with private production studios—he distributed only through state councils of defense. The result proved a startling innovation for the federal government; it had never before played so large a part in making and distributing movies. But even this paled beside Creel's ambition, as he soon launched the CPI on an enterprise representing perhaps its most effective foray into wartime propaganda.[44]

By the late summer of 1917, Creel realized that CPI footage was not being employed to full advantage. Not only, the chairman discovered, did newsreel companies remain inconsistent in their use of Signal Corps material; they also allowed the committee's feature films to miss the bulk of the public. He thus decided to create a CPI Division of Films and to make it responsible, in addition to supervising Signal Corps activities, for investigating new techniques for insuring effective distribution of the committee's motion pictures. Under the direction of the vigorous Charles S. Hart, the Film Division soon considered itself unnecessarily restricted by Creel's desire to avoid commercial competition, and it quickly brought the CPI into the business of making and distributing full-length motion pictures. Hart saw too many limitations in the brief documentaries conceived by Creel; he employed Signal Corps footage to create such magnificent seven-reel features as *Pershing's Crusaders* and *America's Answer* and to transform CPI newsclips into stirring—and entertaining—vehicles of prowar propaganda. Hart also realized that the most effective place to show films was in movie houses, and he established a CPI organization to exhibit its motion pictures in theaters nationwide. He planned a two-part distribution program: first, the films were shown, with considerable fanfare, by a CPI team traveling to major cities; and second, they were leased to local exhibitors across the country. During both phases, the movies received a concerted publicity campaign, including dignitary speakers, posters, and banners, as well as the use of what a CPI official termed "psychological suggestion" to win favorable newspaper editorials. The division ultimately exhibited its features in a larger percentage of movie houses than even the best-promoted commercial films.[45]

Another innovation was the Official War Review. This CPI newsreel proved a great improvement over Creel's hit-and-miss method for distributing Signal Corps war footage. Hart chose to release it through the Pathé exchange, which showed it weekly in a minimum of 25,000 theaters across the country, and the War Review soon became a strong competitor for the attention of regular newsreel audiences. It ultimately turned out to be more than an effective vehicle for disseminating CPI propaganda; it also paid its own way, earning more than a third of a million dollars before the end of the war.[46]

All of this did not make the Film Division popular with commercial movie companies. It seemed bad enough, as film makers saw it, for the CPI to refuse private filming of war-related activities; it was far worse to face direct competition from a government agency. Their many complaints had little effect on Creel, however, who continued to be jealous of the committee's prerogatives in this area. In August 1918 he once again advised Tumulty against granting private producers permission to film the president, suggesting that this should be done only by the Division of Films in order to insure quality and content. Nor did he encourage the president to cooperate in making private documentaries. "If we give permission to one private concern," he wrote Tumulty, "we would have to give permission to all." The CPI's relations with the movie industry thus deteriorated during the war, and not even Tumulty's conciliatory efforts could prevent this from affecting the president's standing with film makers as well.[47]

The motion picture theater also inspired the CPI's most innovative creation—the Four-Minute Men. Chicagoan Donald Ryerson first suggested this organization to Creel, who saw in it an opportunity to take advantage of the nascent industry's capacity for drawing large crowds. The idea was to employ local personalities, performing between shows in neighborhood movie houses, to form a national network of speakers capable of delivering war messages on a day-to-day basis. They spoke originally on the draft and the First Liberty Loan, but their duties soon expanded to include the dissemination of more general CPI propaganda as well.[48]

This division's efforts resulted in a tremendous propaganda success for the CPI. Not only did the Four-Minute Men provide a network for communicating with millions of moviegoers; it also anticipated, by combining message and entertainment, the persuasive potential of radio and television. Nor did the administration fail to see the division's effectiveness. Cabinet members soon buried the organization with requests for publicity, and even Wilson and Creel turned to it for putting across their most important ideas. Another mark of success was the Four-Minute Men's eventual application to other segments of society. By the end of the war there existed a Junior Branch, a Women's Branch—it spoke to matinees —and a group known as the College Four-Minute Men. Any remaining doubts about the usefulness of Ryerson's idea disappeared thirteen years later, when something like the Four-Minute Men reappeared to promote the newly created NRA.[49]

While expanding methods for reaching the general public, the CPI also pioneered the development of techniques for addressing groups previously ignored by presidential publicity. Women formed one such group, and Creel acknowledged their increased importance in time of war by creating a Division of Women's War Work within the CPI. He appointed Clara Sears Taylor to head the division and charged her with mobilizing American women behind the war effort. Taylor quickly put her staff to work publicizing the important role women played in winning the war. She achieved this, primarily, by disseminating news stories, some of which proved good enough to fight their way out of women's sections and onto page one; she also employed such standard CPI propaganda vehicles as magazine features, speeches, and photographs. The women's division ultimately met a sad fate. It was denied funding by Congress in the CPI's June 1918 appropriation—for some, apparently, foreign affairs still represented a man's world—and the Wilson administration returned to its previous disregard for the support of women.[50]

The foreign-born were another group receiving special CPI consideration. Concern for the wartime role of resident aliens did not originate with Creel; it had troubled Wilson even before America's entry. But Creel and the CPI launched the executive's first concerted effort to win alien support for its foreign policies. This originally took the shape of committee cooperation with various foreign-language associations, then being formed to demonstrate the loyalty of hyphenate Americans. By May 1918 the need for more direct methods prompted the creation of a CPI Division of Work among the Foreign-born. This division aimed the bulk of its efforts at the foreign-language press. It distributed large quantities of war news and propaganda to 745 regular publications and maintained close watch on the extent of their use. The division also arranged the publication of foreign-language editions of regular CPI pamphlets, organized parades and speaking tours through predominantly foreign-born districts, and released feature stories to English-language newspapers detailing the contributions of America's resident aliens. It managed throughout to maintain good relations with hyphenate groups— perhaps because it consistently refused to adopt the approach of professional "Americanizers"—and succeeded in presenting the war to the foreign-born.[51]

And finally, the CPI conducted a special campaign for the wartime support of blacks, who had, as Creel realized, plenty of reason for skepticism about the meaning of American motives and ideals. In this case, the CPI departed from its usual practice of creating an independent division for each minority and relied upon the efforts of talented blacks employed by its other propaganda organizations. This produced varied results, including the publication of many news stories and features about black soldiers and citizens, as well as the release of the CPI films *Colored Americans* and *Our Colored Soldiers*. Creel also attempted to serve as Wilson's conscience on the administration's treatment of blacks, reminding him as late as June 1918 that "there are doubts about the way in which the colored population feels about the war" and requesting that he address a CPI conference of black editors scheduled for Washington. The president refused Creel's invitation—he never felt entirely comfortable in the presence of either blacks or newspapermen—but soon demonstrated his agreement with the chairman's concern over the support of black constituents. On 21 July he notified Creel that he intended to deliver an address on the subjects of mob action and lynching and asked the CPI to "prepare the way" for it with a story twenty-four hours in advance. "I am not an expert in publicity, as you know," wrote the president, "but my notion is that a 'story' a day or so in advance" might serve to "fix the attention of the people" on the speech when it was delivered.[52]

It remained one of Creel's fondest contentions that the CPI represented a force for moderation in the troubled years of 1917–18. To some extent this rings true. Most CPI divisions attempted to avoid the worst wartime excesses, and Creel himself supplied the strongest and most consistent voice in Wilson's administration against overzealous application of censorship laws. The CPI had its dark side, however. It seemed occasionally guilty of repeating, if not promoting, the most vicious examples of anti-German propaganda, and it surely helped to create a domestic atmosphere favorable to the persecution of individuals not sharing its enthusiasm for the war. Worse yet, CPI efforts often appeared to lend official sanction to self-appointed censors and patriots, producing the impression that even the most extreme excesses enjoyed the government's support. This was not, of course, what Creel intended—the intentions of local committee representatives remain more difficult to discern—but any evaluation of the CPI must take into account the fact that its powerful propaganda techniques played a significant role, however unwittingly, in generating the kind of wartime immoderation Creel and Wilson abhorred.[53]

Nor should any evaluation overlook the CPI's important contributions to executive techniques for managing opinion. In some ways, of course, the CPI represented nothing more than a temporary aberration in the history of presidential publicity, a wartime expediency that saw many of its programs fall into disuse—indeed, disrepute—after 1919. But it was also, and more importantly, its era's highest expression of executive desire for control and centralization of information, a desire that has permeated presidential thought throughout this century. Not only did Creel's committee enlarge almost beyond imagination the size and scope of executive opinion making—its full-time staff of 395 employees supervised the activities of thousands of volunteers—it also made even skeptical newspapermen and government officials appreciate the value of centralized press relations. And although the CPI began to fade out of existence with the signing of the armistice, its influence on executive public relations continued long into postwar America.[54]

Chapter 8
Experts and Publicists

On December 4, 1918, Woodrow Wilson, the
first President to leave the territory of the
United States during his presidency, sailed for
France on board the *George Washington,*
the most powerful man in the world.
. . . .
he landed at Brest with his staff of experts
and publicists after a rough trip on the *George
Washington.*

John Dos Passos,
Nineteen Nineteen

The *George Washington* nosed out of New York
harbor on the morning of 4 December 1918, carrying the largest and
best-prepared American delegation ever to participate in an international conference. On board, in addition to the president and
his fellow commissioners, were specialists—Wilson called them his
"brains"—on almost every subject the peace conference might touch,
as well as an administrative staff to serve as secretariat to the
mission. Nor, as Dos Passos noted in the passage above, did those
assigning travel accommodations overlook publicity. Their final list
of passengers included George Creel, chairman of the now moribund
Committee on Public Information; Philip Patchin, head of the State
Department's Division of Foreign Intelligence; and representatives
of the three major press associations—L. C. Probert of the Associated Press, Robert Bender of the United Press, and John E. Nevin
of the International News Service. And lest their exclusion from the
president's company provoke hard feelings, other qualified reporters
received special passage aboard the U.S.S. *Orizaba.*[1]
The president's concern for publicity also surfaced on board the
George Washington. Not only did he grant wire service reporters a
number of frank interviews, but he treated them to a rare show of
camaraderie as well. This performance, according to Wilson's physician, left the correspondents "simply carried away with enthusiasm"
for the president's "ideas and plans," and they radioed stories back
to the United States evincing great confidence in the peace mission.

Wilson also found time to discuss publicity with the experienced Creel and to begin formulating press arrangements for Paris.[2]

This represented, by all accounts, an auspicious beginning. But its promise soon faded with presidential neglect of the press after arrival in Europe. No one understood this more painfully than Secretary Tumulty, who fired off numerous cablegrams from Washington warning Wilson of the need for establishing closer press relations. "Keep President in touch with Lawrence, Siebold, press associations, Hills and Gilbert," he cabled three days after Wilson landed at Brest. And "try to get newspapermen Probert, Bender, and Nevin to inject some emotion in stories," he added one day later. But Wilson never seemed to have time for reporters; despite Tumulty's entreaties, he quickly drifted into a state of almost complete isolation from the press. Wilson's aloofness also seemed reflected in his lack of contact with the common people of Europe, adding to Tumulty's concern. "Can't you have President do more mixing with people," he inquired. "Stories . . . only show . . . President as an official living in a palace and guarded by soldiery." There resulted a blast of bad publicity that dulled the edge of Wilson's triumphal procession through Europe and that indicated more closely the situation Wilson faced in Paris than did the halcyon experience of his Atlantic crossing.[3]

Besides Wilson's busy schedule, the biggest problem was his staff's inability to handle publicity. Certainly no one held better qualifications for this task than Creel; indeed, he had been drafted for the European trip to serve exactly this purpose. But his experience as CPI chairman made him seem unacceptable to many correspondents, who feared the continuation in Paris of his wartime activities. That Creel might prove an embarrassment had been suggested earlier by Tumulty and others. At the time of Creel's assignment to the peace mission, Tumulty pointed out that his well-known association with censorship and official publicity might make the Paris conference appear something less than "open" to press and public. Creel denied all charges that he might participate in news suppression at Paris, however, and demonstrated good faith by eliminating the CPI's voluntary censorship regulations. This did not prove sufficient. The press still found his continued tutelage intolerable, and Wilson knew by the time of his sailing that someone other than Creel must handle publicity in Europe.[4]

It was, not surprisingly, the renewed issue of censorship that finally destroyed Creel's usefulness in Europe. The problem stemmed from inadequate Paris cable facilities, which made it necessary for the commission to limit copy sent out by the various reporters and news agencies covering the conference. As head of the CPI, Creel had been introduced to the mysteries of cable communications, and he seemed the logical choice for the job of assigning space and supervising its use. But Creel's acceptance of this position brought out reporters' worst fears of governmental censorship. "There has been sharp criticism that press communiques must pass through Creel," wrote Tumulty around 10 December. "The press will understand the need for rationing wire space, but it must be made clear that this is not the same as censorship." Reporters found this distinction more difficult to grasp than Tumulty believed, however, at least as long as Creel remained in charge of rationing, and the CPI chairman soon became persona non grata in the American press rooms of Paris. Ironically enough, Creel had no intention of using his cable control as a form of censorship; he arranged, in fact, for 3,500 additional words daily over navy wireless. But the bad impression this episode made on the press forced Wilson to find assignments for the chairman far away from American correspondents.[5]

Creel, therefore, did most of his work behind the scenes. In December he employed CPI European personnel to arrange for American newspaper accompaniment of Wilson on visits to England and Italy but played no personal role in publicizing the president's trips. He also utilized his European organization to supply the president with frequent reports outlining the state of continental public opinion. And finally, Wilson charged him with "dissemination and spreading broadcast through the world and the United States of all publicity given out by the commission," a task that reflected only Creel's position as head of the CPI.[6]

With Creel removed from the picture, Tumulty was the administration's most qualified publicity expert. As presidential secretary, he had been personally responsible for conducting the administration's pre-CPI publicity, and he continued to enjoy the kind of amicable press relations that wartime difficulties had rendered impossible for Creel. But Tumulty remained behind in Washington, where he was badly needed as the president's representative in the White House; he could do little to improve the situation developing in Paris. What he might do had been outlined by Wilson before his departure: "Remember," he instructed his secretary, "I shall be far away and what I will want is a frank estimate from you of the state of public opinion on this side of the water. That is what I will find myself most in need of. When you think I am putting my foot in it, please say so frankly." As important as these duties proved, they represented something of a disappointment for Tumulty. He had hoped to accompany Wilson to Paris but accepted with as much enthusiasm as he could muster the task, as he described it, of "keeping" the president "in touch with affairs here."[7]

Despite his absence, Tumulty did not remain content to play a minor role in Wilson's publicity. Not only did he begin to send press clippings—later he would send summaries on the faster cables— while Wilson was still aboard the *George Washington*; he also issued from the White House a seemingly endless stream of suggestions for improved publicity. To expand his effectiveness, Tumulty enlisted the president's personal physician, Rear Admiral Cary T. Grayson, to serve as his liaison with the peace mission, and he subsequently attempted through Grayson to influence virtually every facet of Wilson's overseas public relations. This proved, of course, far from an ideal situation. Imperfect communications produced an inevitable time lag, and this combined with Grayson's inexperience to produce many of the president's initial publicity failures. Still, Grayson developed into an invaluable surrogate for the distant secretary, giving voice to Tumulty's suggestions in Wilson's most intimate counsels. And, taking direction from Washington, he soon supplied the impetus for rescuing the president from his initial publicity doldrums.[8]

Tumulty first wished to enliven Wilson's publicity, and he cabled Grayson detailed instructions for courting the interest of the press. On 16 December he suggested that the president make better use of newsreel cameramen accompanying his travels. "Pathé has two American moving picture photographers in Paris," he informed the doctor, "who were sent out with special instructions to play up American end and particularly to show President in most favorable light. They should be encouraged and given every opportunity to picture the human side of President." It remained, indeed, the presentation of Wilson's "human side" that Tumulty found most lacking in daily press reports; he now made a special point of advising Grayson not to overlook this dimension. Later that same day, he again admonished that "if the President visits hospitals have press representatives with him to get human interest story. Do not let his visits be perfunctory. Let him sit beside bed of common soldiers." And, he reiterated, "don't forget the movie men." For Tumulty, these represented elementary principles of publicity, and he would certainly have rushed to implement them were he in Europe. But he remained an ocean away, and his absence required him to waste valuable time educating Grayson to handle the president's public relations.[9]

For his part, Grayson proved a willing student. "At work on your suggestions," he cabled Tumulty on 21 December. "I hope you will see results in a few days." Not only did Wilson agree to follow his secretary's instructions about visiting hospitals, but he also planned to have "Christmas at the front and dinner with the soldiers." As Tumulty expected, this type of sentimental activity made for friendly columns in the press; by 23 December he could write that "stories appearing in all morning papers reference to President's trip to hospital fine, thrilling. You are doing great work." This kind of favorable publicity went on for the next two weeks, reflecting Grayson's continued efforts on the president's behalf. Tumulty took heart, only to discover that the actual peace conference would require far more than Grayson could deliver.[10]

By the time of his arrival in Paris, Wilson had already given considerable thought to the problem of publicizing the conference. It represented, he recognized, "a matter of more than ordinary importance" that the American delegation maintain contact with the American press. He thus suggested that his four fellow commissioners hold daily meetings with reporters. He also followed the advice of Creel and Commissioner Edward M. House and created a press department within the delegation. "I am also convinced," Wilson wrote on 17 December, "that the preparation of all the press matter that is to be issued from the Commission is a task calling for a particular sort of experienced ability." He thus appointed journalist Ray Stannard Baker to serve as a kind of press secretary—he did not use the term—to the peace delegation and charged him with the task of handling the commission's relations with American correspondents in Paris.[11]

Himself a member of the fourth estate, Baker seemed especially well qualified for the task envisioned by the president. He knew many correspondents covering the peace conference and remained, according to Wilson, "particularly esteemed by the very class of persons to whom it will be most advantageous to us to be properly interpreted." Baker had also spent most of the preceding year in Europe, where he had learned how to get along with French authorities and had, as the president put it, "established relationships which will be of the highest value" in his official duties. The only problem seemed Baker's own reticence to accept the job, which he described in his journal as "this publicity work to which the President wishes to condemn me." In long experience as a journalist, Baker had seen all too clearly the limitations of this kind of position, and he could imagine little hope for gratification in conducting what he called a "nerve-wracking meeting with the newspaper correspondents every day." Still, Baker's misgivings proved no match for the president's blandishments, and he agreed on 18 December to take over the publicity bureau on a trial basis.[12]

Although it proved of little value in his role as press director, Baker demonstrated a shrewd perception of the significance of public opinion. On 20 May 1919 he unburdened himself to his journal, writing that he felt acutely the importance of, as he put it, "the more or less *inarticulate average opinion*." The wise statesman, Baker continued, must consider not only the opinions of publicists and press but must also rely on his sense of "what the great masses will think when *forced* to think." "This," he concluded, "is public opinion," formed by both interest and ideas, intruding uninvited into the mundane life of average citizens. What this signified, Baker understood, was that public opinion had to be created; it did not just wait in the minds of the masses to be discovered. It thus fell to the opinion maker—and none was more potent than the president—to "force" the public to think of vital questions in the most favorable way. This, as the new press secretary understood it, represented the key to successful management of public opinion.[13]

For Baker, too, taking over the press section raised a difficult question: how familiar should he make himself personally with the details of activities he must interpret? Baker first determined he ought to know everything about the peace conference, insisting to Wilson that he should be admitted entirely into the commission's confidence. "This is not," he explained, "because it is necessary to pass all this information to the correspondents—that can be decided later as a matter of expediency," but because he needed to know what was happening before he could become an "intelligent servant." This seems just the kind of progressive position one might expect of a former muckraker; it also expressed Baker's belief in the beneficence of knowledge and maximum disclosure. Within weeks, however, Baker began to realize the impossibility of the task he had set for himself. Time proved the chief difficulty: Baker remained so preoccupied with the demands of his own office that he had little opportunity to study details of the conference. He also found that complete confidence was far too much to expect from a commission that included delegates as used to keeping their own counsel as an army general and a retired diplomat. And finally, the press secretary discovered—as all press secretaries must—that it sometimes proved a serious disadvantage to know too much about his subject.[14]

Despite doubts, however, Baker plunged energetically into his new job. On 19 December he conducted—somewhat prematurely— his first conference with American correspondents and spent the remainder of the day outlining plans for his new organization. Then, having located office space at 4, place de la Concorde, only a few doors from the American delegation's headquarters at the Crillon Hotel, Baker turned his attention to what he termed the "perplexing details" of running a publicity office. These included, first of all, finding a capable administrative staff; Baker chose Arthur Sweetser as his assistant. At the same time, the press secretary faced a seemingly endless array of more substantive problems; they would soon enlarge Baker's duties far beyond the job, as House described it, of "writing clear statements of the aims and purposes of the American Commission."[15]

Baker's most pressing problem seemed the arrangement of communications facilities. The primary source of this difficulty, which the press secretary now inherited from Creel, remained inadequate cable connections with the United States, and there appeared little that Baker could do to prevent this from becoming a serious impediment to press relations. He did manage to avoid the stigma of censorship that had ruined Creel, but even Baker never quite succeeded in convincing the anxious reporters of the need for rationing the cable. Baker tried to placate his disgruntled charges by arranging for the Signal Corps to make wireless transmission of all commission press releases, but its heavy volume of official communications prevented the wireless from adding much to reporters' inadequate word quotas.[16]

Also high on Baker's list of responsibilities was implementing the president's suggestion of daily press conferences. Beginning on 21 December, he arranged meetings for half-past ten each morning in Robert Lansing's quarters at the Crillon, where they attracted as many as fifty correspondents daily. Baker first believed that the press conferences served a useful purpose; they at least provided evidence of the commission's intention to cooperate with newspapermen. But they soon fell far short of reporters' expectations. One problem sprang from the absence of the president himself. As both titular head and moving spirit of the American delegation, Wilson was the only commissioner able to tell correspondents much of what they wanted to know, and his decision to absent himself from meetings immediately circumscribed their usefulness. In addition, the other commissioners quickly found the conferences unpalatable. General Tasker Bliss, for instance, did not say a word during the first five days of press meetings, prompting Baker to observe that the general "hates" publicity and "shrinks from meeting newspaper correspondents." For House, the conferences presented a somewhat different problem: he felt uneasy speaking candidly to reporters in the presence of his fellow commissioners. Eventually, both Bliss and House withdrew from the press meetings, the general to his silence and the colonel to his own daily colloquies with correspondents, and the now "farcical" conferences, as Baker termed them, were halted altogether.[17]

With daily press meetings fast becoming a disappointment, Baker had to find some other means for supplying stories to "clamorous" reporters. This proved especially necessary in the month before the conference's 18 January opening, when the commissioners generated little news of any substance. Compounding the problem was the relative inexperience of the American press corps, which found itself unprepared to write stories interpreting the complex issues soon to be discussed. The solution, as Baker saw it, seemed a simple one: he would utilize position papers already prepared by the commission's experts to provide reporters with background material. These position papers were the fruit of months of study, and they represented the American perspective on the peace. Baker hoped that their release, accompanied by press interviews with the experts themselves, might give correspondents a sense of attachment to the commission as well as some interesting copy.[18]

What Baker did not foresee, however, was the resistance of the commission's more traditionally minded members, who viewed such press releases as potential breaches of security. One such member was Joseph C. Grew, executive secretary to the commission. On 9 January Grew approved Baker's request for information from the commission's Political, Territorial, and Economic Intelligence Section but warned that any press communication based on such information must first be approved by his office. The danger, as Grew described it, was that Baker's plan must inevitably lead to embarrassment "because the newsmen will undoubtedly attribute the information to the Commissioners" themselves. It was not, Grew concluded, for him to decide whether or not to assume this "risk." A similar response came from Grew's assistant, the State Department's Allen W. Dulles. Dulles registered opposition to granting press interviews with members of the Inquiry, despite the fact that Baker, as Dulles put it, "claims to have the approval of the President and Secretary [of State]." Commission officials ultimately agreed to release press memoranda as the less dangerous of two evils; they apparently did not trust experts much more than publicists.[19]

From the first days in office, Baker understood that success depended upon his ability to maintain friendly relations with reporters. It had been, Baker realized, expectation of his success in this area that prompted Wilson to select him for duties with the commission; he now resolved to demonstrate his desire for cooperation. He thus assisted the formation of a peace conference press association— similar to those organized by some groups of Washington correspondents—designed to serve as liaison between his office and the press corps. As Baker might have anticipated, however, this organization proved something of a mixed blessing. It provided tbe press secretary with a valuable means for controlling and disciplining the highly individualistic reporters; it also presented him with a unified lobby intent upon protecting the interests of the 119 correspondents at the conference. Still, the press association was formed in a spirit of cooperation, and this attitude permeated at least its first few weeks of existence.[20]

One of the association's first considerations was the establishment of rules to govern American reporters at the peace conference. On 15 January the American Press Delegation, as the new association called itself, submitted a list of regulations that it hoped might prevent misunderstandings. Most important was a pledge to be signed by each reporter, promising to avoid quotation without expressed permission and denying any connection with the press of a foreign country. The association also suggested that Baker arrange for an army officer to check admittance to news conferences and for an official stenographer to determine the accuracy of quotations given the press. As in most cases of proposed self-regulation, the newspapermen saw much to gain by keeping their own house in order; they certainly hoped to forestall the commission's adoption of even more stringent regulations. Still, their willingness to cooperate made Baker's job undeniably easier.[21]

Using its own rules as a basis, the association also attempted to police the activities of its members. In mid-January, for example, the association's executive committee reported the results of its investigation into an apparent breach of the commission's confidence. The guilty party, it developed, was a journalist named Lewis Styles Gannett, in Paris representing *Survey* magazine, who had passed on a quotation to a foreign correspondent. Gannett pleaded ignorance of any wrongdoing and promised to keep the association's rules in the future. He suffered no punishment other than a warning by his peers.[22]

A more serious breach of confidence occurred a few weeks later, when a correspondent published a direct quotation from the president. The press association did not decide in this case to take on the investigation; it was ordered to do so by the angry commissioners. There followed a more formal process than that utilized in the Gannett case, and the ensuing tension underscored the painful alternative to cooperation. Guilty this time was the *New York Herald*'s Truman Talley, who explained in writing that he had not understood that "Washington rules"—no direct quotation of the president—applied at the peace conference. This had not, he contended, been "made plain to him" by Baker's office, but he apologized anyway for whatever inconvenience he may have caused the commission. Armed with this statement, the association's executive committee reported to Baker that Talley had shown only a lack of caution in quoting the president and recommended only temporary action against him. On 20 February the commission approved the suggested punishment, suspending Talley from all press meetings for two weeks.[23]

Whatever cooperation existed between Baker and the press depended largely upon mutual goodwill, a condition not seriously threatened by the kind of improprieties discussed above. These they invariably resolved amicably, and the occurrence of such imbroglios probably enhanced friendly relations between the two. They certainly added to their confidence in each other's desire for cooperation. The same cannot be said, however, for Baker's other major difficulty with the press association. This was the conference's unwillingness to admit reporters to its daily sessions, a situation that caused, not surprisingly, much press consternation and that came very near to casting Baker and the association as adversaries. Baker did his best to avoid being placed in this position—he did not, of course, sanction the desire for secrecy that underlay the decision to bar reporters—but he found himself unable to prevent this issue from bringing out the inherent conflict between his office and the association.[24]

The secrecy problem first surfaced during the early days of January 1919, when rumors began to circulate that correspondents might be denied access to meetings. No final decision had yet been made, however, and Baker remained optimistic in forwarding a request by reporters—whom he described as "most anxious"—for a public opening of the conference. But Baker soon learned that the wind was blowing in the opposite direction. The commission rejected, ostensibly for "lack of space," the association's request; there remained little for reporters (or Baker) to do but wait for the final blow to fall on their hopes for an open conference. It fell officially on 14 January, when the Associated Powers issued a statement closing all conference sessions to the press. This statement argued that "the Conversations of the Great Powers are far more analogous to the meetings of a cabinet than to those of a legislature" and asserted the impossibility of functioning well in public. This did not mean, the statement continued, that the conference must be conducted in secrecy; the powers desired the press to have, as they put it, "whatever information is compatible with the interests of all in making a just settlement." But necessity clearly required imposing some limits on reporters' activities. The statement thus announced that major decisions would be released when made but that correspondents would not be admitted to actual sessions of the conference.[25]

This explanation was not, of course, altogether disingenuous: excessive publicity might certainly complicate the work of the conference. But the official statement did not satisfactorily describe the Great Powers' deeper motives. For Orlando, Lloyd George, and Clemenceau, secrecy served a political purpose: they could be removed from office for any expression of weakness—or compassion—in their treatment of the Germans and had, therefore, good reason for wishing to conduct the give-and-take of peace negotiations in private. Wilson's case seems somewhat more complex, however. He had nothing to fear politically from publicizing activities of the conference; on the contrary, secrecy for him represented a political liability, at least insofar as the eventual treaty was concerned. In addition, Wilson remained in 1919 the moral leader of the world, a position he might well have enhanced—and turned to advantage— by conducting negotiations in the open. The president had also served in American politics long enough to know that correspondents did not accept rejection gracefully; they would undoubtedly blame him for the peace conference's lack of publicity. And finally, Wilson had long since become identified with, as he put it in Point 1 of the Fourteen Points, "open covenants of peace, openly arrived at," and he might have known that both public and press would find his late attachment to secrecy incomprehensible.[26]

Why, then, did Wilson agree to negotiate in private? One reason, certainly, was his appreciation of difficulties facing other members of the Big Four. Not only did he understand the political dangers they saw in open sessions of the conference; he was also aware that reporters might make them more obdurate in negotiations. But even more important was Wilson's own agreement with the need for closed meetings. Whatever he meant by open diplomacy—and more will be said of this shortly—he did not mean that diplomatic negotiations must be conducted in front of the press. At the conversational stage, Wilson believed, diplomacy remained far too fragile to survive the hammer of publicity, and the quotation above comparing the conference to cabinet meetings bears the marks of his own deft pen. "The issue of publicity," he wrote Tumulty on 20 January, "is being obscured, not cleared, by the newspaper men." "Publicity for the conversations I am holding with the small groups of great powers would invariably break up the whole thing." It was this, more than anything else, that convinced Wilson of the need for private negotiations at the conference. As he perceived diplomacy, nothing else seemed possible.[27]

What, in light of this attitude, could Wilson have meant by "open covenants of peace, openly arrived at"? It clearly represented some sort of commitment to publicity, but it did not mean that every detail should be released to the press. "Openly arrived at" thus signified only that the public should know the general nature of talks being conducted, not that it should be made privy to the substance of conversations themselves. Even this sort of publicity, it must not be forgotten, seemed novel—Baker called it "fire-new"—in 1919, and it is little wonder that Wilson confused even his closest advisers. Tumulty, for instance, grew frantic in Washington over the president's apparent desertion of his principles. And even Baker, on the scene, could see nothing but paradox in Wilson's behavior. "It is an odd thing," wrote the press secretary, "that while the President stands for 'pitiless publicity' and 'open covenants openly arrived at'—a true position if ever there was one—it is so difficult for him to practice it." "He speaks to the masses," Baker concluded, "in terms of the new diplomacy but he deals with the leaders by the methods of the old."[28]

As far as press and public were concerned, Baker's perception of the president could not have been more accurate. How else but as betrayal could they interpret Wilson's apparent acceptance of secrecy? Had he not promised precisely the opposite in the Fourteen Points? Wilson had, to be sure, at least appeared to make such a promise, no matter how circumscribed his actual notion of publicity, and the bulk of the ensuing controversy may be largely attributed to his forceful rhetorical style. The president's problem was one always inherent in adept phrasemaking: powerful words are easily transformed into slogans and seem to mean much more than their author intended. This phenomenon affected many of the Fourteen Points— it accounted, indeed, for their usefulness as propaganda—and led the president into countless difficulties over their application at the peace conference. For representatives of the press, Point 1 had been transformed into a slogan (even Baker misquoted it in the journal entry cited above) that promised an end to negotiations locked outside their gaze, and it is no wonder they flocked to Paris in unprecedented numbers. Wilson made matters worse by showing no inclination to deflate their expectations gently. There had been, of course, no reason for an explanation during the war, but it remains difficult to understand why he kept silent, even in private, after his arrival at the conference.[29]

Wilson's silence soon produced a storm of criticism. On 14 January eleven correspondents wrote in protest over his apparent acquiescence in what they termed a "gag-rule" for the conference. A few days later, Wilson also received a list of resolutions passed by representatives of the Allied and American press—except the French, who received ample news through official leaks in their own delegation—that called for opening all conference sessions to reporters. By 16 January Tumulty saw the results of Wilson's silence in the newspapers; he now warned Grayson it would be "fatal" for the president to accept secrecy. "He could have afforded to go to any length," Tumulty chided, "even to leaving the conference rather than submit to this ruling." Tumulty resided an ocean away, however; Baker sat at the center of the storm. For the press secretary, closed negotiations signaled the end of his honeymoon with reporters, who now unified in their determination to garner information he could not give them. Baker also became the fulcrum for correspondents' efforts to pry open the doors of the conference, serving as their advocate with the commission and as their personal contact with the president. In this position, Baker soon discovered that goodwill helped little on an issue as vital to the press as secrecy.[30]

There remained, however, considerable irony in the fact that Wilson received blame for maintaining conference secrecy. Not only was he publicity's most consistent advocate in meetings of the Big Four; he also succeeded in wresting major concessions from the more secretive Europeans. Wilson took personal responsibility for releasing press communiqués—the reporters' most consistent source of conference news—on a day-to-day basis. He also made arrangements for journalists to receive occasional firsthand looks at the conference by opening plenary sessions to the press. Of course, neither concession proved satisfactory to reporters: the daily statements soon became as bland as a dozen private secretaries could make them, and opening plenary sessions only relegated them to window dressing. But it still seems noteworthy that the Big Four adopted such forms of publicity, which went far beyond those practiced at previous international conferences, only at the prodding of the much-maligned Wilson. Still, the president had also done more than anyone to enlarge reporters' expectations, and there remained perhaps no way for him to avoid the consequences of failing to deliver on his promises. And it certainly did not help that Wilson refused to inform correspondents of his efforts on their behalf, an item of news that any experienced press secretary—Tumulty, for instance —would have made sure the president's reticence did not obscure.[31]

To varying degrees, secrecy remained a problem throughout the conference. Reporters generally found the issue subordinate to their more mundane concerns of identifying sources and gathering news, but they grew angry enough on several occasions to cause Baker great consternation. One occasion was the 7 May presentation of the peace treaty to the Germans, to which the Big Four admitted a restricted number of correspondents only after reversing its initial decision to bar them altogether. The reason was ostensibly a lack of space in the Trianon Palace, where the ceremonies were conducted, but the real difficulty was the Big Four's—in this Wilson must be included—seemingly unalterable distrust of the press. The delegates now feared that reporters might be used unwittingly as agents of German propaganda; the depth of their concern appeared in their decision, even after reconsidering on press representation at the meeting itself, to maintain their ban on any personal contact between correspondents and German delegates. This quarantine ultimately proved ineffectual as a result of poor French security, but its obvious pettiness served to heighten the pique of many journalists.[32]

By May, however, Wilson could have done little to improve his relations with the press; the time to do that had come—and passed unused—in the hectic days of January. No one understood this better than the vigilant Tumulty, who cabled on 13 January that "the trend of newspaper despatches from Paris has indicated a misunderstanding of your general attitudes towards the problems pending at the peace conference." This "could easily be remedied," the secretary continued, "if you would occasionally call in the three press association correspondents who crossed with you on the *George Washington*" and give them "an understanding of the developments as they occur." Similar suggestions also came from Baker, who shared Tumulty's appreciation of the need for better press relations at the conference, as well as from Creel, but none of the president's advisers succeeded in arousing their chief to additional effort.[33]

Wilson's failure requires some explanation: why, upon receipt of such sound advice, did he neglect to establish closer relations with the press? One reason, surely, was his long-standing distaste for the company of many correspondents, as well as for the profession they represented. Only Tumulty's efforts had held this personality conflict to a minimum at the White House; it ran more or less unchecked after Wilson's arrival in Europe. The president could also find little time in his already crowded schedule for meetings with correspondents. With so much work to be done, and so little time to do it, it is small wonder that Wilson rejected the additional responsibility of talking to the press—a task he at any rate did not enjoy. A final reason may be adduced from the reporters' own behavior. On at least one occasion, Wilson did hold a press conference, but it resulted, or so he saw it, in the deliberate betrayal of his confidence. This incident, which occurred in mid-February, confirmed the president's low opinion of newspapermen, and he made no effort to meet them again.[34]

Tumulty apparently realized he could do little to prevent deterioration of press relations in Paris; he soon shifted his emphasis to the United States, where he could maintain personal control over Wilson's publicity. On 7 January he cabled for permission to schedule a large public reception upon the president's return. "The time of your return," the secretary admonished, "is the hour for you to strike in favor of the League of Nations." Tumulty understood that the bad press Wilson was receiving might hurt the treaty's chances in the Senate, where criticism of its proposed provisions—especially the League of Nations—had already begun to surface. Clearly, something was needed to offset damaging reports from Paris, and Tumulty proposed a full-blown publicity campaign to begin with Wilson's arrival in the United States. Such a campaign, the secretary argued, might mobilize public opinion behind the president's efforts and silence senatorial critics of the treaty. What Tumulty had in mind was a direct presidential appeal to the people, for which Wilson harbored a well-known predisposition and to which he would be drawn as a panacea when news from Paris—and the treaty's chances—later deteriorated.[35]

For the time being, however, Wilson found his secretary's plans a bit premature. His work at the conference remained far from finished, he told Grayson on 25 January, and any demonstrations of popular support should wait until the deliberations were completed. It was also now apparent, Wilson continued, that his mid-February return to the United States would be only temporary. A second trip to the peace conference remained necessary, and he preferred to postpone a public appeal until after his final return. In part, Wilson was here expressing a genuine concern for the propriety of advance publicity—he did not think it correct to generate support for his successes until after he achieved them. But this seemed less important than the president's desire to avoid controversy in the United States during the crucial period of negotiations, which he feared might suffer from any semblance of disunity. This view contained, to be sure, considerable wisdom from the standpoint of negotiations, but it helped produce a potentially disastrous publicity vacuum at home.[36]

Tumulty remained only too aware of this danger, following up his publicity proposal with even more persistence than usual. On 30 January he wrote Wilson a seven-page letter to discuss the need for intensifying his fight for public opinion, in which he argued that any difficulties might be overcome by "plenty of publicity." The way to achieve this, Tumulty believed, was through public appearances while the president was in the United States. He thus proposed that Wilson instruct the *George Washington* to land in New England—the backyard of Senator Henry Cabot Lodge, the league's chief antagonist—where the secretary could arrange a welcoming reception, and he disclosed plans for a parade and celebration to mark Wilson's return to Washington.[37]

Despite Tumulty's efforts, plans for a presidential reception soon grew tangled. The first problem stemmed from the ocean separating the secretary and the president; even by cable the two of them could not communicate with sufficient speed and ease. As a result, Tumulty often lacked the kind of details he needed to complete his arrangements (he did not know as late as 17 February, for instance, the date of Wilson's expected arrival) and could not deal with inevitable difficulties as they developed. Wilson's busy schedule compounded these difficulties. Tumulty had to rely excessively upon information supplied by the inexperienced Grayson, whose own eleventh-hour arrangements with Boston's Mayor Andrew Peters only magnified the confusion. The chief problem, however, proved the president himself, who continued to resist Tumulty's schemes for creating favorable publicity. Not only did Wilson express an original preference for landing at Hampton Roads instead of Boston; he also rejected the idea of a Washington celebration—at least until Tumulty presented it to him, with distinct lack of candor, as only a parade of ex-servicemen. At the last minute, he even decided to cancel an evening address in Boston, informing Tumulty that he was afraid it might seem staged and that, anyway, an extemporaneous speech in the afternoon stood a better chance of making the morning papers. Tumulty must have been less than delighted to see his concern for full publicity turned against his own plans. At any rate, the nervous—and apparently exasperated—secretary soon slammed the door on further presidential wavering by announcing that any decision to alter plans for the new afternoon address would be "embarrassing" and possibly "misinterpreted."[38]

Despite these difficulties, the president's ship met an enthusiastic crowd when it pulled into Boston harbor on 24 February. Tumulty had laid his plans thoroughly, traveling north himself to see to such final details as closing schools and business houses, and the secretary's skillful hand showed unmistakably in the proceedings. Wilson did his part as well, inspiring thousands who packed Mechanics' Hall with his customary eloquence and provoking cheers of support with a statement of his determination to fight for the League of Nations. The overall impression seemed exactly what the secretary envisioned: public opinion, even in Massachusetts, appeared to support the efforts of the president. This was a point that, Tumulty hoped, no one in the country—and especially in the Senate—might miss, and he considered the administration's opening salvo an unequivocal success. Tumulty was badly mistaken, however, if he believed the reception might dent the resolve of such critics as Senator Lodge, who would in later months demonstrate the fallacy of attempting to influence the Senate with a belated public appeal.[39]

The Boston speech proved, unfortunately, the highlight of Wilson's brief visit to the United States. The president did not share his secretary's desire to make his stay in Washington a public relations campaign, and he thus failed to exploit the popularity uncovered by his reception. His halfhearted attempt to win senatorial backing by inviting the Foreign Relations Committee to a White House dinner also proved disastrous, despite Tumulty's efforts to produce a good press for the event. And not even his mammoth send-off from New York City, accompanied by a stirring address at the Metropolitan Opera House, could rekindle the kind of enthusiasm generated by his landing ten days earlier. As a result, Wilson returned to France on 5 March without creating any major support for his beloved League of Nations; the next few months alone would determine its fate.[40]

Ray Stannard Baker has observed that "the President's real difficulties began when he returned to Paris." Not least of these difficulties, Baker realized, was continued deterioration of the commission's already fragile press relations. As usual, Tumulty's cablegrams provided tbe best barometer of the president's publicity; they grew increasingly shrill following his second arrival at the conference. "There appears to be a complete breakdown in publicity at that end," he chided Grayson on 14 March. "Is there anyone in charge? Now that you are in Paris we look for better results." On the same day, he warned Wilson that "publicity from European end doing great damage here."[41]

In part, Tumulty's alarm resulted from the new willingness of the press corps to criticize negotiations about the League of Nations itself. "Country greatly disturbed," he cabled on 13 March, "over

stories appearing Paris and elsewhere under Associated Press head
that League of Nations is not to be included in peace treaty." Such
stories proved, of course, accurate: House and Lansing had agreed in
the president's absence to separate the League of Nations from a
"preliminary" peace treaty. But they conveyed a message exactly
the opposite of the one Wilson had carried to the United States, and
reporters grew sharply critical of the commission's failure to win the
league a place in the actual treaty. Tumulty wanted the matter
clarified—he hoped with a denial—and petitioned the president to
take appropriate action with American correspondents in Paris. For
once, Wilson quickly followed his secretary's advice. On the morning
of 15 March, he called Baker via the secret American telephone
circuit and instructed him to deny reports that the League of Nations would not be included in a preliminary treaty. Baker realized
the "vital importance," as he put it, of this message, and he submitted his draft to the president for personal approval before releasing it that afternoon. The result was just what Tumulty desired—a
clear statement of the president's intention to retain the League of
Nations—and he cabled Wilson his approval.[42]

Tumulty may have been satisfied with his success on this occasion; he soon stepped up requests for additional publicity. On 16
March he cabled—once again—that the time had come for Wilson to state America's position on the League of Nations. And on
25 March he asked the president to deny newspaper stories that the
league was stalling the conference's deliberations. Wilson had been
hearing similar requests from Baker for several days; on 27 March
he finally agreed to let the press secretary draft a statement. Baker
made the mistake, however, of trying "to tell too much truth" about
what he termed "obstructionist groups" at the conference and saw
the president blue-pencil most of his effort. Nevertheless, his final
press release, which he not only distributed to correspondents but
also cabled to Compub in New York City, exculpated the league of
detaining the conference and made, according to Tumulty, a "fine
effect" in the United States.[43]

Such successes did not sate Tumulty's desire for publicity, however. Through March and April he continued to hammer home the
need for more public leadership, using mounting opposition to the
League of Nations as a flag to catch Wilson's attention. On 30 March
he warned that press dispatches from Paris, hitherto optimistic, now
seemed "touched with deep pessimism." "I fear your real position in
Council is not understood here," the secretary admonished, "and
that lack of publicity [is] strengthening many false impressions."
On 5 April he tried to alert Grayson to the dangers involved in

Wilson's failure to take public charge of the convention, informing him that "only publicity of a dramatic kind can now save the situation." Tumulty's efforts made little impact on the president, however, despite the successes discussed above; the League of Nations received nothing like the kind of publicity made possible by Wilson's presence in Paris.[44]

Baker also attempted to pick up the pace of publicity in the peace conference's second phase. Unlike Tumulty, the press secretary remained dissatisfied with Wilson's denial of reports that the league was holding up negotiations, and he asked for a more explicit statement of reasons for the conference's inactivity. This the president refused for fear of alienating the French, who were primarily responsible for stalling negotiations. Baker then suggested he be allowed to "leak" the information to some American correspondents. "Well," Wilson responded, "if some of them are indiscreet enough to tell the truth I shall have no objections." Baker thus told several friendly newspapermen, including Herbert B. Swope, Richard V. Oulahan, and the representatives of press associations, the story of how excessive French demands prevented completion of the treaty; they soon had dispatches to that effect on the cable to the United States. This represented one of the few times that information leaked officially from the American delegation, even though its success in this instance might have provided ample recommendation for further use. Baker, certainly, must have realized the value of this technique, and Wilson's failure to approve it on other occasions gives a good indication of his stiff perception of publicity. It seems ironic, moreover, that the president chose this particular instance to loosen his principles; the French, whose official delegation leaked at every seam, could hardly have been fooled by his all-too-apparent subterfuge.[45]

Baker also attempted to expand his own usefulness to reporters by meeting daily with the president. He hoped, in this way, to provide more inside information but soon discovered Wilson unwilling to let him relate even the subjects of their discussions to waiting journalists. For Wilson, in fact, the importance of these evening colloquies seemed unrelated to publicity; it is more likely that he saw in Baker a replacement for the alter ego lost with House's fall from favor. As a result, Baker often expressed frustration over Wilson's indifference to his requests for releasing information. "I was allowed," he wrote on 21 April, "to tell almost nothing to the correspondents this evening," an occurrence that the journalists themselves perceived as less the exception than the rule. From a publicity standpoint, of course, the ideal situation would have been for the president to meet directly with reporters—the use of an intermediary proved, perhaps intentionally, far too oblique—but Wilson had ruled out such a possibility in the first days of the peace conference. It remained, no doubt, to Baker's credit that he made the most of a difficult situation; yet his evening sessions with the president paid few dividends in either better publicity or improved press relations.[46]

For all their efforts, Baker and Tumulty did not persuade Wilson to take the initiative in publicity. As a result, the commission's public relations proved essentially reactive, dealing with criticisms discovered in the press—often several days after they were made. On 19 April, for example, Tumulty informed Wilson that the *Sun*'s headlines depicted an American alliance with Great Britain and France and warned him that "now is the time to kill these vicious stories." The time to kill this story had passed, in fact, several days earlier, when Wilson had learned from commissioner Henry White that the veteran diplomat had been trapped, in the course of a press interview, into giving out this information. But then the president had decided, as usual, to take no action on the commissioner's report; any attempt to defend his security treaty with England and France had to wait until after attacks appeared against it—that is, until after much of the damage was already done. It seems unlikely, of course, that anything Wilson might have said in 1919 could have earned a favorable reception for the alliance, but simply taking the initiative on 16 April might have mitigated the resounding criticism it received.[47]

Only slightly more satisfactory was publicity on the Shantung question. Wilson realized that the decision to award this German leasehold to Japan might unleash a storm of criticism in the United States; it might even imperil the treaty's chances in the Senate. He thus decided to prepare advance publicity, cabling Tumulty a statement labeled, "for public use at such time as the matter may come under public discussion." Wilson made clear, however, that this explanation must not be given out as a quotation from him; it might only be used, as he put it, "in some other form for public information at the right time." By "the right time" Wilson meant only after the issue was raised by his critics, and he took pains to insure that Tumulty did not mistake his cablegram for a press release. He took similar precautions with Baker, who received a copy of Wilson's statement from confidential secretary Gilbert F. Close on the same day. According to Close, Baker might use Wilson's explanation only for discussions with correspondents and—once again—only after the general subject appeared in the press. The statement existed, in short, for the purpose of answering criticism, not forestalling it.[48]

Baker did not like this arrangement, however, and he finally persuaded the president to give the press a preemptive statement, "to prevent them," as he put it, "from getting it garbled from the Japanese." The danger, Baker realized, was that Japan might present the Shantung decision as an unadulterated victory, rather than as the best possible compromise of a difficult question. It was in this latter fashion, of course, that Wilson perceived all the conference's efforts, and it was in this way that he hoped Baker might persuade journalists to understand it. He therefore agreed to an advance explanation. Still, Baker realized he courted disaster by talking with reporters, even with the president's approval, and confided in his journal that "I had to choose my words carefully in reporting it" to them. His care soon paid dividends. On the next day, he informed Wilson that openness with the press corps had made a favorable impression and that many correspondents were now writing friendly articles defending the Shantung decision as "the only practical decision." Tumulty soon found the going surprisingly easy in the United States. On 2 May he informed Wilson of a sympathetic *New York World* editorial and concluded that it did not now appear necessary to release the president's statement. The remarkable thing here—and it represents a good example of poor coordination among Wilson's publicity personnel—is that Tumulty still did not know, three days after the event, that Baker had released the statement he was now withholding from the press.[49]

Of the commission's many publicity failures, none proved more damaging than its refusal to release the treaty before it was signed. Not only did this decision underscore the destructive issue of secrecy; it also produced a negative effect on the treaty's chances in the Senate. This problem did not arise for lack of awareness; even Lansing—a traditionalist in these matters—warned Wilson more than two months in advance that, as he put it, "to attempt to suppress [the treaty] will increase the irritation of the press and public as to secret agreements." Baker also perceived the importance of early publication, raising the issue with Wilson on 17 April, only to be rebuffed with the observation that Britain and France would never allow release even a day early. This proved ultimately to be the case—the Allies did remain insistent upon secrecy—but much responsibility for the difficulties delay caused in the United States must be attributed directly to Wilson himself.[50]

This was true, largely, because Wilson came personally to believe

—if he did not originally—in the correctness of maintaining the treaty's secrecy. The strength of Wilson's commitment to confidentiality became apparent in early May, when he subjected Lansing to a severe dressing down for what he regarded as insufficient care in the State Department's handling of the treaty. The department's Washington offices had remained, in fact, incredibly confused for several weeks about the document's publication status, a situation for which Wilson's own failure to issue a public statement was largely responsible. Now the president wanted to make certain that confusion did not result in a leak of the treaty's contents. "I am clear in my judgment," he informed the secretary of state, "that no sentence of the official text ought to be given to the press until the treaty is signed." Wilson had learned, however, that Patchin had been permitted to send the entire treaty to the United States—and that, worse, he had actually sent some of it "plain," uncoded. "I hope," he instructed Lansing with pointed redundancy, "that the Department of State will be warned by you, yourself, to observe the utmost care to keep the treaty to itself." There resulted increased caution in handling the treaty, and its secrets remained safe in the United States several weeks after they circulated freely in Europe.[51]

The bright spot in this otherwise dismal episode proved the composition of advance treaty summaries, designed to give the press and public some idea of what the actual document might contain. Released 7 May, these summaries were written by the combined British, French, and American press bureaus and represented as such the peace conference's best example of international cooperation. Their distribution also seemed something of a technical achievement for Baker's office, which sent them not only to the United States but also throughout North and South America. And finally, Baker cabled the summaries to Compub in New York City a day before their scheduled release, demonstrating the kind of cooperation possible between the commission and the press. These efforts soon paid dividends, and the summaries' publication represented, as Tumulty put it, a "great triumph" for the president.[52]

This triumph proved short-lived, however, as criticism of Wilson's refusal to release the treaty continued to mount. On 22 May Tumulty cabled that "there is an intense feeling in the Senate in favor of the publication of the terms of the treaty. Can anything be done to straighten this out?" Wilson replied with a reaffirmation of his commitment to secrecy, which he now explained by describing the treaty as only a first draft. "Senators anxious for treaty publication," he instructed both Tumulty and Lansing, "should be told frankly that the matter is not yet settled, that some portions of the treaty are still subject to reconsideration." There existed, to be sure, considerable merit in this explanation: the release of unfinished treaties remained far from standard procedure in 1919. But the president had clearly not calculated his remarks to have a favorable effect on senators already angry over their exclusion from the conference. Wilson also should have known—indeed, Baker warned him—that the treaty's terms were about to come out anyway. By the end of May, copies could be purchased cheaply at any European newsstand; it remained only a matter of time before an American newspaper published it. Although technically correct, Wilson's refusal to release the still unfinished treaty only deepened his political difficulties.[53]

The extent of Wilson's error became apparent on 9 June when the text of the treaty was published in the *Congressional Record*. It had already appeared, a few days earlier, in the *Chicago Tribune* and was now reprinted at the request of Senator William Borah, who no doubt delighted in the stealing of a presidential prerogative. The matter proved considerably more serious than Borah's personal animosity, however, because several senators were already questioning how it happened that the press—and others, including denizens of Wall Street—had received access to a treaty held secret from their own deliberations. Hoping to embarrass the president, the Senate soon passed a resolution to investigate the treaty's leak, which many charged had occurred within the commission itself. Overall, Wilson's decision to withhold the treaty exacted a heavy price: it reintroduced the damaging issue of secrecy, fueled the Senate's anger over presidential neglect of its authority, and made Wilson appear needlessly stubborn and unyielding in defending his position. The difficult process of treaty ratification, it could not be doubted, was off to a very bad start.[54]

The treaty's vulnerability to such contretemps stemmed largely from the commission's poor handling of publicity. We have already seen several reasons for this failure, including the secrecy decision and Wilson's lack of contact with the press, but other factors also contributed to the severity of the situation. Among these, perhaps most important was the strain Wilson's distance from Washington placed on his leadership of public opinion: he was, as Tumulty feared from the beginning, out of "touch" with affairs at home. Part of this problem came from the slowness of most communication across the Atlantic, which prompted Wilson to complain on 2 April that he had not received White House mail for over ten days. And even the speedier cable, which supplied the president with news and editorial summaries from a variety of sources, could not convey the depth or intensity of public sentiment, leaving Wilson unable to evaluate the real impact of his publicity. Perhaps more damaging still was the absent president's inability to make his normal impression on the thinking of the American people. As usual, the perceptive Tumulty expressed the problem, informing Wilson on 16 June that "your absence here has been a tremendous handicap to us" and that he looked forward to the "psychological value" of the president's return.[55]

Another reason for the commission's poor publicity was a lack of coordination within its highly complex organization structure. While still on board the *George Washington*, Grayson already found himself at loggerheads with officials of the State Department, whom he accused of attempting to "hog" all the best accommodations. Such battles over authority—and its perquisites—were not uncommon among individuals charged with handling publicity, and they soon proved a decided impediment to smooth-running public relations. On 23 December Grayson reported to Tumulty that, although he was personally doing his best with reporters, he found his efforts hampered by what he termed "poor cooperation from the army and State Department." This particular disagreement stemmed from the State Department's excessive concern for security—Acting Secretary Frank Polk even went so far as to suggest that someone read all press reports before they were cabled—but it pointed to the more general problem of conflicting viewpoints among the commission's publicity staff.[56]

A similar conflict existed between Baker and Creel, resulting in two "somewhat stormy" interviews on 21 December. This episode occurred at a time when Creel's influence with Wilson was on the wane; it represented his determination to place his personal stamp on the commission's press office. Within a week, reports filtered back to Tumulty that Creel had departed the conference in a "huff" over the affair—an eventuality, by the way, that would have caused the secretary few regrets—but the fact remained that Creel was being eased out of Paris by the president.[57]

Tumulty also felt the sting of poor coordination among the commission's public relations personnel. In early January he learned from the AP that one of Wilson's ambassadors had resigned, a piece of information that he had been instructed to withhold from reporters. Errors of this nature seemed to abound while Wilson remained in Paris, and they soon prompted Tumulty to comment that "I wish we could have better cooperation on matters of publicity." Confusion prompted Tumulty to take more upon himself; he often attempted to insure staff coordination from Washington. He did so, for example, on 18 May, when he cabled Grayson that "I am handling the President's message [to the special session of Congress] here and using every means to prevent a leak. Hope you will not intimate to any newspaper man what message contains." Tumulty could rely on Grayson's studied discretion, but he was in no position to control the rest of the commission. He found, therefore, that the timing of releases from Paris rarely met his high standards for optimum publicity.[58]

This lack of coordination also plagued the State Department, which attempted to conduct its own publicity at the peace conference. It was just these efforts, of course, that led it into difficulty with both Grayson and Baker—and that accounted for the department's frequent omission from publicity distribution lists. When the treaty summaries were cabled to Compub, for example, the commission advised Acting Secretary of State Polk to ask the New York press bureau for a copy, an arrangement he could hardly have found satisfactory. Polk generally suffered most for the department's disagreements with other publicity personnel, and he often expressed his anxiety in cablegrams beseeching cooperation.[59]

This problem also showed in the commission's inability to prevent leaks to the press—even on the part of some of its most important members. "Publicity matters are hard to handle over here," Grayson wrote Tumulty on 10 April. "Colonel House, Secretary Lansing and others are constantly giving out statements that do not agree with the President's viewpoints." House, especially, went well beyond the mere issuance of contradictory remarks; he also undermined Wilson's position by admonishing reporters against taking the president's statements too seriously. House also enlarged his influence with correspondents by taking them into his confidence at morning press meetings, a practice responsible for several of the more serious leaks at the conference. Grayson quickly perceived the dangers inherent in this personal conduct of publicity, warning Tumulty on 19 May that the colonel "confers with newspapermen daily and gives out information of which we have no knowledge." This seemed weak coordination indeed, and although much of what Wilson termed "the extraordinary indiscretion of the American delegation" represented only his associates' desire to compensate for his failures, it made nevertheless for poor public relations.[60]

The primary cause of these difficulties was the proliferation of public relations personnel at the conference. Besides Baker, Grayson, and Tumulty, several other individuals played more or less important roles in managing publicity and press relations, a situation almost certain to result in conflict and confusion. Such seemed the result, surely, of Creel's presence in Paris. The CPI chairman appeared unable to resist dabbling in the affairs he had so ably directed in wartime Washington; small wonder, then, that Baker could not wait to see him assigned duties requiring his absence from the city. Also handling the commission's public relations were Maximilian Foster, the president's personal press liaison; Gilbert F. Close, Wilson's confidential secretary at the conference; Philip Patchin, the former State Department press officer now in the position of executive secretary to the commission; and the already ubiquitous representatives of military intelligence. Among such diverse individuals, there existed an obvious need for centralized authority. But the president was the only one in a position to supply or assign it, and he never even seemed to realize the problem. There soon developed, predictably enough, the inevitable wire crossings and bureaucratic jealousies always present in large, decentralized organizations.[61]

It remains difficult, under the circumstances, to understand Wilson's apparent complacency: why did he demonstrate so little concern over the commission's poor publicity? One reason, surely, was his crushing schedule at the peace conference; another was his distance from the United States, where the actual damage to the treaty was being inflicted. Most important, however, was the president's deep belief in his personal support among the American people, in his ability to win them over with a personal appeal. He expressed this view on 17 June, when he informed Tumulty that he had known, as he put it, "instinctively" all along that the conference's problems were ephemeral; he would easily set the situation right after his return. Whatever its merits, this remained one of Wilson's most firmly held beliefs. For Wilson, a personal campaign might overcome a multitude of publicity sins, and it was his strong resolve, as he informed Lansing, "to take a most militant and aggressive course . . . the minute I get back" that best explained his neglect of public relations during the conference itself.[62]

Tumulty, of course, shared this view of presidential power; he had begun in January to push Wilson for a vigorous campaign of personal publicity. By the end of April, Tumulty had decided on the way this should be done. He now proposed that Wilson tour the country on behalf of the treaty and the league. "It would be a great stimulant," he declared, "and [would] mean the utter rout of your political enemies." Contrary to Tumulty's later dramatized version, this suggestion—like the president's acceptance of it on 2 May—did not result from a sudden impulse. The idea of a "swing around the circle" had been discussed by Wilson and Tumulty for several months and had been rumored in the press as early as Wilson's February return to the United States. Nor did it represent the fruit of desperation; even with the tour trump unplayed, both Wilson and his secretary remained decidedly sanguine—at least in the spring of 1919—about the treaty's acceptance in America. Still, they knew the commission's work must face a stiff challenge in the Senate, where opposition to the League of Nations had already begun to crystallize; there seemed an obvious need for all the public support the president could generate.[63]

Tumulty began accordingly to lay plans for a presidential tour, one he hoped might "turn the tide" in favor of the treaty. His first need seemed an itinerary, and Tumulty constructed one—described as "tentative and speculative"—that covered 10,000 miles and twenty-six cities in twenty-seven days. He soon gave second thought to some of his proposed stops, cabling Wilson that he now wanted to cover more of the Northwest and less of the South, which he thought aleady favorable to the treaty. This decision represented an assumption found throughout the preparation of Wilson's plans: speeches should be made in the states of questionable senators, who might be convinced to vote favorably by evidence of treaty support among their constituents. At best dubiously accurate, this still represented conventional Washington wisdom, and Wilson received similar advice from friendly senators as well as from Polk and Lansing. It also seemed important to coordinate the president's trip with speaking tours of other treaty advocates, such as former President Taft, already on the hustings. This task fell likewise to Tumulty, and he soon acted to establish the White House as a kind of clearing center for protreaty propaganda. By the end of June, Tumulty had prepared a tentative program for the month following Wilson's arrival, including a reception in New York City, a personal address to Congress, and within two or three weeks an extended speaking tour of the country.[64]

Wilson was also thinking of plans for an appeal to the public. On 5 June he cabled Tumulty for his opinion of a proposed trip to Saint Louis and asked him to consider the advisability of other stops along the way. Wilson also raised this issue with Thomas W. Lamont, who responded with a list of suggestions for increasing the tour's publicity. Plans for the trip, according to Lamont, should be announced immediately upon Wilson's departure from Europe and should be "played up" in order "to get the country keyed up with expectation." The White House should also put Taft's "machinery" into operation and coordinate his speeches with the president's plans, pointing everything toward a public relations explosion upon Wilson's return. And finally, the president's staff should take pains to secure the attendance of dissenters as well as supporters at public meetings. To Wilson, all this made a great deal of sense; he appeared finally ready to throw off the shackles of restraint imposed by his presence at the conference. Now, he wrote Lamont on 23 June, seemed the "psychological moment to strengthen the tide" in favor of the treaty and the league.[65]

This was, of course, precisely Tumulty's opinion; he now proposed a number of ideas for focusing public attention on the president's achievements. On 25 June he suggested Wilson prepare a message of congratulations to the American people, to be released at the time of the conference's conclusion. What Tumulty had in mind was to make the treaty's signing a national day of celebration—a peace jubilee—with executive departments closing and demonstrations by the army and navy. The secretary also proposed that Wilson receive a hero's welcome in New York City, where he might take the opportunity to deliver his first address on the treaty's behalf. Wilson quickly agreed, cabling Tumulty—who must have been relieved after his experience in February—that he also thought it a mistake to pass through to Washington unnoticed, and the secretary made plans for the president's second reception in the United States.[66]

This time preparations went more smoothly. Not only did Tumulty have Wilson's cooperation, but he also felt more confident in his own control of public relations. The result proved a welcome like that given, as Baker put it, to "no homecoming American ever before in our history," complete with dreadnoughts, airplanes, and dirigibles. Wilson landed in Hoboken, New Jersey, on 8 July and motored through crowded streets to New York's Carnegie Hall, where he delivered a major address to 4,000 electrified admirers. And although he made no direct reference to the controversial League of Nations, Wilson left little doubt of his intention to fight.[67]

Next on Tumulty's timetable came the treaty's submission to the Senate, a duty the secretary perceived primarily as public relations. He thus linked the president's Senate message with his strategy of a nationwide speaking tour, suggesting in a June memorandum that Wilson employ the same arguments in each instance. The issues to stress, Tumulty contended, were peace with the treaty or war without it and the importance of the League of Nations to stop the spread of disorder and bolshevism. Tumulty also pointed out that Wilson must take the offensive and never relinquish it. His speeches must have the kind of punch and language capable of bringing the reasons for the league home to what Tumulty termed the "ordinary man." And finally, Wilson must take care to "satisfy every kind of opinion in this country" and to appeal to every occupational group.

Confident that the president would follow his advice, Tumulty soon took charge of making publicity arrangements for Wilson's Senate address. "For publicity purposes," he cabled on 3 July, the speech ought to be given to reporters on the morning before its delivery, "in order to reach all over the country, especially [the] country press." This might insure maximum publicity—always the goal of prior release—and allow the president to use the Senate chambers as a kind of national sounding board for the treaty and the league.[68]

For all Tumulty's efforts, however, the Senate speech proved something of a disappointment. It dealt almost entirely in generalities, with Wilson clearly failing to assume the sort of offensive position Tumulty suggested. This represented, to be sure, a characteristic Wilsonian approach, one that had served him well on several previous occasions, but it could not supply the punch needed to arouse public opinion for the treaty and the league. The speech also suffered from weak presentation, at least by the president's standards. Perhaps Wilson sensed hostility in his audience, or perhaps he was simply tired from long labors at the conference; whatever the cause, he experienced unusual difficulties delivering his address to the Senate. Only at the end did he seem to hit his stride, laying aside his prepared remarks and speaking with eloquence about the league as the fulfillment of America's promise to the world. These words were greeted, tellingly, with thunderous applause from the galleries —and with icy silence from the Republican side of the Senate.[69]

With this, the stage seemed set for Wilson's tour of the country; it would remain set for almost two months, while the treaty languished before the Senate Foreign Relations Committee. There existed, undoubtedly, good reasons for this delay: Wilson's health was questionable, domestic problems were pressing, and the president was required in Washington to marshal senatorial support for the treaty. Still, Wilson sensed the momentum slipping from his position and understood that nothing he could do in the capital—short of compromise—might allow him to regain it. He therefore spoke more and more of touring the country, of appealing to "Caesar," as he called the people. In this he received encouragement from his advisers, who began to see only too clearly the trouble brewing on the Hill. Tumulty, for instance, wrote on 15 August that he hoped the president might follow up his Senate meetings "by an appeal to the country." House sent similar advice through Lansing, citing flagging popular interest as a reason for attempting what he termed "a resurrection of the ideals America fought for." Only Grayson, now more interested in his patient's health than in publicity, continued to demur, and he was soon overruled by the president's own disregard for his personal safety. By September, the time had clearly come for Wilson to play his final card; he announced that he was taking his case to the people.[70]

Tumulty hastily completed the plans he had drawn up in June. He made a few changes in the itinerary, primarily to secure coverage of the most important areas, and omitted, at the president's insistence, a week's vacation at the Grand Canyon. He also discovered that the president's train was too small to accommodate the party he had envisioned, forcing the elimination of several economic and political leaders. Tumulty refused to budge, of course, on inclusion of the press, and he assigned space to approximately twenty journalists and motion picture cameramen in a special press car. The secretary also made all arrangements for publicity. He asked local supporters to prepare detailed schedules—he called them "maneuver sheets"—covering every facet of the president's visit and distributed them to newspapermen twenty-four hours before each stop. He insured local publicity by employing advance men in each community and by assigning them the responsibility of supplying promotional information to the press. As usual, Tumulty's plans proved thorough; the rest was up to Wilson.[71]

The train left Washington on 3 September, heading for the Midwest and Wilson's first speech at Columbus, Ohio. During the next three days, Wilson delivered major addresses at Indianapolis, Saint Louis, and Kansas City, attracting large crowds wherever he appeared. This represented, no doubt, the fruit of Tumulty's preparations—he had, for instance, scheduled a speech at the Indiana State Fair—as well as the drawing power of the president. But it should not be supposed that large audiences reflected Wilson's effectiveness on the stump. Only at Saint Louis, where his reception seemed surprisingly friendly, did he rise to the occasion and deliver an aggressive peroration. This pattern continued throughout the Midwest; Wilson received a warm but not hysterical welcome and responded with addresses clearly lacking in effectiveness.[72]

Nor did things improve as Wilson headed west. This seems, perhaps, predictable: the president was now moving into the heart of enemy territory—the home states of Senators William Borah (Idaho), Miles Poindexter (Washington), and Hiram Johnson (California). Still, Wilson's desire to assail his antagonists in their own bailiwicks had inspired his trip in the first place, and he might have been expected to take a more aggressive position on this leg of the journey. Such did not prove the case, however; Wilson reiterated his earlier tone and arguments in addresses at such places as Coeur d'Alene and Spokane. There soon developed considerable concern among Wilson's advisers, and some began to wonder if the idea of a western trip had been such a good one after all.[73]

As always, Tumulty remained in the thick of these considerations. Before leaving the capital, he had instructed Rudolph Forster, staying behind at the White House, to keep him abreast of Washington comment; he soon solicited similar information from Bernard Baruch in New York City. Tumulty also maintained close contact with correspondents accompanying the president, requesting their impressions of crowd response at every stop. He thus grew increasingly aware of the journey's shortcomings and eventually found it necessary to make recommendations for its improvement. The most important of these related to Wilson's addresses, which Tumulty realized were falling consistently short of their objectives. On 12 September he submitted the first of several memorandums on this subject, proposing three specific arguments he believed might strengthen the president's position. Wilson should, according to Tumulty, show that the League of Nations fulfilled America's reasons for entering the war; he should also present the league as an institution above partisanship; and he should, finally, describe the league as an instrument for eliminating war. Within a few days, Tumulty added an attack on isolation to the president's list and informed Wilson that he was sending back to Washington for a copy of McKinley's famous "age of isolation" speech. The secretary also now began—cautiously—to criticize the president's delivery. "Frankly," he wrote after Wilson's speech at Salt Lake City, "Your punch did not land last night. . . . As a newspaperman put it this morning, you simply pushed the ball; there was no snap in your stroke." Tumulty played an increasingly important role in designing Wilson's speeches, until by the end of the journey he composed draft passages for the president to consider.[74]

At least partly due to Tumulty's efforts, Wilson's addresses soon won more favorable response. This seemed most evident in Los Angeles, where the audience finally reacted with enthusiasm. Wilson may have been only, as the *New York Times*'s Charles Grasty suggested, now "getting the cumulative effect of his missionary work," but there existed no doubt among accompanying reporters that Los Angeles represented the high point of the trip. Even David Lawrence, whose crowd reports had been pessimistic, now believed that Wilson might be able to return to Washington in triumph.[75]

This trend continued as the train pointed eastward. The president received huge ovations in Utah and Wyoming—sometimes reminiscent of his receptions in Europe—and he moved into Colorado with rejuvenated confidence. At Pueblo, he gave the most moving speech of his entire tour, reminding the audience that, as he put it, "there is one thing that the American people always rise to and extend their hand to, and that is the truth of justice and of liberty and of peace. We have accepted that truth," he concluded, "and it is going to lead us, and through us the world, out into pastures of quietness and peace such as the world never dreamed of before." This seemed, even for Wilson, unwonted eloquence, and it left his auditors tearful. There proved, however, no chance for Wilson to repeat this success; he was stricken later that evening with the illness that incapacitated him for several months. Immediately, the train returned to Washington—and to Wilson's showdown with the Senate.[76]

The trip had clearly not succeeded. No matter what effect it had on public opinion—and it did appear to uncover some support for the League of Nations—the tour did nothing to diminish the strength of senatorial opposition. Indeed, it probably had the opposite effect, increasing the resolve of bitter-enders, especially from the states Wilson visited, to defeat his treaty in the Senate. This result seemed, moreover, predictable; Wilson should have known better than to undertake this kind of tour in the first place. He had previously written, in *Constitutional Government in the United States*, that although the House of Representatives might be influenced by public appeal, "the President has not the same recourse when blocked by the Senate. . . . The Senate is not so sensitive to opinion," he explained, "and is apt to grow, if anything, more stiff if pressure of that kind is brought to bear upon it." Perhaps Wilson's White House experience had expanded his opinion of the president's publicity power, or perhaps he simply needed the vindication of evoking popular support. He might, at any rate, have done better to follow his own earlier advice and to improve his personal relations with undecided senators. For several reasons, first of temperament, then of illness, he rejected this solution. The result was his treaty's rejection by the Senate.[77]

Years later, Ray Stannard Baker wondered if Wilson had not waited until it was, as he put it, "too late to influence a recalcitrant political opposition. Was he not attempting an enlightenment of the people that should have been started while we were at Paris? Had we all been too sanguine?" These remained understandably difficult questions for the former press secretary, but they still point directly to the major flaw in Wilson's conception of the treaty's publicity. If public opinion might have had any impact at all on the Senate's decision to approve or reject the finished document, it should have been won over while the treaty—and the senators' opinion of it—remained in the process of formulation. The time to do this came, naturally, during the peace conference itself; by the summer of 1919 it had grown, as Baker realized, simply "too late."[78]

Conclusion

Power and the
People

the President at the White House microphone,
the Senators, Congressmen, spokesmen, at
    microphones—
Each and all have a target.
Each one aims for the ping ping
the bling bling of a sharpshooter.
    Here is a moving colossal show,
a vast dazzling aggregation of stars and hams
selling things, selling ideas, selling faiths,
selling air, slogans, passions, selling history.
    The target is who and what?
        The people, yes—

Carl Sandburg, *The People, Yes*

By 1921 the White House had developed "by
degrees" into the most productive news source in Washington. "It is
so," according to journalist J. Frederick Essary, "because, since the
days of McKinley, Presidents have more and more realized the high
value of inspired publicity," bringing under control the generation of
news and opinion. Wilson's White House would have seemed strange
indeed to his nineteenth-century predecessors: not only did reporters now have a workroom of their own, but they were ministered to
by a press staff—when not by the president himself—outnumbering
Grant's entire entourage in the mansion. For better or worse, presidential management had become an established part of the Washington news scene, and there could be no doubt that "inspired
publicity" now represented an important influence on the public's
perception of foreign affairs.[1]

This change occurred, as Essary noted, over the course of several
administrations. McKinley supplied the foundation, and his efforts
in this dimension—as in others—unlocked doors that later presidents pushed widely ajar. Roosevelt demonstrated how presidential

publicity could be enhanced by a nose for news, as he employed his ebullient personality and radiant style to maintain himself in the spotlight. Considering their different approaches, it is not surprising that historians have portrayed Roosevelt rather than McKinley as the originator of executive publicity, yet TR's role seems in many ways secondary to his more reticent predecessor's. The two also formed an almost perfect complement: according to Max Weber's classifications, McKinley developed a "bureaucratic leadership" of press and public, relying upon rationalization and routinization to accomplish his goals, while Roosevelt—employing McKinley's techniques—brought all the attributes of "charismatic leadership" into the White House.[2]

Taft's public relations failures—and they were prodigious—highlighted the perils awaiting any president who disregarded publicity. As Roosevelt's successor, Taft may have been doomed to suffer by comparison, but he only made things worse by rejecting his staff's proposals for influencing the public. The result proved devastating, instructing future presidential aspirants in the need for a good press. Wilson, at least, seemed convinced; his well-known pledge of "pitiless publicity" represented the first step in a public relations program that resulted in the introduction of regularly scheduled press conferences. This innovation soon fell prey to Wilson's mistrust of reporters, but its objectives found fruition in the remarkably comprehensive Committee on Public Information.

There existed, as we have seen, several reasons for this enlarged interest in press and public opinion. One was the improved technology of the late nineteenth century, as the development of speedier printing processes and advanced telegraphy transformed the daily newspaper into a potent medium of public information. Viewed from the White House, this appeared as both threat and opportunity: more news from the capital increased public scrutiny of presidential behavior, but it also made it possible for the judicious chief executive to present his policies in favorable perspective. The development of national wire services enhanced this opportunity by dominating transmission of Washington news; they soon made it possible for the president to influence headlines and front pages nationwide through contact with only a handful of correspondents. What the president required was a system for controlling the stories of Washington reporters; it was for this reason that McKinley enlarged the size of his staff and innovated practices to bring newspapermen to him for daily information. As they developed, other technological innovations were also incorporated into the president's arsenal for managing opinion. Still photographs and motion pictures were soon utilized in this way, and—although they fall beyond the purview of this study—the same proved later true of radio and television.[3]

Another factor was the importance of public opinion to American expansion. This appeared, to some extent, during the administrations of Cleveland and Harrison but did not produce significant changes until McKinley became president. Then America's larger destiny became manifest—and so did the need for more careful management of public opinion. No longer could the president be satisfied with minimum public approval; he now required support to pursue new policies of national aggrandizement. Such proved, as later presidents would understand, the problem with imperial democracy; McKinley dealt with it by tightening his grip on the levers of news and opinion. This process—like many others—accelerated during wartime, when the need for unity required a more thorough orchestration of sentiment. In 1898, McKinley faced this need with a fledgling organization; twenty years later, Wilson proved better prepared, creating in the powerful Creel committee this era's apotheosis of public opinion management. Thus if, as Arthur Schlesinger, Jr., has written, "the Imperial Presidency was essentially the creation of foreign policy," no less can be said for the executive's efforts to control the press and public opinion.[4]

And finally, there remains the impact of progressivism on the presidents' perceptions of public opinion. To some extent, this twentieth-century ideology resembled its counterpart in the Age of Jackson; both, at least, stressed the people's role in national affairs. But progressivism's effect on public opinion management hardly represented an extension of Jacksonian democracy. There seems, of course, considerable irony in this situation: progressivism was supposed to enhance popular participation in government, not to increase the executive's control over public opinion. But there also existed in the progressive creed articles supporting opinion management. One was faith in a strong chief executive; another was belief in the applicability of sound management to all fields of administrative endeavor. These elements combined with heightened awareness of public opinion to produce a melancholy reversal of the avowed spirit of progressivism.

Nor did the usefulness of opinion management escape the notice of progressive theorists. They described it, in a number of books and articles, as supplying the means of "social control" for improving national life and took every opportunity to praise its implementation by a strong chief executive. What the progressives did not seem to apprehend, of course, was the danger involved in what Graham

Wallas described as "the creation of opinion by the deliberate exploitation of subconscious non-rational influence" or the possibility of its application to goals they did not share. They failed throughout, in fact, to grasp the situation in quite this way. When, in the years before the First World War, progressivism began to break down, it retained its faith in management long after its belief in popular wisdom had started to disappear. Thus, Richard T. Ely and Walter Lippmann joined Herbert Croly in calling for expanded executive latitude, and the informed administrator replaced the popular will as the arbiter of national policy. Ultimately, of course, war participation (under the expert tutelage of the CPI) discredited the public altogether, prompting Lippmann's scathing indictment of democratic public opinion and allowing progressivism to embrace at last the implications of its premises.[5]

This conclusion may have caused the theorist some soul-searching; the same cannot be said for progressive presidents. For them, public opinion management seemed primarily a practical concern, and it is little wonder that they suffered few second thoughts about employing progressivism to justify their activities. This is not to say, of course, that these presidents were altogether cynical; they saw the release of favorable information as a kind of public education. But neither did they consider entrusting the formulation of policy to anything as unpredictable as the public will. The dilemma that drove Walter Lippmann into the camp of conservatism thus had no significance in Roosevelt's "bully pulpit," and its lack of interest for Wilson seems best demonstrated by his wartime conception of the avowedly propagandist CPI.

The result of these changes proved a decided increase in executive ability to manage opinion. With an enlarged staff and rapidly improving publicity techniques, the president was now able to take greater advantage of what V. O. Key has called "the prominence of his position" to "command the attention of all the media" with his release of information. No longer did the president remain substantially outside the process of opinion formulation; he now played an active—and daily—role in composing the news and editorials that nurtured it. If, as another student of public opinion has written, "the substantial power of the press is in its selectivity—its definition of 'news,'" that power now resided in the White House, where more often than not the president himself initiated foreign policy "news." In so doing, he made use of reporters' incessant need for information, and he soon found it possible to define national issues, to regulate the timing of their release, and to suggest the context in which they should be considered. By 1921 such concerns had become standard

White House procedure, and correspondents were transformed, albeit unwittingly, into a kind of adjunct to the president's publicity staff. This did not mean, of course, that there existed no truth at all to the popular conception of the press as a check on executive activity. On occasion, reporters remained a source of considerable presidential pain and embarrassment; this study, indeed, abounds with such occasions. But the common interest of both parties in disseminating news kept the president-reporter relationship from becoming the adversary one usually depicted by democratic theorists.[6]

Our study has also cast doubt on another aspect of democratic theory: the importance of public opinion in formulating foreign policy. As Melvin Small has pointed out, historians have had no choice but to "assume" that the threat of popular disapproval plays a major part in the shaping of presidential policy; there is no real proof one way or the other. The compelling charm of democratic theory has, in fact, led historians to assign a role to public opinion— the broad definition of objectives—that remains manifestly unverifiable and has allowed them to ignore the more available information that does not support this pleasing hypothesis. Such information seems abundant for the years of this study. We have taken a close look at foreign policy deliberations of presidents from McKinley to Wilson and have found none affected to any significant degree by considerations of public opinion. This is not to say, of course, that presidents have shown no concern at all for popular approval, but it is to say that this concern had little impact on the actual process of policy formulation. In most cases, the issue of public support entered executive discussions only after policy decisions were made; it was generally related solely to questions of implementation. There existed, to be sure, variations in this pattern, usually caused by the nearness of elections or by the unreliability of Congress, but there can be no doubt that public opinion ranked last among presidential considerations in making foreign policy.[7]

Still, the role assigned to public opinion remains part of what Bernard Cohen has termed "the folklore of our time," and its acceptance by otherwise trustworthy commentators deserves at least hasty explanation. We have seen already the significance of this interpretation for democratic doctrine and can perhaps understand its appeal to historians as a kind of theoretical wish fulfillment. For the press, moreover, its acceptance has filled an even stronger need: journalists have long supposed their newspapers supplied a vital link between public and policy maker; to deny a leading role to public opinion would rob the press of its primary function in democratic society. Newspapermen have thus been understandably unwilling to acknowledge any limitations upon the power of the people, and they remain among the most fervent in ascribing public opinion—and themselves—an important place in executive decision making. Presidents have had perhaps the strongest motive for paying homage to this interpretation. They have comprehended, quite correctly, the role played by public opinion in the "folklore" of democracy and have been understandably loath to contradict a myth so fundamental to their own continuation in power. They have also made, not surprisingly, the repetition of statements about the importance of public approval into a kind of presidential ritual. This does not mean, certainly, that American chief executives are nothing more than cunning Machiavellians—the ritualizers of any faith, even democracy, are often its most devout believers—but it does offer an explanation for the distance between presidential statements and behavior on the place of public opinion in foreign policy making.[8]

This distance did not narrow during the twenty-five years of our investigation. Changed conditions may have increased the president's awareness of public opinion, but they did not enhance the public's voice in making foreign policy. They seem, in fact, almost certain to have produced the opposite effect; the development of management techniques moved the president's relationship with the people even farther from the democratic ideal. Public opinion had never, of course, played a large role in the process of foreign policy making, but the theorist could always take solace, at least, in the unimportance of foreign affairs in the average citizen's daily life. By 1921 this seemed increasingly untrue, as America's participation in world affairs catapulted foreign policy into an important place in the national consciousness. Yet it could not be said that public opinion had any more genuine impact on the making of policy than it had enjoyed in 1897. This, then, represented the real significance of public opinion management: in a time of increasingly vital foreign policy decisions, it allowed the executive to neutralize the danger of public disenchantment and to behave, in making its decisions, largely as it had twenty-five years before. If public opinion seemed a more frequent topic of White House discussion in 1921, it remained a minor consideration in policy deliberations. Nothing more was required; techniques now existed to insure the president of public support.

This seems, indeed, the purpose for which opinion management was developed. Presidential publicity had been a valued instrument as early as the Grant administration, but it found only rare and sporadic implementation through the nineteenth century. For presidents of that era, publicity—like foreign policy—filled only limited needs; it was the onset of heightened international responsibilities that made their lack of sophistication a problem. McKinley and Roosevelt saw in opinion management a way to eliminate this new danger. Their goal was enhanced control over the vicissitudes of public opinion; the result proved a marked increase in the executive's ability to guide public perceptions of foreign affairs.

It should not be supposed, however, that any president achieved total control. Even White House reporters, with their seemingly insatiable need for news, have found at times the independence to treat executive information with skepticism, and the existence of other countervailing factors has been demonstrated by several well-known authorities. This may qualify our conclusions. Yet presidential opinion management remains an important element in administering foreign policy, and its continued—indeed, widened—use suggests that chief executives perceive its contribution to be valuable. It has succeeded, to a remarkable extent, in freeing presidents from the potential constraint of public opinion that came with the nation's larger role in world affairs, so that today's chief executives seem no more shackled than their nineteenth-century counterparts by the supposed force of popular perceptions. Public opinion has demonstrated, in fact, increasing support for the president in times of crisis, and this implies a degree of freedom that chief executives— armed with techniques for shaping public opinion—have been far from the last to understand.[9]

It remains unclear, of course, whether or not an unfettered executive should be considered a salutary development. In one sense, surely, the management of public opinion represents an enlargement of presidential leadership; it will appeal as such to those concerned, like so many latter-day progressives, over the tendency of democracy to drift in time of crisis. Such an answer seems a bit simplistic, however, and we shall have to look farther to determine the ultimate impact of this new power on the health of democratic institutions. There has been, for one thing, a stunning decline in the public's independence in perceiving foreign affairs. No matter how totally they distrusted the public's wisdom, nineteenth-century presidents had neither facilities nor inclination to control the popular debate over questions of foreign policy, and there often developed, at least in the press, lively if not acrimonious exchanges of ideas about international relations. This has proved less true for the twentieth century, when chief executives have consistently displayed the ability—and the desire—to manipulate increasingly complex foreign policy information to forestall, at least temporarily, the development of contradictory interpretations. This has come about, to a significant extent, because the White House's undoubted authority has combined with the executive's control over timing to enable the president to define the boundaries of foreign policy debates, a power often used to preempt the arguments of his most dangerous detractors. The result has been a marked increase in the public's tendency to take its direction from the executive and to see questions of foreign affairs in terms spelled out for it not by the "independent" press of democratic theory but by statements of policy makers themselves.

The existence of management techniques has also prompted the president to grow unduly concerned about the appearance, as opposed to the substance, of even the most important foreign policies. Chief executives have come increasingly to define the problem of administration in terms of public relations, resulting in a willingness to change official explanations and policy pronouncements— but not policies themselves—to accord with perceived wishes of the people. This has often tempted presidents to play fast and loose with the truth, and there can be little doubt that the ultimate result can be only a shadow—or mirror image—of what is usually meant by the term *democracy.*

There remains, finally, the matter of what might be called the Lippmann fallacy. "The unhappy truth," according to Walter Lippman, "is that the prevailing public opinion has been destructively wrong at the critical junctures. The people have imposed a veto upon the judgment of informed and responsible officials" and "have compelled" the government to follow policies consistently in error. Such imputations, also found in much of the historiography of foreign affairs, are more than "unhappy"; they are also false. No matter how benighted public opinion may, in fact, have been "at the critical junctures," it played little part in making foreign policy decisions—and errors—during the period covered by this study. In many cases, the views of the public were simply ignored; in others, where this did not seem expedient, they were molded by deliberate use of the executive's managerial techniques. On the basis of such evidence, it makes little sense to accuse public ignorance of causing deficiencies in foreign affairs, although this theory has, to be sure, supplied presidents—and their intellectual supporters— with a valuable rationalization for their failures in conducting foreign policy. It should be clear that whatever has gone wrong with America's position in the world remains the sole responsibility of executive officials. They, not public opinion, have had the authority to make decisions; no real power has ever been given to the people.[10]

Notes

Introduction

1. See Arthur M. Schlesinger, Jr., *The Imperial Presidency*; and Joseph A. Califano, Jr., *A Presidential Nation*, pp. 100–21.

2. See Robert W. Desmond, *The Press and World Affairs*, pp. 63, 96–98; Bertrand R. Canfield, *Public Relations*, pp. 21–22; and Scott M. Cutlip and Allen H. Center, *Effective Public Relations*, pp. 24–45. Between 1890 and 1909, the total circulation of daily newspapers in the United States nearly tripled, and the circulation per household increased from 0.66 to 1.23. See table in Melvin L. De Fleur, *Theories of Mass Communication*, p. 20.

3. See Schlesinger, *Imperial Presidency*, pp. 82–90; Nelson W. Polsby, "The Institutionalization of the U.S. House of Representatives," pp. 144–68; and Robert L. Beisner, *From the Old Diplomacy to the New, 1865–1900*.

Chapter 1

1. The quotations are from James A. Garfield, *The Works of James Abram Garfield*, 2:49–50; and from the *World* to James Creelman, 3 January 1896, ser. 2, Cleveland Papers. See also Hamilton Fish Diary, 22 February, 1, 2, 13, 17 June 1870, Box 314, Fish Papers; Memorandum, "Associated Press," 6 December 1892, ser. 1, Harrison Papers; James G. Blaine to Chester A. Arthur, 3 February 1882, ser. 1, Arthur Papers; and Henry Watterson to Walter Q. Gresham, 12 November 1893, Box 41, Gresham Papers.

2. The quotations are from Rutherford B. Hayes Diary, 12 March 1878, Hayes Papers; and from Pierrepont to Fish, 24 November 1873, Box 98, Fish Papers; the emphasis is Pierrepont's. See also Fish Diary, 26 October 1870, Box 316, Fish Papers; and Elijah Halford Diary, 9 April 1889, ser. 15, Harrison Papers.

3. "Samoa" Scrapbook, Box 228, Bayard Papers; Scrapbooks, ser. 7, Grant Papers; Richard Weightman to Bayard, 7 April 1887, Box 187, Bayard Papers; Cleveland to George F. Parker, 10 December 1889, ser. 2, Cleveland Papers; Richard Olney to Josiah Patterson, 12 February 1896, Box 7, Olney Papers; Edna M. Colman, *White House Gossip*, p. 118; and Bernard C. Cohen, "The Relationship between Public Opinion and Policy Maker," p. 71.

4. Hamilton Fish, "Regulations of the Department of State," 20 October 1869, quoted in Graham H. Stuart, *The Department of State*, pp. 142–45; and "A Day in the White House," unnamed newspaper, 27 April 1889, in Scrapbooks, ser. 16, Harrison Papers.

5. Irwin H. Hoover, *Forty-Two Years at the White House*, p. 21; Ida Tarbell, "President McKinley in War Times," p. 214; Orlando O. Stealey, *Twenty Years in the Press Gallery*, pp. 34–35; James E. Pollard, *The Presidents and the Press*, pp. 558, 565; and Margaret Leech, *In the Days of McKinley*, p. 231. Although Porter's briefings did not eliminate the correspondents' need for additional inside information, for which they continued their traditional habit of interviewing the president's callers, they did offer a steady source of information that allowed reporters to become increasingly dependent on the secretary for both facts and interpretation.

6. The quotation is from Edward G. Lowry, *Washington Close-ups*, p. 127. See also George B. Cortelyou Diary, 22, 25 March 1898, Box 62, Cortelyou Papers; and Leech, *McKinley*, p. 231.

7. Leech, *McKinley*, p. 126; H. Wayne Morgan, *William McKinley and His America*, pp. 305–7; and Leonard D. White, *The Republican Era*, p. 102.

8. Stuart, *Department of State*, pp. 184, 194; and Paolo E. Coletta, "Prologue: William McKinley and the Conduct of American Foreign Relations," p. 18.

9. The quotation is from David S. Barry, "News-Getting at the Capital," p. 286. See also J. Frederick Essary, *Covering Washington*, p. 87; David S. Barry, *Forty Years in Washington*, p. 237; Tarbell, "President McKinley," p. 214; *Ohio State Journal*, 30 November 1897, in ser. 12, McKinley Papers; and Morgan, *McKinley*, p. 85.

10. Cortelyou Diary, 12 August 1898, Box 52, Cortelyou Papers; Charles Willis Thompson, *Presidents I've Known and Two Near Presidents*, pp. 16, 73; and Pollard, *Presidents and the Press*, p. 566.

11. Albert Halstead, "The President at Work," p. 2080; "Current Comment" Scrapbook, ser. 12, McKinley Papers; Cortelyou Diary, 30 July 1898, Box 52, Cortelyou Papers; and Morgan, *McKinley*, pp. 322–23.

12. The quotation is from the *Washington Post*, 5 April 1897. See also Lester D. Langley, *The Cuban Policy of the United States*, pp. 90–98; Morgan, *McKinley*, p. 335; and Walter La Feber, *The New Empire*, pp. 326–36.

13. "Current Comment" Scrapbook, ser. 12, McKinley Papers; Letters to McKinley, ser. 1, McKinley Papers; and John L. Offner, "President McKinley and the Origins of the Spanish-American War," pp. 104, 109. McKinley's failure to see Cuba as an important political issue was not limited to his first few months in office. Throughout the crisis, he showed more concern over the role that public opinion could play in the execution of his policy—especially in the event of war—than with the possible political ramifications of opposing the public's wishes. Despite the existence in 1896 of what everyone seemed to perceive as intense public interest in Cuba, the island had not been an issue in that year's election, and McKinley probably saw no reason to suppose that things would be any different in 1900. Congress supplied the greatest public expression of expansionist sentiment in this period, but McKinley's silence indicates that, for the time being at least, he did not feel threatened by its fulminations.

14. "Current Comment" Scrapbook, ser. 12, McKinley Papers; Letters to McKinley, ser. 1, McKinley Papers; Cortelyou Diary, undated but early April 1898, Box 52, Cortelyou Papers; Offner, "President McKinley," p. 134; Morgan, *McKinley*, p. 350; and La Feber, *New Empire*, p. 135. Again Congress was providing a discordant note, but McKinley knew that it would soon be stilled by adjournment.

15. The quotation is from Sherman to Dupuy de Lôme, 26 June 1897, in U.S., Department of State, *Foreign Relations of the United States, 1897*, pp. 507–8; see also Morgan, *McKinley*, p. 342.

16. Sherman to Woodford, 16 July 1897, Instructions to Spain, vol. 22, Record Group 59, National Archives, Washington, D.C.

17.The quotations are from Woodford to Sherman, 20 September 1897, Despatches from Spain, vol. 131, Record Group 59, National Archives, Washington, D.C.; and Assistant Secretary of State William R. Day to Woodford, 1 October 1897, Instructions to Spain, vol. 22.

18. "Current Comment" Scrapbook, ser. 12, McKinley Papers; and Letters to McKinley, ser. 1, McKinley Papers. From 2 June to 1 December 1897, McKinley received only three letters from the public dealing with Cuba.

19. Morgan, *McKinley*, pp. 344–45.

20. Woodford to Sherman, 26 October and 27 November 1897, and Woodford to McKinley, 14 November 1897, Despatches from Spain, vol. 132; La Feber, *New Empire*, pp. 340–41; and Morgan, *McKinley*, p. 347.

21. The quotations are from Cortelyou Diary, 16 November 1897, Box 52, Cortelyou Papers; and Message to Congress, 6 December 1897, in George Washington et al., *A Compilation of the Messages and Papers of the Presidents, 1789–1905*, 10:30–38. See also Offner, "President McKinley," pp. 169–71.

22. Porter to McKinley, 7 December 1897, ser. 1, McKinley Papers; and "Current Comment" Scrapbook, ser. 12, McKinley Papers.

23. Fitzhugh Lee to Day, 12–15 January 1898, Consular, Havana, Record Group 59, National Archives, Washington, D.C.; and Offner, "President McKinley," pp. 184–86.

24. The quotation is from Sherman to Woodford, 23 February 1898, Instructions to Spain, vol. 22. See also de Lôme to Don Jose Caralejas, 15 January 1898, in Department of State, *Foreign Relations, 1898*, pp. 1007–8.

25. Offner, "President McKinley," pp. 209–10.

26. The tenders of service are in ser. 1, McKinley Papers; see also Cortelyou Diary, 18 March 1898, Box 52, Cortelyou Papers; Sherman to Woodford, 1 March 1898, and Day to Woodford, 3 March 1898, Instructions to Spain, vol. 22.

27. The quotation is from Day to Woodford, 3 March 1898, Instructions to Spain, vol. 22.

28. James Creelman, "Mr. Cortelyou Explains President McKinley," pp. 572–74, in ser. 12, McKinley Papers; and Morgan, *McKinley*, p. 362.

29. The Root quotation is from Charles S. Olcott, *The Life of William McKinley*, 2:346. See also Cortelyou Diary, 31 July 1898, Box 52, Cortelyou Papers; and Morgan, *McKinley*, p. 276.

30. Long's statement was quoted in the *Washington Evening Star*, 16 February 1898; and see Porter to Long, 16 February 1898, ser. 2, McKinley Papers.

31. The quotations are from Reid to McKinley, 8 March 1898, Reel 72, Reid Papers; and Lodge to McKinley, 21 March 1898, ser. 1, McKinley Papers.

32. Cortelyou Diary, 28, 29 March and 2 April 1898, Box 52, Cortelyou Papers; Stealey, *Twenty Years*, p. 9; Essary, *Covering Washington*, p. 21; and Leech, *McKinley*, pp. 230–31.

33. *Washington Post*, 25, 26, 27 February 1898.

34. *Washington Post, 2 March 1898; Washington Evening Star*, 3 March 1898; Cortelyou Diary, 19, 22 March 1898, Box 52, Cortelyou Papers; and Offner, "President McKinley," pp. 226–27.

35. The quotations are from Cortelyou Diary, 28 March 1898, Box 52, Cortelyou Papers. See also Cortelyou Diary, 25 March 1898, Box 52, Cortelyou Papers; and Message to Congress, in Washington et al., *Messages of the Presidents*, 10:52–55.

36. The quotation is from the Asher C. Hinds Diary, 9 March 1898, quoted in Offner, "President McKinley," p. 238. See also L. White Busbey, *Uncle Joe Cannon*, pp. 186–98; and U.S., Congress, *Congressional Record*, 55th Cong., 2d sess., pp. 2602–21.

37. The quotations are from Cortelyou Diary, 26 March and 16 April 1898, Box 52, Cortelyou Papers. See also "Current Comment" and "Foreign Affairs" Scrapbooks, ser. 12, McKinley Papers; Letters to McKinley, ser. 1, McKinley Papers; and Porter to John Hay, 14 March 1898, ser. 2, McKinley Papers. Ira T. Smith, who worked in the White House mail room, has written that McKinley received large quantities of mail—much of it abusive—urging him to go to war. If Smith was correct, most of the letters he described were not retained in the McKinley Papers. Perhaps the explanation for this lies in Smith's admission that very few letters actually reached the

president; it is possible that only mail seen by McKinley was retained in his files. I have, at any rate, accepted this explanation and taken McKinley's papers as a better indicator than Smith's estimates of the president's own perception of public opinion. Ira T. Smith, *Dear Mr. President*, pp. 3–4, 12, 46. Even Theodore Roosevelt, who believed that the public favored war, noted that there were "multitudes" of what he called "peace-at-any-price" telegrams coming into the White House from all sections of the country. Roosevelt to Elihu Root, 5 April 1898, Box 162, Root Papers.

38. The quotations are from Reid to McKinley, 8 March 1898, Reel 72, Reid Papers; and Walden to McKinley, 1 March 1898, Box 56, Cortelyou Papers. See also Reed to McKinley, 16 March 1898, and Woodward to Reed, 14 March 1898, Box 52, Cortelyou Papers; and Frederick Holls to McKinley, 2 March 1898, ser. 1, McKinley Papers.

39. Joseph E. Wisan, *The Cuban Crisis as Reflected in the New York Press*; and George Auxier, "Middle-Western Newspapers and the Spanish-American War," pp. 523–34.

40. The quotations are from *Des Moines Leader*, 23 February 1898; and *Dubuque Daily Times*, 18 February 1898. See also *Mount Vernon Hawk-Eye*, 18, 25 February 1898; and *Davenport Daily Democrat*, 23 February 1898.

41. The quotations are from *Council Bluffs Nonpareil*, 3 March 1898; and *Davenport Daily Democrat*, 14 March 1898. See also *Des Moines Daily Leader*, 24 February and 9, 11 March 1898; *Keokuk Daily Gate City*, 5, 9, 12 March 1898; *Mount Vernon Hawk-Eye*, 4, 11 March 1898; *Dubuque Daily Times*, 26 February and 8 March 1898; and *Lansing Mirror and Chronicle*, 11 March 1898.

42. See, for example, *Dubuque Daily Times*, 19, 22 April 1898.

43. The quotations are from *Weekly Northern Vindicator* (Estherville), 31 March and 14 April 1898. See also *Clinton Age*, 15 March and 1 April 1898; and *Waukon Standard*, 23 March and 6 April 1898.

44. The quotation is from Cortelyou Diary, 16 April 1898, Box 52, Cortelyou Papers. See also "Current Comment" and "Foreign Affairs" Scrapbooks, ser. 12, McKinley Papers; Cortelyou Diary, 17 February 1899, Box 52, Cortelyou Papers; and Offner, "President McKinley," pp. 71–74.

45. Cortelyou Diary, 16 April 1898 and 17 February 1899, Box 52, Cortelyou Papers; Charles F. Manderson to McKinley, 28 February 1898, ser. 1, McKinley Papers; Reid to McKinley, 8 March 1898, Reel 72, Reid Papers; and Day to Woodford, 3 March 1898, Instructions to Spain, vol. 22.

46. Alger to McKinley, 5 April 1898, ser. 1, McKinley Papers; Charles G. Dawes, *A Journal of the McKinley Years*, p. 146; and La Feber, *New Empire*, pp. 402–3.

47. Woodford to McKinley, 11 April 1898, Despatches from Spain; and Message to Congress, 11 April 1898, in Washington et al., *Messages of the Presidents*, 10:560–67.

48. The quotation is from Cortelyou Diary, 12 April 1898, Box 52, Cortelyou Papers. See also Message to Congress, 11 April 1898, in Washington et al., *Messages of the Presidents*, 10:560–67; "Current Comment" Scrapbook, ser. 12, McKinley Papers; and Dawes, *America of Yesterday*, p. 176.

49. Cortelyou Diary, 25 April 1898, Box 52, Cortelyou Papers.

Chapter 2

1. David S. Barry, *Forty Years in Washington*, pp. 253–54; Cortelyou Diary, 17 September 1899, Box 52, Cortelyou Papers; and Henry L. Stoddard, *As I Knew Them*, pp. 252–53.

2. Charles H. Brown, *The Correspondents' War*, p. 202; Margaret Leech, *In the Days*

of McKinley, pp. 207, 228; and Message to Congress, in George Washington et al., *A Compilation of the Messages and Papers of the Presidents, 1789–1905*, 14:6298–99.

3. Ida Tarbell, "President McKinley in War Times," p. 214; Leech, *McKinley*, pp. 230–31; and Brown, *Correspondents' War*, p. 141.

4. Brown, *Correspondents' War*, pp. 225–27; copy of telegram from Melville Stone, general manager of the Associated Press, to C. A. Boynton, AP Washington manager, 19 July 1898, ser. 1, McKinley Papers; and Cortelyou Diary, 22 May 1898, Box 52, Cortelyou Papers.

5. The quotation is from Cortelyou Diary, 22 May 1898, Box 52, Cortelyou Papers. See also Frank Freidel, "Dissent in the Spanish-American War and the Philippine Insurrection," pp. 74–75; and J. Frederick Essary, *Covering Washington*, p. 219.

6. Resolution Adopted by the Board of Directors of the Associated Press, 17 May 1898, Box 68, Cortelyou Papers.

7. H. Wayne Morgan, *William McKinley and His America*, pp. 383–85, 395; and Resolution Adopted by the Board of Directors of the Associated Press, 17 May 1898, Box 68, Cortelyou Papers.

8. McKinley to Merritt, 19 May 1898, in U.S., War Department, *Correspondence Relating to the War with Spain*, 2:676–78; and Daniel B. Schirmer, *Republic or Empire*, pp. 68–73.

9. Morgan, *McKinley*, pp. 387–88; Brown, *Correspondents' War*, p. 416; Message to Congress, in Washington et al., *Messages of the Presidents*, 14:6302; and "Current Comment" Scrapbook, ser. 12, McKinley Papers.

10. See, for example, Ernest R. May, *Imperial Democracy*, pp. 258–59; and Julius W. Pratt, *Expansionists of 1898*, pp. 336–37.

11. See, for example, Paolo E. Coletta, "The Peace Negotiations and the Treaty of Paris," p. 143; Morgan, *McKinley*, pp. 388–89, 397, 402–7; and Foster Rhea Dulles, *The Imperial Years*, pp. 158–61. Charles S. Olcott's *The Life of William McKinley* is an older work that shared this view; see 2:348–50.

12. Herman H. Kohlsaat, *From McKinley to Harding*, p. 68. With respect to McKinley, at least, many of Kohlsaat's "recollections" appear to have been apocryphal.

13. The quotation is from Morgan, *McKinley*, pp. 396–97. See also Cortelycu Diary, 31 July 1898, Box 52, Cortelyou Papers.

14. Note, initialed and in McKinley's hand, dated 26 July 1898, ser. 1, McKinley Papers.

15. U.S., Department of State, *Foreign Relations of the United States, 1898*, pp. 828–30.

16. Quoted in Olcott, *McKinley*, 2:345; and U.S., Government Printing Office, *Spanish Diplomatic Correspondence and Documents, 1896–1900*, pp. 206–7. See also Day to Alvee Adee, 18 November 1898, in Department of State, *Foreign Relations, 1898*, pp. 955–57.

17. The quotation is from Cortelyou Diary, 20 July 1898, Box 52, Cortelyou Papers. See also Cortelyou Diary, 2, 12 August 1898, Box 52, Cortelyou Papers; Letters to McKinley, ser. 1, and Scrapbooks, ser. 12, McKinley Papers.

18. Cortelyou Diary, 12 August 1898, Box 52, Cortelyou Papers.

19. See Letters to McKinley, ser. 1, and Scrapbooks, ser. 12, McKinley Papers; Whitelaw Reid, *Making Peace with Spain*, pp. 14–15; George F. Hoar, *Autobiography of Seventy Years*, 2:312; and Leech, *McKinley*, p. 329. Besides appointing a majority of expansionists, McKinley also appointed a majority of senators to the commission, disregarding the advice of Senator William Chandler of New Hampshire that senators ought not to make treaties for their own approval. McKinley was certainly

aware of the conflicts of interest that his appointments would create; he was counting on them to smooth approval of the treaty in the Senate. See Chandler to McKinley, 17 August 1898, ser. 1, McKinley Papers. McKinley raised another interesting constitutional issue, and further demonstrated his shrewdness, by approaching several Supreme Court justices with offers of commission posts. Inclusion of the justices, all of whom declined appointment, would have given the treaty prior sanction by members of all three federal branches; it would also, McKinley hoped, put to rest public doubts about the constitutionality of acquiring the Philippines.

20. Reid Diary, 16 September 1898, Reel 2, Reid Papers; and Instructions to Peace Commission, 16 September 1898, in Department of State, *Foreign Relations, 1898*, pp. 904–8.

21. Cortelyou Diary, 8 June 1898, Box 52, Cortelyou Papers; and Instructions to Peace Commission, 16 September 1898, in Department of State, *Foreign Relations, 1898*, pp. 904–8.

22. The quotation is from Cortelyou Diary, 9 September 1898, Box 52, Cortelyou Papers. See also McKinley to Daniel W. Jones, governor of Arkansas, 7 September 1898, Box 57, Cortelyou Papers; Olcott, *McKinley*, 2:349–50; Morgan, *Making Peace*, pp. 14, 102, n.

23. Charles Truax, president, National Peace Jubilee, Chicago, to Porter, 30 September 1898, and Porter to Truax, 4 October 1898, Box 57, Cortelyou Papers; Albert Halstead, "The President at Work," p. 2082; and numerous "Associated Press Bulletins," especially of speech at Cedar Rapids, Iowa, 11 October 1898, ser. 4, McKinley Papers. Written on the Cedar Rapids bulletin preserved with McKinley's papers, and apparently in the handwriting of one of his secretaries, are the words, "Collect press rate [the *Sun*] New York." See also James Ford Rhodes, *The McKinley and Roosevelt Administrations, 1897–1909*, p. 103, n.

24. Speech at Tama, Iowa, 11 October 1898, ser. 4, McKinley Papers; Olcott, *McKinley*, 2:349–50; and Charles Emory Smith, "McKinley in the Cabinet Room," p. 7.

25. Speech at Omaha, Nebr., 12 October 1898, ser. 4, McKinley Papers.

26. McKinley's speeches at Chariton, Iowa, 14 October 1898, Springfield, Ill., 15 October 1898, Chicago, 18 October 1898, Tipton, Ind., 21 October 1898, and Columbus, Ohio, 22 October 1898, ser. 4, McKinley Papers; and McKinley to Day, 25 October 1898, ser. 1, McKinley Papers.

27. Coletta, "Peace Negotiations," p. 143; Olcott, *McKinley*, 2:349–50; A. W. Dunn, *From Harrison to Harding*, 2:279; and Cyrenus Cole, *I Remember I Remember*, pp. 282–83.

28. Clipping from *Saint Louis Globe-Democrat*, 16 October 1898, ser. 12, McKinley Papers; and Medill to McKinley, 17 October 1898, ser. 1, McKinley Papers. As Cyrenus Cole put it: "When President McKinley spoke in Clinton [Iowa] he still seemed to be in doubt about annexation, but when he made a more important speech in Cedar Rapids, he left no doubt in the minds of those who heard him as to the fate of the islands." Cole, *I Remember*, p. 283.

29. The quotations are from Hay to McKinley, 19 October 1898, Box 57, Cortelyou Papers; McKinley to Day, 25 October 1898, ser. 1, McKinley Papers; and Hay to Day, 28 October 1898, in Department of State, *Foreign Relations, 1898*, pp. 937–38. See also Letters to McKinley, ser. 1, and Scrapbooks, ser. 12, McKinley Papers; and McKinley to Reid, 31 October 1898, Reid Papers.

30. Barnard's memorandums and clippings, Reel 74, and Reid to McKinley, 15 November 1898, Reel 73, Reid Papers; the quotation is from Reid Diary, 4 October 1898, Reel 2, Reid Papers. Barnard's services for Reid and the commission were

similar to those supplied the American delegation to the Paris conference of 1918–19 by what was left of the European offices of the Committee on Public Information.

31. The quotations are from Reid to McKinley, 15, 1 November 1898, Reel 73, Reid Papers; and clippings from *New York Tribune*, 6 November 1898, of a front-page editorial, "Will You Vote to Aid Spain?" Reel 74, Reid Papers.

32. Day to McKinley, 10 December and 19 November 1898, ser. 1, McKinley Papers; and U.S., Congress, *Congressional Record*, 55th Cong., 3d sess., p. 20.

33. The speeches are in William McKinley, *The Speeches and Addresses of William McKinley*, pp. 158–84. See also Leech, *McKinley*, p. 349; Coletta, "Peace Negotiations," p. 163; and Morgan, *McKinley*, p. 415.

34. William Jennings Bryan, *The Memoirs of William Jennings Bryan*, pp. 121–22; Dulles, *Imperial Years*, p. 174; and Paolo E. Coletta, "Bryan, McKinley, and the Treaty of Paris," pp. 131–46. The final tally on the treaty was 57–27, one vote over the necessary two-thirds majority.

35. *Congressional Record*, 55th Cong., 3d sess., pp. 20, 93–96, 493–502, 959, 1530; the quotation is from p. 498. See also U.S., Congress, Senate, *Journal of the Executive Proceedings of the Senate*, 55th Cong., pp. 1161–284. One of the resolutions, offered by Senator S. D. McEnery of Louisiana, did actually pass the Senate. Voted on after the treaty was already approved, it was the weakest of the resolutions, calling only for the eventual emancipation of the Philippines. Nominally a joint resolution, however, it was never approved by the House and did not go into effect. *Congressional Record*, 55th Cong., 3d sess., pp. 1830–47.

36. Scrapbooks, ser. 12, McKinley Papers; Barry, *Forty Years*, p. 260; Schirmer, *Republic or Empire*, p. 97; Senate, *Executive Proceedings*, 55th Cong., p. 1284; the quotations are from Cortelyou Diary, 4 February 1899, Box 52, Cortelyou Papers, and Schirmer, *Republic or Empire*, p. 130.

37. Cortelyou Diary, 4 February 1899, Box 52, Cortelyou Papers. The term "foolish" was McKinley's.

38. Cortelyou Diary, 15 February 1899, Box 52, Cortelyou Papers.

39. The quotation is from Cortelyou Diary, 16 February 1899, Box 52, Cortelyou Papers.

40. McKinley, *Speeches and Addresses*, pp. 185–93; and Scrapbooks, ser. 12, McKinley Papers.

41. The quotations are from *Boston Evening Transcript*, 15 February 1899; and "Speech at Commercial Club Reception," ser. 4, McKinley Papers. See also Schirmer, *Republic or Empire*, chaps. 7, 10.

42. The quotations are from McKinley's speeches at Springfield, Mass., 21 June 1899, Cliff Haven, N.Y., 15 August 1899, and Pittsburgh, Pa., 28 August 1899, ser. 4, McKinley Papers. See also other speeches in this series.

43. The quotations are from McKinley's speeches at Vincennes, Ind., 11 October 1899, Red Wing, Minn., 12 October 1899, and Minneapolis, Minn., 12 October 1899, ser. 4, McKinley Papers. See also speeches at Quincy, Ill., 6 October 1899, and Pittsburgh, Pa., 28 August 1899, as well as others in this series.

44. The quotation is from Cortelyou Diary, 17 September 1899, Box 52, Cortelyou Papers. See also Morgan, *McKinley*, pp. 470–71, 499.

45. The quotations are from Cortelyou Diary, 17 September 1899, Box 52, Cortelyou Papers. See also *Boston Journal*, 5 March 1900, ser. 12, McKinley Papers. Although McKinley took advantage of his acceptance of the Republican nomination to call the antiimperialists "obstructionists," he made no other real campaign speech, leaving the heavier attacks to other party spokesmen. Secretary of War Elihu Root, for example, called Aguinaldo "a half-breed Chinese" and accused Bryan of aiding the

enemy. See *Philadelphia Inquirer*, 13 July 1900, and *Washington Post*, 25 October 1900, ser. 12, McKinley Papers.

46. Scrapbooks, ser. 12, McKinley Papers: McKinley to Hay and Hay to McKinley, 14 September 1900, ser. 1, McKinley Papers; and Thomas J. McCormick, *China Market*, pp. 156–75.

47. Scrapbooks, ser. 12, McKinley Papers; see also the quotation from *New York World*, 18 July 1899.

48. See clippings in Scrapbooks, ser. 12, McKinley Papers, especially *Cleveland Plain Dealer*, 16 July 1899, *New York Tribune*, 18 July 1899, *New York World*, 18 July 1899, and, for an example of McKinley's support, *Commercial Advertiser*, 18 July 1899.

49. See Scrapbooks, ser. 12, McKinley Papers, particularly *New York Herald*, 21 July 1899; Cortelyou Diary, 13 July 1899, Box 52, Cortelyou Papers; and Schirmer, *Republic or Empire*, pp. 173–74.

50. The quotation is from Leech, *McKinley*, p. 231. See also Cortelyou Diary, 4 January 1900, Box 54, Cortelyou Papers; and Halstead, "The President at Work," p. 2081.

51. The quotation is from Tyler Dennett, *John Hay*, p. 198. See John S. Dickey, "The Secretary and the American Public," p. 149; Norman L. Hill, *Mr. Secretary of State*, p. 93; and Stuart, *Department of State*, p. 201.

52. Cortelyou Diary, 13, 18 March 1900, Box 54, Cortelyou Papers; and Morgan, *McKinley*, pp. 450–51.

Chapter 3

1. David S. Barry, *Forty Years in Washington*, pp. 267–69.

2. J. Frederick Essary, *Covering Washington*, p. 88; James E. Pollard, *The Presidents and the Press*, pp. 569–72; and W. W. Price, "How the Work of Gathering White House News Has Changed," in *Washington Star*, 16 December 1902, ser. 15, Roosevelt Papers.

3. The quotation is from Edward G. Lowry, *Washington Close-ups*, pp. 127–28. See also *Washington Star*, 25 September 1902, and *Chicago Tribune*, 25 September 1902, ser. 15, Roosevelt Papers; Press Releases, ser. 6, Roosevelt Papers; and John M. Blum, *The Republican Roosevelt*, p. 69.

4. The quotation is from Lowry, *Washington Close-ups*, pp. 127–28. Later, Roosevelt would find that even a cabinet office was a waste of Cortelyou's talent, and he had him appointed chairman of the Republican party for the election of 1904. Following the election, Cortelyou was returned to the cabinet as postmaster general. William Loeb, Cortelyou's successor as secretary to the president, found the job to be a difficult one. Lacking Cortelyou's careful attention to detail, he frequently had to shoulder the responsibility for presidential blunders. In consequence, "Loeb Takes the Blame" became a common newspaper headline during Roosevelt's second term in office. See Lowry, *Washington Close-ups*, p. 128.

5. The quotation is from Archie Butt, *Taft and Roosevelt*, 1:30–31. See also Pollard, *Presidents and the Press*, p. 569; Nicholas Roosevelt, *Theodore Roosevelt*, p. 39; Charles Willis Thompson, *Presidents I've Known and Two Near Presidents*, p. 114; and Joachim Tinker, "How the President Earns His Salary," in *Public Opinion*, 4 March 1905, ser. 15, Roosevelt Papers.

6. The quotation is from Pollard, *Presidents and the Press*, p. 570.

7. The quotation is from Roosevelt to Bonaparte, 1 August 1905, ser. 4, Roosevelt

Papers. See also George Mowry, *The Era of Theodore Roosevelt and the Birth of Modern America, 1900–1912*, pp. 89–95; Richard Hofstadter, *The American Political Tradition and the Men Who Made It*, pp. 269–70; reprint of editorial by Norman Hapgood, in *Collier's*, 1905, ser. 15, Roosevelt Papers; and *Washington Star*, 20 July 1902, in ser. 15, Roosevelt Papers.

8. The quotations are from Edward A. Ross, *Social Control*, pp. 101–3; see also chap. 10.

9. The quotations are from Roosevelt to Ross, 19 September 1907, ser. 4, Roosevelt Papers; and clipping of Roosevelt's address to the Periodical Publisher's Association, from *Washington Post*, 8 April 1904. See also Roosevelt's address before the National Editorial Association, Jamestown, Va., 10 June 1907, ser. 5C, Roosevelt Papers. Roosevelt's views on public opinion closely paralleled those set forth by Ross, although he placed the greatest emphasis on the role of the elites. He did not neglect the other possibilities for change, however, but hoped that they would find fruition under the tutelage of "the wise."

10. The quotations are from Roosevelt to Bonaparte, 10 February, 1906, ser. 4, Roosevelt Papers; and Blum, *Republican Roosevelt*, p. 139. See also Roosevelt to Alfred Henry Lewis, head of Washington bureau of the *New York Journal*, in Theodore Roosevelt, *The Letters of Theodore Roosevelt*, 5:157.

11. The quotation is from Samuel Haber, *Efficiency and Uplift*, p. 54. See also Samuel P. Hays, *Conservation and the Gospel of Efficiency*, pp. 266–76.

12. The quotations are from Roosevelt to Sir George Trevalyan, 19 June 1908, ser. 4, Roosevelt Papers; and clipping of "At the White House," in *Washington Star*, 7 March 1902, ser. 15, Roosevelt Papers; see also "At the White House" clipping for 19 December 1902.

13. See "At the White House," in *Washington Star*, especially 6 October, 3 November, and 26 December 1905 and 25 October 1907, ser. 15, Roosevelt Papers.

14. Roosevelt to Loomis, 1 July 1903, Roosevelt to Postmaster General Henry Clay Payne, 25 June 1903, and the quotation is from Roosevelt to Wilson, 2 April 1902, ser. 4, Roosevelt Papers.

15. Roosevelt to John Robert Proctor, 30 July 1902, ser. 4, Roosevelt Papers. See also Butt, *Taft and Roosevelt*, 1:30–31.

16. N. Roosevelt, *Theodore Roosevelt*, p. 39; Ira T. Smith, *Dear Mr. President*, p. 62; Essary, *Covering Washington*, p. 88; and Pollard, *Presidents and the Press*, pp. 573–78.

17. The quotations are from Oscar K. Davis, *Released for Publication*, p. 128. See also Lincoln Steffens, *The Autobiography of Lincoln Steffens*, p. 509; Essary, *Covering Washington*, p. 121; and typescript of article for *New York Times*, 6 March 1913, Thompson Papers.

18. The quotation is from Steffens, *Autobiography*, p. 515. See also Justin Kaplan, *Lincoln Steffens: A Biography*, pp. 145–46; and *New York Times*, 15 February 1906.

19. The quotations are from Isaac Marcosson, *Adventures in Interviewing*, pp. 87–88; and Charles W. Thompson to Mrs. Thompson, 8 September 1912, Thompson Papers. See also Essary, *Covering Washington*, p. 88; and Pollard, *Presidents and the Press*, pp. 575–76.

20. The quotation is from Thompson, *Presidents I've Known*, p. 118. See also Pollard, *Presidents and the Press*, pp. 578–79.

21. The quotations are from Davis, *Released for Publication*, pp. 123–24. See also Barry, *Forty Years*, p. 271; and Thompson, *Presidents I've Known*, p. 119.

22. The quotations are from Essary, *Covering Washington*, p. 88; and Thompson, *Presidents I've Known*, p. 119.

23. See press releases in ser. 6, Roosevelt Papers, especially those relating to Roosevelt's western trip beginning 1 April 1903, the one dated 9 November 1906, and another of 4 February 1909, from which the quotation is taken. See also "At the White House," in *Washington Star*, 28 January 1905, ser. 15, Roosevelt Papers; Roosevelt to George Cary Eggleston of *New York World*, 20 April 1902, ser. 4, Roosevelt Papers; and Thompson, *Presidents I've Known*, p. 143.

24. Pollard, *Presidents and the Press*, pp. 570–72; and *New York Herald*, 5 December 1904, ser. 15, Roosevelt Papers, from which the quotation is taken. On other occasions, Roosevelt simply asked publishers to remove the offending correspondents. See Roosevelt to Paul Dana of the *New York Sun*, 30 July 1902, ser. 4, Roosevelt Papers; and *New York World*, 21 June 1903, ser. 15, Roosevelt Papers.

25. Barry, *Forty Years*, pp. 270–71. See also Pollard, *Presidents and the Press*, pp. 572–73. Roosevelt also continued McKinley's efforts to facilitate contact with reporters by including a press room in plans for tbe 1902 refurbishment of the White House.

26. The quotations are from Roosevelt to Hay, 17 August 1903, and Roosevelt to Albert Shaw, 7 October 1903, ser. 4, Roosevelt Papers. See also *Philadelphia Press*, 18 August 1903, ser. 15, Roosevelt Papers; Roosevelt to William H. Taft, 15 September 1903, ser. 4, Roosevelt Papers; Henry F. Pringle, *Theodore Roosevelt*, pp. 218–34; Foster Rhea Dulles, *The Imperial Years*, pp. 243–53; and William D. McCain, *The United States and the Republic of Panama*.

27. The quotations are from Roosevelt to Shaw, 7 October 1903, and Roosevelt to Kermit Roosevelt, 4 November 1903, ser. 4, Roosevelt Papers. See, in addition, Roosevelt to Shaw, 10 October 1903, Roosevelt to Jacob Gould Shurman, 10 September 1903, and Roosevelt to Long, 12 October 1903, ser. 4, Roosevelt Papers; *Outlook* 74 (1903): 961; and Mowry, *Era of Theodore Roosevelt*, p. 151.

28. Press release, 3 November 1903, ser. 6, Roosevelt Papers.

29. Press release, 6 November 1903, ser. 6, Roosevelt Papers, from which the quotation is taken; paper by Moore, ser. 5, Roosevelt Papers; *New York Times*, 25 March 1911; Memorandum by Oscar Straus, enclosed in Roosevelt to Hay, 6 November 1903, in Roosevelt, *Letters*, 3:648; and Pringle, *Theodore Roosevelt*, pp. 223–24.

30. Roosevelt to Theodore Roosevelt, Jr., 9 November 1903, ser. 4, Roosevelt Papers, from which the quotation is taken; "At the White House," in *Washington Star*, 9 November 1903, ser. 15, Roosevelt Papers; and article by William Henry Thorne, in *Philadelphia Record*, 14 November 1903, "Current Events," ser. 15, Roosevelt Papers. See also James Ford Rhodes, *The McKinley and Roosevelt Administrations*, Addenda, pp. 272–73. On one other occasion, Roosevelt received muckraker criticism of his foreign policy, and it apparently bothered him a great deal. In the 13 May 1905 edition of *Collier's* there appeared an article by Richard Harding Davis entitled "The Asphalt Scandal," linking the president's policy in Venezuela to the "asphalt trust." On the same day the article appeared, Roosevelt wrote to Davis, endeavoring to set him straight on what he saw as a number of errors in the piece. Perhaps this involvement in foreign policy questions was one of the potential muckraker abuses that Roosevelt became increasingly aware of in the following year and that led to his famous "man with the muckrake" speech of 14 April 1906. See Davis, "The Asphalt Scandal," in *Collier's*, 13 May 1905, ser. 15, Roosevelt Papers; Roosevelt to Davis, 13 May 1905, and Roosevelt to William H. Taft, 15 March 1906, ser. 5, Roosevelt Papers.

31. The quotation is from Roosevelt to George B. Harvey, 19 December 1903, ser. 4, Roosevelt Papers. See also Roosevelt to Otto Gresham, 30 November 1903, ser. 4, Roosevelt Papers; Lawrence F. Abbott, *Impressions of Theodore Roosevelt*, p. 139;

Dulles, *Imperial Years*, pp. 251–52; and "Current Comment" clippings, ser. 15, Roosevelt Papers.

32. Roosevelt to Charles W. Eliot, 22 September 1906, ser. 4, Roosevelt Papers; press release, 12 October 1904, ser. 6, Roosevelt Papers; "At the White House" clippings, 20 May and 18 October 1904, ser. 15, Roosevelt Papers; and press releases, 20 January and 19 February 1906, 7 February 1908, and 27 April 1907, from which the quotation is taken, ser. 6, Roosevelt Papers.

33. The quotation is from Roosevelt to Root, 18 August 1906, Box 163, Root Papers; and Special Message to Congress concerning the Panama Canal, 17 December 1906, ser. 5, Roosevelt Papers. See also press clippings, ser. 15, Roosevelt Papers.

34. Theodore Roosevelt, *Autobiography*, p. 524; and press clippings, ser. 15, Roosevelt Papers. For an assessment of Roosevelt's role in the revolution, see Pringle, *Theodore Roosevelt*, pp. 224–30.

35. Lester D. Langley, *The Cuban Policy of the United States*, pp. 127–28; the quotation is from press release, 14 September 1906, ser. 6, Roosevelt Papers.

36. Roosevelt to Taft, 26 September 1906, ser. 4, Roosevelt Papers. The emphasis is mine.

37. Roosevelt to Taft, 28 September 1906, ser. 4, Roosevelt Papers, from which the quotation is taken; and press releases, ser. 6, Roosevelt Papers.

38. Roosevelt to Taft, 21 August 1907, Box 163, Root Papers.

39. Roosevelt to Francis Butler Loomis, 1 July 1903, ser. 4, Roosevelt Papers; and press releases, 13 February 1906 and 28 February 1907, ser. 6, Roosevelt Papers.

40. The quotations are from *New York Tribune*, 8 March 1905, and "At the White House," in *Washington Star*, 16 May 1906, ser. 15, Roosevelt Papers. See also "At the White House," in *Washington Star*, 9 December 1903 and 17 February 1905, ser. 15, Roosevelt Papers; and Roosevelt to Secretary of the Navy Bonaparte, 10 February 1906, ser. 4, Roosevelt Papers.

41. Addresses at Annapolis, Md., 24 April 1906, Saint Louis, Mo., 2 October 1907, from which the quotation is taken, and Cairo, Ill., 3 October 1907, ser. 5C, Roosevelt Papers; and press release of address at Naval War College, 22 July 1908, ser. 6, Roosevelt Papers.

42. Press release, 14 April 1904, ser. 6, Roosevelt Papers, from which the quotation is taken; *Washington Post*, 30 May 1904, and *New York Herald*, 30 May 1904, ser. 15, Roosevelt Papers; and Roosevelt to Bonaparte, 1 August 1905, ser. 4, Roosevelt Papers. The later disaster was the explosion of the *Bennington*, in which more than fifty sailors were killed.

43. Press releases, 24 December 1907, from which the quotation is taken, and 3 January 1908, ser. 6, Roosevelt Papers; and Roosevelt to the Reverend Lyman Abbott, 17 January 1908, ser. 4, Roosevelt Papers. Brownson resigned rather than carry out Roosevelt's directive to appoint a medical officer as captain of a hospital ship, raising such issues as naval discipline and the willingness of officers to be under civilian control.

44. Roosevelt to Bonaparte, 6 August 1906, and Roosevelt to Root, 18 August 1906, ser. 4, Roosevelt Papers. See also Roosevelt, *Letters*, 5:343, n.

45. The quotations are from Roosevelt, *Autobiography*, pp. 564–65; and Abbott, *Impressions of Roosevelt*, p. 110. See also Roosevelt to Root, 13 July 1907, Box 163, Root Papers, Howard K. Beale, *Theodore Roosevelt and the Rise of America to World Power*, p. 285; and for the best account of the cruise, Thomas A. Bailey, *Theodore Roosevelt and the Japanese-American Crises*, pp. 211–27, 261–303.

46. *Boston Evening Transcript*, 1, 5 July 1907; *New York Times*, 3, 5 July 1907, from which the quotation is taken; and Bailey, *Theodore Roosevelt*, pp. 213–15.

Although it is not known for certain who was responsible for the 1 July leak to the press, Roosevelt generally dealt personally with this sort of thing. This would also explain why the reporters made no attempt to identify their source.

47. *New York Times*, 5 July and 2, 24 August 1907. In fact, the destination of the fleet after it left San Francisco was not made public by a reliable source until February 1908. See Bailey, *Theodore Roosevelt*, p. 263.

48. Roosevelt to Newberry, 10 August 1907, ser. 4, Roosevelt Papers.

49. Roosevelt to Newberry, 17 August 1907, from which the quotations are taken, and Brownson to Roosevelt, 17 August 1907, ser. 4, Roosevelt Papers.

50. The quotations are from Roosevelt to Taft, 3 March 1909, ser. 4, Roosevelt Papers; and Henry L. Stoddard, *As I Knew Them*, p. 298. See also Bailey, *Theodore Roosevelt*, p. 298; and Franklin Matthews, *With the Battle Fleet* (New York: Century Co., 1909) and *Return to Hampton Roads* (New York: Century Co., 1909). Criticism of sending the fleet to the Pacific had approached what Roosevelt termed hysteria in the late summer of 1907. See Roosevelt to Root, 31 July 1907, and to Hermann Speck von Sternberg, 16 July 1907, ser. 4, Roosevelt Papers; and Bailey, *Theodore Roosevelt*, pp. 225–27. Nevertheless, Roosevelt thought as early as September 1907 that "public opinion was extremely well pleased at my sending the fleet to the Pacific." Roosevelt to Henry Cabot Lodge, 2 September 1907, ser. 4, Roosevelt Papers.

51. The quotations are from Roosevelt to Taft, 21 August 1907, Box 163, Root Papers; and Roosevelt to Joseph Lincoln Steffens, 6 February 1906, ser. 4, Roosevelt Papers.

Chapter 4

1. Henry F. Pringle, *The Life and Times of William Howard Taft*, 1:394, 397; and Walter V. Scholes and Marie V. Scholes, *The Foreign Policies of the Taft Administration*, p. 4, n.

2. James Pollard, *The Presidents and the Press*, p. 604; Charles Willis Thompson, *Presidents I've Known and Two Near Presidents*, pp. 228–31; Donald F. Anderson, *William Howard Taft*, p. 202; Oscar K. Davis, *Released for Publication*, p. 95; and Archie Butt, *Taft and Roosevelt*, 2:724, from which the quotation was taken. It is ironic, considering Taft's failure to understand the needs and problems of the press, that his first job was as reporter on his brother's *Cincinnati Times*. See Pollard, *Presidents and the Press*, p. 601.

3. Both quotations are from Butt, *Taft and Roosevelt*, 1:26. See also Pollard, *Presidents and the Press*, p. 606.

4. The quotation was taken from Taft to W. D. Foulke, 29 November 1909, ser. 8, Taft Papers. See also Pollard, *Presidents and the Press*, pp. 608–9.

5. Pollard, *Presidents and the Press*, p. 612; Pringle, *Taft*, 1:260, 416; Butt, *Taft and Roosevelt*, 1:29–31; Anderson, *Taft*, pp. 218–19; Paolo E. Coletta, *The Presidency of William Howard Taft*, p. 54; and Davis, *Released for Publication*, p. 178.

6. Pringle, *Taft*, 1:416; and Butt, *Taft and Roosevelt*, 1:31.

7. Butt, *Taft and Roosevelt*, 1:29–31; Pollard, *Presidents and the Press*, pp. 603, 606; and Lafayette Young of the *Des Moines Capital* to Charles D. Norton, secretary to the president, 24 October 1910, ser. 6, file 309, Taft Papers.

8. The quotation is from Arthur W. Dunn, *From Harrison to Harding*, 2:111. See also Coletta, *Presidency*, p. 262.

9. The quotations are from Thompson, *Presidents I've Known*, p. 235; and Taft to Roosevelt, 21 March 1909, ser. 8, Taft Papers. See also Anderson, *Taft*, p. viii.

10. The quotations are from Taft to White, 20 March 1909, ser. 8, Taft Papers; and Butt, *Taft and Roosevelt*, 1:26. See also Coletta, *Presidency*, p. 55.

11. The quotations are from Coletta, *Presidency*, p. 260.; and Butt, *Taft and Roosevelt*, 1:3, 5. See also Dunn, *From Harrison to Harding*, 2:206–7.

12. The quotation is the subtitle to Anderson, *Taft*; see also Scholes and Scholes, *Foreign Policies*, p. 27.

13. The quotations are from William H. Taft, *Our Chief Magistrate and His Powers*, pp. 145, 144.

14. The quotaions are from Taft to White, 20 March 1909, ser. 8, Taft Papers; and Coletta, *Presidency*, p. 261.

15. Quoted in Coletta, *Presidency*, p. 261; see also Taft to Henry S. Brown of the *New York Herald*, 1 April 1909, ser. 8, Taft Papers.

16. Butt, *Taft and Roosevelt*, 1:30.

17. Taft to Pierce, 14 April 1910, and Taft to O'Brien, 28 June 1910, ser. 8, Taft Papers.

18. Taft to J. H. Cosgrave, editor of *Everybody's Magazine*, 23 February 1910, ser. 8, Taft Papers.

19. The quotation was taken from Butt, *Taft and Roosevelt*, 1:29–30.

20. The quotations are from Butt, *Taft and Roosevelt*, 2:775; see also Anderson, *Taft*, pp. 233–34.

21. Edward H. Butler to Charles D. Hilles, 10 September 1912, in U.S., Department of State Decimal File (hereafter, DSDF) 811.911/2, National Archives, Washington, D.C.; and the quotation is from Taft to Charles P. Taft, 1 March 1912, ser. 8, Taft Papers.

22. The quotations are from Davis, *Released for Publication*, p. 184.

23. Coletta, *Presidency*, pp. 54–55; Anderson, *Taft*, p. 219; the quotation is from Davis, *Released for Publication*, p. 184.

24. Edward G. Lowry, *Washington Close-ups*, p. 125; and Coletta, *Presidency*, p. 55.

25. The quotations are from Young to Norton, 25 October 1910, ser. 6, file 309, Taft Papers. See also Anson Phelps Stokes to Norton, 10 November 1910, ser. 6, file 96, Taft Papers; and George F. Authier of the *Minneapolis Tribune* to Norton, 20 September 1910, ser. 6, file 309, Taft Papers.

26. The quotations are from Young to Norton, 25 October 1910, and Wilson to Norton, 27 October 1910, ser. 6, file 309, Taft Papers. The emphasis is Wilson's. See also John A. Schleicher to Norton, 31 October 1910, ser. 6, file 309, Taft Papers.

27. The quotations are from an unsigned memorandum, ser. 6, file 309, Taft Papers.

28. The quotation is from a White House memorandum, for filing with the Young letter and initialed W.L.S., ser. 6, file 309, Taft Papers.

29. The quotation is from Francis M. Huntington Wilson, "The American Foreign Service," *Outlook*, vol. 82, no. 9 (3 March 1906), Reel 1, Huntington Wilson Papers. See also Memorandum on Reorganization, 1906, Reel 1, Huntington Wilson Papers; Graham H. Stuart, *The Department of State*, pp. 206–7, 212; Scholes and Scholes, *Foreign Policies*, p. 15; and Francis M. Huntington Wilson, *Memoirs of an Ex-Diplomat*, p. 171.

30. Stuart, *Department of State*, p. 217; Scholes and Scholes, *Foreign Policies*, p. 26; Memorandum on Reorganization, 1906, Reel 1, Huntington Wilson Papers; and Records of Information Series, Boxes 39–43, Knox Papers.

31. John S. Dickey, "The Secretary and the American Public," p. 142; Stuart, *Department of State*, p. 217; Records of Information Series, Boxes 39–43, Knox Papers; and Memorandum for Patchin, Reel 1, Huntington Wilson Papers. That Patchin's skill in dealing with the public did not go unnoticed during his tenure as

chief of the Information Division is suggested by the fact that he was named, during much more difficult times, to serve as its cohead when it was enlarged and renamed the Division of Foreign Intelligence in May 1917. See Stuart, *Department of State*, p. 243.

32. Memorandum on Reorganization, 1906, Reel 1, Huntington Wilson Papers.

33. See press releases and Huntington Wilson to Knox, 3 July 1910, Reel 1, Huntington Wilson Papers; J. Frederick Essary, *Covering Washington*, p. 169; and Huntington Wilson to Brown, 11 June 1909, Reel 1, Huntington Wilson Papers, from which the quotation was taken.

34. Memorandum, Huntington Wilson to Taft, 22 February 1910, Reel 1, Huntington Wilson Papers.

35. Philip Jessup, *Elihu Root*, 1: 457; Joseph Grew, *Turbulent Era*, 1:76–77; Scholes and Scholes, *Foreign Policies*, p. 16; and Huntington Wilson to Brown, 11 June 1909, Reel 1, Huntington Wilson Papers, from which the quotation was taken.

36. The quotation is from Scholes and Scholes, *Foreign Policies*, pp. 11–12; and see press release, 1 August 1912, Reel 1, Huntington Wilson Papers.

37. William Bayard Hale et al. to Knox, 3 March 1912, Box 17, Knox Papers.

38. See Pringle, *Taft*, pp. 682–83; Anderson, *Taft*, pp. 261–62; and Scholes and Scholes, *Foreign Policies*, pp. 106–7.

39. The quotations are from an undated memorandum, in "Confidential File," Reel 1, Huntington Wilson Papers; "Arbitration Treaties," address at Sacramento, Calif., 13 October 1911, Addresses, vol. 24, Taft Papers; and Address to Third National Peace Conference, Baltimore, Md., 4 May 1911, Reel 1, Huntington Wilson Papers. See also William O. Manson to Taft, 12 August 1912, ser. 6, file 102, Taft Papers; press clippings, Reel 1, Huntington Wilson Papers; and Message to Congress, December 1912, in George Washington et al., *A Compilation of the Messages and Papers of the Presidents, 1789–1905*, 18:8150.

40. The quotation is from undated memorandum, in "Confidential File," Reel 1, Huntington Wilson Papers.

41. The quotations are from Address to American Arbitration and Peace League, March 1910, and Address at Connecticut State Fair, 17 September 1911, Addresses, 18:127–218, 21:276–77, Taft Papers. Taft also invited senatorial anger by failing to instruct Knox to consult that body when drawing up the actual treaties. As a result, numerous senators charged that in approving the treaties they would be acquiescing in the surrender of their powers without even taking part in the deliberations. See Address to Methodist Conference, Ocean Grove, N.J., 15 August 1911, Addresses, 21:215, Taft Papers; and Francis B. Loomis to Dr. Nicholas Murray Butler, 31 October 1911, Box 78, Root Papers.

42. The quotation is from Butt, *Taft and Roosevelt*, 2:635.

43. The quotations are from Butt, *Taft and Roosevelt*, 2:769, 730.

44. The quotations are from Taft to Bryan, 16 January 1912, ser. 8, Taft Papers; and Butt, *Taft and Roosevelt*, 2:635. See also Addresses, vols. 22–24, Taft Papers; letter and memorandum, C.F.W. to Knox, 2 November 1911, Box 16, Knox Papers; and Taft to R. A. Taft, 27 August 1911, ser. 8, Taft Papers. The treaties were eventually emasculated by Senate amendments, including one that left the question of justiciability to the Senate itself, and passed in March 1912 by a vote of 76 to 3. The result was a hard slap in the face for the president. See Pringle, *Taft*, 2:754–55.

45. Taft to Marburg, 31 January 1910, ser. 8, Taft Papers.

46. Taft to Knox, 11 March 1911, and Taft to Roosevelt, 22 March 1911, ser. 8, Taft Papers. See also Scholes and Scholes, *Foreign Policies*, pp. 84–86.

47. Taft to Roosevelt, 22 March 1911, ser. 8, Taft Papers; Scholes and Scholes, *Foreign Policies*, p. 86; and Pringle, *Taft*, 2:702.

48. Taft to Wood, 12 March 1911, ser. 8, Taft Papers. See also Taft to Knox, 11 March 1911, and Taft to Roosevelt, 22 March 1911, ser. 8, Taft Papers; Butt, *Taft and Roosevelt*, 2:603; and Anderson, *Taft*, pp. 267–68.

49. Taft to Williams, 28 March 1911, ser. 6, file 95A, Taft Papers.

50. Huntington Wilson to Knox, 10 March 1911, Reel 1, Huntington Wilson Papers.

51. Anderson, *Taft*, pp. 269–70; Scholes and Scholes, *Foreign Policies*, p. 88; newspaper clippings, ser. 6, file 95B, Taft Papers; Taft to James L. Slaydon, 12 September 1912, ser. 6, file 95C, Taft Papers; N. G. Turk to Taft, 22 February 1912, ser. 6, file 95B, Taft Papers; and W. B. Howard to Taft, 30 July 1912, ser. 6, file 95C, Taft Papers.

52. Taft to Stimson, 17 October 1911, DSDF, 812.00/2416/2295; Taft to Stimson, 4 February 1912, ser. 8, Taft Papers; Memorandum of Hilles's statement, 24 February 1912, ser. 6, file 95C, Taft Papers; and Huntington Wilson to Woodrow Wilson, 24 February 1912, Box 40, Knox Papers.

53. Memorandum, Gibson to Secretary of State, 12 November 1910, Reel 1, Huntington Wilson Papers, from which the quotation was taken; and Huntington Wilson Memorandum, 24 February 1912, DSDF, 812.00/2797A. See also Scholes and Scholes, *Foreign Policies*, p. 90.

54. Taft to Wickersham, 9 August 1912, and Wickersham to Taft, 12 August 1912, ser. 6, file 95B, Taft Papers. See also petition from residents of Nogales, Ariz., to Taft, 23 July 1912, ser. 6, file 95B, Taft Papers.

55. Press statement by Secretary Hilles, 23 February 1913, ser. 6, file 95B, Taft Papers; U.S., Department of State, *Foreign Relations of the United States, 1913*, p. 730; and Memorandum, Acting Secretary of State to President, 22 February 1913, ser. 6, file 95B, Taft Papers, from which the quotation was taken.

56. Butt, *Taft and Roosevelt*, 2:605.

Chapter 5

1. The quotations are from Woodrow Wilson, *Constitutional Government in the United States*, p. 68; and Ray Stannard Baker, *Woodrow Wilson*, 3:181. See also Arthur S. Link, *Woodrow Wilson and the Progressive Era*, pp. 25–53; and John Morton Blum, *Woodrow Wilson and the Politics of Morality*, p. 41.

2. Arthur S. Link, *Wilson: The Road to the White House*, pp. 82–83, 229; Baker, *Woodrow Wilson*, 4:228; and Arthur W. Dunn, *From Harrison to Harding*, p. 214.

3. The quotations are from Wilson to Oswald Garrison Villard, 2 January 1911, in Ray Stannard Baker Papers; and Joseph P. Tumulty, "In the White House Looking Glass," p. 13. See also James Pollard, *The Presidents and the Press*, p. 632; Blum, *Woodrow Wilson*, p. 67; and David Lawrence, *The True Story of Woodrow Wilson*, pp. 89–90.

4. The quotation is from *New York Tribune*, 5 March 1913. See also Pollard, *Presidents and the Press*, p. 632.

5. The quotations are from Pollard, *Presidents and the Press*, p. 630; and Dunn, *From Harrison to Harding*, p. 214.

6. John Morton Blum, *Joe Tumulty and the Wilson Era*, p. 62; Datebook, 1913, ser. 1, Wilson Papers (Library of Congress); and Philippa Strum, *Presidential Power and American Democracy*, p. 63. Taft scheduled his press meetings for late in the afternoon and often put them off until six or half-past six in the evening, making the reporters cool their heels until he could fit them in. Wilson, on the other hand, called his first conference for 12:45 and although he changed the time periodically was always punctual with the correspondents. See Dunn, *From Harrison to Harding*, p. 235; and Datebooks, 1913, 1914, 1915, ser. 1, Wilson Papers (Library of Congress).

7. The quotations are from Edward G. Lowry, *Washington Close-ups*, p. 19; and David S. Barry, *Forty Years in Washington*, p. 309. See also Baker, *Woodrow Wilson*, 4:230, 232; Pollard, *Presidents and the Press*, p. 631; Charles Willis Thompson, *Presidents I've Known and Two Near Presidents*, pp. 273–74; and Dunn, *From Harrison to Harding*, pp. 235–36.

8. Typescript of story for *New York Times*, 16 March 1913, and Oulahan to Thompson, 28 April 1913, Thompson Papers.

9. The quotations are from typescript of story for *New York Times*, 16 March 1913, Thompson Papers; and Baker, *Woodrow Wilson*, 4:230, 229. See also Diary of Head Usher at White House, 1913–21, ser. 1, Wilson Papers (Library of Congress); Baker, *Woodrow Wilson*, 4:231; and Barry, *Forty Years*, p. 309.

10. The quotations are from handout of speech by Wilson at press conference, 22 March 1913, copy in Box 4, Tumulty Papers. See also Diary of Head Usher, 22 March 1913, ser. 1, Wilson Papers (Library of Congress); and transcripts of the press conferences, Swem Papers.

11. Quotations are from Fowler to Tumulty, 22 July 1913, ser. 4, file 671, Wilson Papers (Library of Congress); Oulahan to Tumulty, 22 July 1913, ser. 4, file 690, Wilson Papers (Library of Congress).

12. The quotations are from Oulahan to Baker, quoted in Baker, *Woodrow Wilson*, 4:232; and transcript of press conference, 2 February 1915, Swem Papers. See also Elmer E. Cornwell, Jr., "The Press Conferences of Woodrow Wilson," pp. 292–300.

13. George Creel, "Woodrow Wilson," p. 37.

14. The quotation is from Thompson to Mrs. Thompson, 5 September 1912, Thompson Papers. See also Thompson to Mrs. Thompson, 6 September 1912, Thompson Papers.

15. The quotation is from transcript of press conference, 22 December 1914, Wilson Papers (Firestone); see also transcripts of press conferences, 26 May 1913, Wilson Papers (Firestone); and 17 August 1914, Swem Papers.

16. The quotations are from transcripts of press conferences, 11 April 1913, Swem Papers; 16 October and 20 November 1913, Wilson Papers (Firestone); and from Link, *Wilson: Road to the White House*, p. 2. See also Thompson to Mrs. Thompson, 6 October 1912, Thompson Papers; and transcripts of press conferences, 13 July 1913 and 26 March 1914, Swem Papers; and 22 June 1915 and 8 December 1913, Wilson Papers (Firestone).

17. The quotation is from transcript of press conference, 24 November 1914, Wilson Papers (Firestone). See also transcript of press conference, 12 June 1913, Wilson Papers (Firestone).

18. The quotations are from transcripts of press conferences, 22 May and 25, 11 August 1913, Wilson Papers (Firestone). See also transcripts of press conferences, 9 June 1913 and 24 November 1914, Wilson Papers (Firestone).

19. The quotations are from transcripts of press conferences, 11 June 1914, 18 September 1913, and 23 July 1914, Wilson Papers (Firestone). See also transcripts of press conferences, 8 December 1913, Wilson Papers (Firestone), 26 March 1914, Swem Papers.

20. The quotation is from transcript of press conference, 15 May 1913, Swem Papers. See also transcript of press conference, 3 August 1914, Swem Papers.

21. The quotations are from transcript of press conference, 13 July 1913, Swem Papers.

22. The quotations are from transcripts of press conferences, 5 June 1913, 24 August 1914, and 5 January 1915, Wilson Papers (Firestone). See also transcripts of press conferences, 20 November 1913, 22 January and 21 September 1914, Wilson Papers (Firestone).

23. The quotation is from transcript of press conference, 12 January 1915, Swem Papers.

24. The quotation is from transcript of press conference, 21 April 1913, Swem Papers. See also transcripts of press conferences, 28 April and 8 May, 1913, Wilson Papers (Firestone).

25. The quotation is from J. Frederick Essary, *Covering Washington*, p. 99; see also Datebooks, 1913, 1915, ser. 1, Wilson Papers (Library of Congress); Memorandum, Tumulty to Wilson, 25 September 1914, ser. 4, file 690, Wilson Papers (Library of Congress); and Blum, *Tumulty*, p. 62.

26. The quotations are from Tumulty's memorandum of 18 November 1916, and Tumulty to Wilson, with Wilson's replies, 6 December 1916, ser. 4, file 690, Wilson Papers (Library of Congress). The emphasis is Wilson's. See also Datebook, 1916, ser. 1, Wilson Papers (Library of Congress).

27. The quotation is from Wilson to S. R. Bertron, 18 April 1918, ser. 4, file 690, Wilson Papers (Library of Congress). See also Datebooks, 1917, 1918, 1920 (1919 is missing), ser. 1, Wilson Papers (Library of Congress); and Wilson to George Creel, 29 July 1918, ser. 4, file 690, Wilson Papers (Library of Congress).

28. The quotations are from Blum, *Tumulty*, p. 62; and Lawrence, *True Story*, p. 89. See also Tumulty, "White House Looking Glass," p. 13.

29. Tumulty to Wilson, 27 April 1914, ser. 4, file 117, Wilson Papers (Library of Congress); Tumulty to Wilson, 26 January 1918, ser. 4, file 2510, Wilson Papers (Library of Congress); Wilson to Noyes and Stone, 27 April 1914, ser. 4, file 117, Wilson Papers (Library of Congress); Wilson to Brisbane, 26 January 1918, ser. 4, file 2510, Wilson Papers (Library of Congress); and Blum, *Tumulty*, p. 64.

30. The quotation is from Tumulty to Smith, 14 July 1913, ser. 4, file 103, Wilson Papers (Library of Congress). See also Smith to Tumulty, 15 July 1913, ser. 4, file 103, Wilson Papers (Library of Congress); Tumulty to Farrelly, 16 March 1913, ser. 4, file 116, Wilson Papers (Library of Congress); and Thompson to Tumulty, 14 July 1913, ser. 4, file 103, Wilson Papers (Library of Congress). These complaints of improper procedure contained an element of competition among the press associations. It was invariably the smaller and less technologically sophisticated wire service that found itself in trouble with the administration, and the charges were almost always lodged by a member of one of the major associations.

31. Jackson Evertt, Associated Press correspondent, to Tumulty, 28 June 1916, ser. 4, file 117, Wilson Papers (Library of Congress).

32. Blum, *Tumulty*, pp. 63–64; Wilson to Randolph Marshall, 2 September 1915, ser. 3, Wilson Papers (Library of Congress); and Tumulty to Wilson, 15 September 1915, ser. 2, Wilson Papers (Library of Congress).

33. Link, *Wilson and Progressive Era*, pp. 35–36; Dunn, *From Harrison to Harding*, p. 222; Joseph Maille to Wilson, 8 April 1913, and Augustus Johnson to Wilson, 8 April 1913, ser. 2, Wilson Papers (Library of Congress).

34. The quotations are from *New York Times*, 28 January 1914. See also Arthur S. Link, ed., *The Papers of Woodrow Wilson*, 29:180–84.

35. For another example of Wilson's use of the news leak, see Link, *Papers of Wilson*, 30:39–42.

36. The quotations are from Wilson's note on William Phillips to Tumulty, 6 June 1914, and Wilson to Tumulty, 18 August 1916, ser. 2, Wilson Papers (Library of Congress). See also Tumulty to Wilson, 16 August 1916, ser. 2, Wilson Papers (Library of Congress).

37. The quotations are from Edward G. Lowry, "What the President Is Trying to Do for Mexico," pp. 261–66. See also Link, *Papers of Wilson*, 29:92.

38. The quotations are from Ida Tarbell, "A Talk with the President of the United

States," pp. 5–6, 40; the emphasis is Tarbell's. See also Samuel G. Blythe, "A Talk with the President," pp. 3–4, 37–38; Ray Stannard Baker, "Wilson," pp. 5–6; and Link, *Papers of Wilson*, vol. 31 (forthcoming): 5 December 1914.

39. The quotations are from Wilson to Eliot, 1 June 1914, ser. 3, Wilson Papers (Library of Congress). The ultimate result was the Committee on Public Information, a direct outgrowth of the publicity bureau idea. See Baker, *Woodrow Wilson*, 4:235, n.

40. The quotation is from Wilson to Eliot, 1 June 1914, ser. 3, Wilson Papers (Library of Congress). See also Bryan to Wilson, 30 July 1913, ser. 4, file 40, Wilson Papers (Library of Congress); and Bertram D. Hulen, *Inside the Department of State*, p. 144.

41. The quotations are from Bryan to Wilson, 30 July 1913, ser. 4, file 40, Wilson Papers (Library of Congress). See also Dunn, *From Harrison to Harding*, pp. 226–27.

42. The quotations are from Bryan to Wilson, 30 July 1913, ser. 4, file 40, Wilson Papers (Library of Congress).

43. The quotations are from Bryan to Wilson, 30 July 1913, ser. 4, file 40, Wilson Papers (Library of Congress).

44. The quotation is from Wilson to Bryan, 31 July 1913, ser. 4, file 40, Wilson Papers (Library of Congress). See also Pollard, *Presidents and the Press*, p. 649.

45. Bryan to Wilson, 18 February 1915, ser. 2, Wilson Papers (Library of Congress); Wilson to Tumulty, 20 February 1915, ser. 3, Wilson Papers (Library of Congress); and Tumulty to Wilson, 20 February 1915, ser. 2, Wilson Papers (Library of Congress).

46. The quotation is from Tarbell, "Talk with the President," p. 6. See also Arthur S. Link, *Wilson the Diplomatist*, p. 27; Pollard, *Presidents and the Press*, p. 645; and Wilson, *Constitutional Government*, p. 68.

47. Link, *Wilson and Progressive Era*, pp. 82–83; and Pollard, *Presidents and the Press*, p. 644. It is ironic that one of Huntington Wilson's innovations in the State Department—the Division of Information—was assigned to study press comment on the assistant secretary's resignation and found that "he receives but little comfort from public opinion." According to the division's report, most of the country's editors believed that he should have overlooked President Wilson's slight in the matter of the Chinese loan; there was thus little cause for real concern over the affair. See report dated 1 April 1913, Division of Information, Department of State, Record Group 59, Box 38, NA. The division also reported that the newspapers were supporting with "hearty approval" Wilson's refusal to continue backing of the Six-Power loan. See report dated 31 March 1913, Division of Information, Department of State, Record Group 59, Box 37, National Archives, Washington, D.C.

48. The quotations are from Bryan to Wilson, 20 July 1913, and Memorandum, Bryan to Wilson, 20 July 1913, ser. 2, Wilson Papers (Library of Congress). Bryan's plan also discussed the alternative of "recognition" of the Huerta regime.

49. The quotations are from Bryan to Wilson, 2 August 1913, ser. 4, file 95, Wilson Papers (Library of Congres).

50. The quotations are from Bryan to Wilson, 9 August 1913, ser. 4, file 40, Wilson Papers (Library of Congress); and see Kenneth J. Grieb, *The United States and Huerta*, p. 91; and *Washington Post*, 25 July 1913.

51. The quotations are from Wilson to Bryan, 11 August 1913, ser. 4, file 95, Wilson Papers (Library of Congress).

52. Bryan to Wilson, 10 August 1913, ser. 2, Wilson Papers (Library of Congress); Wilson, Address to Congress, 27 August 1913, ser. 9, Wilson Papers (Library of Congress); Moorfield Storey to Wilson, 28 August 1913, ser. 4, file 95A, Wilson Papers (Library of Congress); *New York Times*, 28 August 1913; Grieb, *United States and Huerta*, pp. 90, 100–1; and transcripts of press conferences, 21, 25, 28 August 1913,

Swem Papers. Although, as Grieb has pointed out, the idea for the inclusion of the phrase "watchful waiting" came from Senator Augustus O. Bacon, chairman of the Senate Committee on Foreign Relations, the term itself, with its qualities of brevity and alliteration, was the work of the president. From a publicity standpoint, Wilson's well-chosen words were what made the headlines. See Bryan to Wilson, 26 August 1913, in Correspondence of Secretary of State Bryan with President Wilson, 1913–15, 1:177; and Grieb, *United States and Huerta*, p. 100.

53. The quotations are from Garrison to Wilson, 11 March 1914, and press release, 11 March 1914, ser. 4, file 95, Wilson Papers (Library of Congress). See also Arhut Call to Wilson, 24 March 1914, ser. 4, file 95, Wilson Papers (Library of Congress).

54. The quotation is from Lane to Wilson, 6 April 1914, ser. 4, file 95, Wilson Papers (Library of Congress). See also Wilson to Lane, 7 April 1914, ser. 4, file 95, Wilson Papers (Library of Congress).

55. The quotations are from *New York World*, 14 April 1914; and *New York Times*, 16 April 1914. See also *New York Times*, 12 April 1914; Robert E. Quirk, *An Affair of Honor*, pp. 18–33, 40; and transcripts of press conferences, 14 April 1914, Wilson Papers (Firestone); and 16 April 1914, Swem Papers.

56. The quotations are from Wilson's Address to Congress, in U.S., Department of State, *Foreign Relations of the United States, 1914*, pp. 474–76. See also Baker, *Woodrow Wilson*, 4:319; letters to Wilson, ser. 4, file 95, Wilson Papers (Library of Congress); Quirk, *Affair of Honor*, p. 75; and transcripts of press conferences, 20, 23 April 1914, Swem Papers. Although Arthur S. Link has argued that the public was opposed to war with Mexico during the incident, this does not appear to have been the case with either newspaper editors or letter writers to the president. In any event, the seizure of Veracruz was almost unanimously applauded, at least among those communicating with Wilson. See Link, *Wilson and Progressive Era*, p. 125, n.

57. The quotations are from Tumulty, *Wilson*, p. 153; and Quirk, *Affair of Honor*, p. 114. See also Henry Cabot Lodge, *The Senate and the League of Nations*, p. 18; and Grieb, *United States and Huerta*, p. 154.

58. The quotation is from press release, 24 March 1916, ser. 4, file 95, Wilson Papers (Library of Congress).

59. The quotation is from press release, 24 March 1916, ser. 4, file 95, Wilson Papers (Library of Congress). See also letters to Wilson, ser. 4, file 95, Wilson Papers (Library of Congress); and Link, *Wilson and Progressive Era*, pp. 142–44. That newspaper cooperation was something less than total, however, was indicated by Wilson in a letter to Arizona senator Marcus A. Smith. In response to Smith's concern over press reports intimating a quick withdrawal of troops, Wilson remarked that "you may rest assured that the Press knows absolutely nothing about what is intended in Mexico, and that what it contains is not only conjecture, but invention." See Smith to Wilson, 23 April 1916, and Wilson to Smith, 25 April 1916, ser. 4, file 95, Wilson Papers (Library of Congress).

60. The quotations are from Statement for the Press by Secretary of War Baker, 10 March 1916, no. 2638774, Record Group 94, War Department Records; and Statement for the Press by Secretary Lansing, 13 March 1916, DSDF, 812.00/17743. See also Link, *Papers of Wilson*, vol. 36 (forthcoming): 13 March 1916.

61. The quotations are from Baker to Funston, 13 March 1916, file 2377632, AGO doc. file, Record Group 94, National Archives, Washington, D.C.

62. The quotations are from Lansing to Wilson, 21 June 1916, DSDF, 812.00/18533A.

63. The quotations are from Remarks to the New York Press Club, 30 June 1916, in Link, *Papers of Wilson*, vol. 37 (forthcoming): 30 June 1916.

Chapter 6

1. The quotation is from transcript of press conference, 3 August 1914, Swem Papers.

2. The quotation is from Secretary of the Navy Josephus Daniels to Wilson, 6 August 1914, ser. 2, Wilson Papers (Library of Congress); see also James Pollard, *The Presidents and the Press*, p. 648, Arthur S. Link, *Wilson and the Progressive Era*, p. 148, n.; and Ray Stannard Baker, *Woodrow Wilson*, 5:17.

3. The quotations are from Wilson's Proclamation, in Woodrow Wilson, *The Public Papers of Woodrow Wilson*, 3:157–59. See also Baker, *Woodrow Wilson*, 5:19; Letters to Wilson in ser. 4, files 324, 1645G, Wilson Papers (Library of Congress); and Wilson to Otto J. Krampikowsky, 14 December 1914, ser. 4, file 1645G, Wilson Papers (Library of Congress).

4. The quotation is from Memorandum, 3 September 1914, ser. 4, file 1645H, Wilson Papers (Library of Congress).

5. The quotations are from Roper to Wilson, 4 September 1914, ser. 4, file 1645, Wilson Papers (Library of Congress). See also Ben G. Davis, chief clerk, State Department, to Tumulty, 17 September 1914, ser. 4, file 1645G, Wilson Papers (Library of Congress); and chap. 8, below. For other, even more direct, forerunners of the *Official Bulletin* idea, see William L. Cheney to Wilson, 1 October 1914, and Thomas Pendel to Wilson, 9 May 1916, ser. 4, file 143, Wilson Papers (Library of Congress).

6. The quotation is from Bryan to Wilson, 10 September 1914, ser. 4, file 1645G, Wilson Papers (Library of Congress). See also Wilson to Bryan, 11 September 1914, and Karl Harriman of the *Ladies' Home Journal*, to Bryan, 8 September 1914, ser. 4, file 1645G, Wilson Papers (Library of Congress); and J. Cohn of Universal Films to Tumulty, 30 October 1914, ser. 4, file 72, Wilson Papers (Library of Congress).

7. The quotations are from Wilson to Lansing, 1 October 1914, ser. 4, file 40, Wilson Papers (Library of Congress). See also Graham H. Stuart, *The Department of State*, pp. 244–45.

8. The quotation is from McAdoo to Wilson, 29 October 1914, ser. 4, file 1645D, Wilson Papers (Library of Congress). See also McAdoo to Wilson, 28 October 1914, and McAdoo's order to the collectors of customs of the same date, ser. 4, file 1645D, Wilson Papers (Library of Congress); and Pollard, *Presidents and the Press*, p. 648.

9. The quotations are from Joseph Tumulty, *Woodrow Wilson as I Know Him*, p. 233. See also Robert Lansing, *The War Memoirs of Robert Lansing*, pp. 22–24.

10. The quotations are from *New York Times*, 9 May 1915; Wilson, *Public Papers*, 3:321; and transcript of press conference, 11 May 1915, Swem Papers. See also Tumulty, *Wilson*, p. 237; and Baker, *Woodrow Wilson*, pp. 333–34.

11. The quotations are from Bryan to Wilson, 12 May 1915, Bryan-Wilson Correspondence, vol. 4, and William Jennings Bryan, *The Memoirs of William Jennings Bryan*, p. 400. See also Baker, *Woodrow Wilson*, pp. 338–39; and Bryan to Ambassador James W. Gerard, 13 May 1915, Bryan Papers.

12. The quotations are from "Proposed Notice for Publication," enclosed in Wilson to Bryan, 13 May 1915, ser. 3, Wilson Papers (Library of Congress); and John Morton Blum, *Joe Tumulty and the Wilson Era*, p. 97. See also Lawrence, *The True Story of Woodrow Wilson*, pp. 145–46; and Bryan, *Memoirs*, pp. 401–2. It was this unissued tip that provoked the well-known "postscript" controversy during the election campaign of 1916. Responding at that time to charges leveled by Senator Henry Cabot Lodge, Wilson claimed that "no postscript or amendment to the *Lusitania* note was ever written or contemplated by me." Strictly speaking, Wilson was telling the truth with this denial, for his explanatory gloss was neither postscript nor amendment, but he

neglected, in describing the tip proposal, to divulge how close he had actually come to its release. The quotation is from Wilson to Walter Lippman, 30 October 1916, ser. 4, file 3257, Wilson Papers (Library of Congress); and see Henry Cabot Lodge, *The Senate and the League of Nations*, pp. 44–54.

13. Bryan to Wilson, 2, 3, 4, 5, 8 June 1915, Bryan-Wilson Correspondence, vol. 4; Bryan, *Memoirs*, pp. 420–21; David F. Houston, *Eight Years with Wilson's Cabinet, 1913–1920*, 1:137–39; and the analysis by Charles Willis Thompson in *New York Times*, 30 May 1915.

14. The quotations are from Bryan to Wilson, 5 June 1915, Bryan-Wilson Correspondence, vol. 4; Bryan, *Memoirs*, p. 423; and Bryan to Wilson, 8 June 1915, Bryan-Wilson Correspondence, vol. 4. See also Baker, *Woodrow Wilson*, 5:356–60; and Lawrence W. Levine, *Defender of the Faith, William Jennings Bryan*, p. 4.

15. The quotation is from Levine, *Bryan*, p. 18. See also Levine, *Bryan*, pp. 22, 31, 34, 60; Lansing, *War Memoirs*, p. 49; Ellsworth R. Bathrick to Lansing, 31 July 1915, Box 11, Lansing Papers; and Arthur S. Link, *Wilson: The Struggle for Neutrality*, pp. 425–26. The contumely heaped upon the former secretary of state by the press was sometimes so excessive as to be humorous. Henry Watterson of the *Louisville Courier-Journal*, for example, argued that "men have been shot and beheaded, even hanged, drawn and quartered, for treason less heinous" than Bryan's, whom he accused of having "the mind of Barnum and the soul of Tittlebat Titmouse." *Louisville Courier-Journal*, 12 June 1915.

16. The quotation is from Wilson to Oswald G. Villard, 7 September 1915, ser. 3, Wilson Papers (Library of Congress). See also Wilson to Garrison, 21 July and 19 August 1915, ser. 4, file 1935, Wilson Papers (Library of Congress); Wilson to Thomas Dixon, 7 September 1915, ser. 3, Wilson Papers (Library of Congress); Arthur W. Dunn, *From Harrison to Harding*, pp. 302–3; Tumulty, *Wilson*, p. 239; and Arthur S. Link, *Wilson: Confusions and Crises*, pp. 15–54.

17. The quotations are from Garrison to Wilson, 12 August 1915, ser. 4, file 1935, Wilson Papers (Library of Congress).

18. The quotations are from Wilson to Garrison, 16 August 1915, ser. 4, file 1935, Wilson Papers (Library of Congress); and Wilson to Galt, 18 August 1915, ser. 3, Wilson Papers (Library of Congress). See also Link, *Wilson: Confusions and Crises*, p. 16; and Wilson to Garrison, 18 August 1915, ser. 4, file 1935, Wilson Papers (Library of Congress).

19. The quotation is from Joseph P. Tumulty, "In the White House Looking Glass," p. 13.

20. The quotation is from Wilson to Garrison, 16 August 1915, ser. 4, file 1935, Wilson Papers (Library of Congress).

21. The quotation is from Wilson to Garrison, 18 August 1915, ser. 4, file 1935, Wilson Papers (Library of Congress). See also Garrison to Wilson, 17 August 1915, ser. 4, file 1935, Wilson Papers (Library of Congress); and Lindley M. Garrison, "Reasonable Preparation," pp. 226–27.

22. The quotations are from Wilson to Garrison, 19 August 1915, ser. 4, file 1935, Wilson Papers (Library of Congress); see also Wilson to Garrison, 17 January 1916 and 10 February 1916, ser. 3, Wilson Papers (Library of Congress).

23. The quotation is from Tumulty to Wilson, 4 October 1915, ser. 4, file 1935, Wilson Papers (Library of Congress). The emphasis is Tumulty's. See also Dunn, *From Harrison to Harding*, p. 296; *New York Times*, 3 September 1915; Wilson to Tumulty, 9 September 1915, Box 4, Tumulty Papers; and Tumulty to Wilson, 27 July 1915, ser. 4, file 470, Wilson Papers (Library of Congress).

24. The quotations are from Wilson's address, in Wilson, *Public Papers*, 3:384–90.

25. See letters to Wilson, ser. 4, file 1935, Wilson Papers (Library of Congress);

Wilson's Message to Congress, in Wilson,*Public Papers*, 3:406–28; and Link, *Wilson: Confusions and Crises*, pp. 22–39. As early as 27 July, Tumulty was convinced that the president's interest in preparedness had struck a responsive chord in public opinion. On that date he informed Wilson, who was vacationing in Cornish, N.H., that "I think the effect of our [preparedness] story of Friday night has been remarkable. It seems that we put it out at the psychological moment." Tumulty to Wilson, 27 July 1915, ser. 4, file 470, Wilson Papers (Library of Congress).

26. The quotations are from Tumulty to Wilson, 17 January 1916, ser. 4, file 1935, Wilson Papers (Library of Congress).

27. The quotation is from Wilson to Glass, 18 January 1916, ser. 3, Wilson Papers (Library of Congress). See also *New York Times*, 19 January 1916.

28. The quotations are from Wilson, *Public Papers*, 4:1–121; and Dunn, *From Harrison to Harding*, pp. 300–1. See also *New York Times*, 30 January and 3 February 1916; and Link, *Wilson: Confusions and Crises*, pp. 46–49. That Wilson was embarrassed by his Saint Louis outburst about the navy was made apparent by his decision to change, for the official version, the wording of his statement to read, "incomparably the most adequate navy in the world." See Wilson, *Public Papers*, 4:114.

29. The quotations are from Wilson to S. R. Bertron, 23 February 1916, ser. 4, file 1935, Wilson Papers (Library of Congress); Allan L. Benson, "The Politics of 'Preparedness,'" p. 246; and *New Republic* 6 (1916):1–2. See also Letters to Wilson, ser. 4, file 1935, Wilson Papers (Library of Congress).

30. Secretary of State to Diplomatic Officers in European Countries, in U.S., Department of State, *Foreign Relations of the United States, 1916, Supplement*, p. 170; U.S., Congress, *Congressional Record*, 64th Cong., 1st sess., p. 2756; and *New York Times*, 16, 18, 23 February 1916.

31. The quotations are from Wilson to Stone, 24 February 1916, ser. 3, Wilson Papers (Library of Congress). See also Tumulty to Wilson, 24 February 1916, Box 4, Tumulty Papers; and *New York Times*, 25 February 1916.

32. *New York Times*, 25, 26, 27 February 1916; Link, *Wilson: Confusions and Crises*, pp. 173–78; and Lansing, *War Memoirs*, pp. 101, 116–17.

33. Lansing to J. H. Hammond, 17 January 1917, Box 24, Lansing Papers; and Blum, *Tumulty*, p. 123. It was this episode that gave rise to the well-known "leak" investigation of 1917, in which Republicans accused Tumulty and other administration insiders of Wall Street profiteering from knowledge of government plans. These charges, eventually disproven, were made to seem incredible by Wilson's close security and must have seemed especially galling to Tumulty, who had been kept in ignorance of the president's intentions. See Blum, *Tumulty*, pp. 122–29.

34. The quotations are from Dunn, *From Harrison to Harding*, p. 350. See also Wilson to Lansing, 21 December 1916, ser. 3, Wilson Papers (Library of Congress); Lansing to Edward N. Smith, 21 January 1917, Box 24, Lansing Papers; and Blum, *Tumulty*, pp. 123–24. Evidence supporting the accuracy of Lansing's first statement can be found in Lansing's letter to Smith and in a "semiofficial" White House statement quoted in Dunn, *From Harrison to Harding*, p. 350.

35. The quotations are from Tumulty, *Wilson*, pp. 254–55; and Wilson's address to Congress, 3 February 1917, in Wilson, *Public Papers*, 4:422–26. See also "Memorandum on the Severance of Diplomatic Relations with Germany," in Lansing Diary, 4 February 1917, Lansing Papers; and Edward M. House, *The Intimate Papers of Colonel House*, 2:443, 451.

36. The quotations are from Page to Secretary of War, 24 February 1917, in Department of State, *Foreign Relations, 1917, Supplement 1*, pp. 147–48; and Wilson's address to Congress, 26 February 1917, in Wilson, *Public Papers*, 4:428–32.

See also Tumulty to Lansing, 19 February 1917, Box 24, Lansing Papers.

37. The quotations are from House to Wilson, 27 February 1917, in House, *Intimate Papers*, 2:452; and Memorandum by Lansing, 4 March 1917, in Lansing, *War Memoirs*, p. 227. See also *New York Times*, 27 February 1917.

38. The quotations are from Memorandum by Lansing, 4 March 1917, in Lansing, *War Memoirs*, pp. 228–29. Although Lansing may have dramatized his own part in reaching this decision, the fact that he wrote this memorandum only a few days after the event suggests that he probably recalled the administration's motives correctly.

39. The quotation is from *New York Times*, 5 March 1917. See also Lansing, *War Memoirs*, pp. 229–32; and Tumulty to Wilson, 8 March 1917, Box 5, Tumulty Papers.

40. The quotation is from Link, *Wilson and Progressive Era*, p. 276. See also *New York Times*, 19, 20, 21, 23, 25 March 1917; Tumulty to Wilson, 24 March 1917, Box 5, Tumulty Papers; and Thomas B. Smith, mayor of Philadelphia, to Wilson, 28 March 1917, Box 25, Lansing Papers.

41. The quotations are from Wilson's message to Congress, 2 April 1917, in Wilson, *Public Papers*, 5:6–16.

42. The quotation is from Smith to Wilson, 16 April 1917, ser. 4, file 103, Wilson Papers (Library of Congress). See also letters to Wilson in ser. 2, Wilson Papers (Library of Congress), as well as letters of public support in the Lansing and Tumulty Papers; and Lansing, *War Memoirs*, p. 243. There were some who continued to dissent, however, including six senators and fifty congressmen who voted against the resolution of war. In the opinion of Lansing, moreover, opposition in the House would have been greater "had not the overwhelming majority in the Senate [served] as an indication of popular opinion." Lansing to Edward N. Smith, 7 April 1917, Box 26, Lansing Papers.

43. The quotation is from Wilson to House, 18 May 1916, in Baker, *Woodrow Wilson*, 6:216–17. See also Link, *Wilson: Confusions and Crises*, pp. 18–26; and Arthur Walworth, *Woodrow Wilson*, 2:36–39.

44. The quotations are from Address before the League to Enforce Peace, 27 May 1916, in Wilson, *Public Papers*, 4:184–88.

45. The quotations are from ibid.

46. The quotations are from Memorial Day Address, 30 May 1916, ibid., pp. 191–96.

47. The quotations are from Address at Shadow Lawn, 2 September 1916, ibid., pp. 275–91.

48. The quotations are from Addresses at Omaha, Nebr., 5 October 1916, Indianapolis, Ind., 12 October 1916, and Cincinnati, Ohio, 26 October 1916, ibid., pp. 344–49, 356–63, 376–82.

49. The quotations are from Address at Shadow Lawn, 4 November 1916, ibid., pp. 384–94.

50. The quotations are from Address to the United States Senate, 22 January 1917, ibid., pp. 407–14.

51. The quotations are from Second Inaugural Address, 5 March 1917, ibid., 5:1–5.

52. The quotations are from Address before a Joint Session of Congress, 2 April 1917, ibid., pp. 6–16.

53. The quotations are from the Fourteen Points Speech, 8 January 1918, ibid., pp. 155–162.

54. The quotations are from Address to Congress, 1 February 1918, ibid., pp. 177–84.

55. The quotations are from Address at Mount Vernon, 4 July 1918, ibid., pp. 231–35.

56. The quotations are from Address opening the campaign for the Fourth Liberty

Loan, 27 September 1918, ibid., pp. 253–61.

57. The quotations are from Address to Congress, 11 November, 1918, ibid., pp. 294–302.

Chapter 7

1. The quotation is from John L. Heaton, *Cobb of "The World*," pp. 267–69. There is some disagreement over when this conversation occurred. See Arthur S. Link, *Wilson: Campaigns for Progressivism and Peace*, p. 399, n.

2. The quotation is from Josephus Daniels, *The Cabinet Diaries of Josephus Daniels, 1913–1921*, p. 109. See also Daniels, *Cabinet Diaries*, pp. 111, 115, 116, 131; Walton E. Bean, "George Creel and His Critics," pp. 22–23; and James R. Mock, *Censorship, 1917*, pp. 41–44.

3. Daniels, *Cabinet Diaries*, pp. 127, 131, 133; James R. Mock and Cedric Larson, *Words That Won the War*, pp. 48–50; and Lansing, Baker and Daniels to Wilson, 13 April 1917, ser. 4, file 3856, Wilson Papers (Library of Congress).

4. The quotations are from Lansing, Baker, and Daniels to Wilson, ser. 4, file 3856, Wilson Papers (Library of Congress). See also Mock and Larson, *Words That Won the War*, pp. 50–51; and Datebook, 1917, entry for 13 April, ser. 1, Wilson Papers (Library of Congress).

5. Mock, *Censorship, 1917*, pp. 48–54; Mock and Larson, *Words That Won the War*, pp. 48–50; Creel to son, 21 March 1931, Box 1, Creel Papers; Datebook, 1917, ser. 1, Wilson Papers (Library of Congress); Tumulty to Wilson, 20 April 1917, and Wilson to Arthur Brisbane, 25 April 1917, Box 5, Tumulty Papers.

6. George Creel, *Rebel at Large*, pp. 50, 94, 96–98; Edwin Markham, Benjamin Lindsey, and George Creel, *Children in Bondage*; *New York Times*, 16 April 1917; Bean, "Creel and His Critics," pp. 5, 24; Robert Lansing, *The War Memoirs of Robert Lansing*, p. 323; and Mock and Larson, *Words That Won the War*, pp. 52–60.

7. The quotations are from Creel, *Rebel at Large*, pp. 149, 153. See also George Creel, *Wilson and the Issues*, Box 23, Creel Papers; Bean, "Creel and His Critics," pp. 19–22; and Mock and Larson, *Words That Won the War*, p. 59. Wilson had been sufficiently impressed with Creel's efforts on his behalf to offer him an administration job in 1916, but it was an offer that the impecunious journalist could not afford to accept. Creel, *Rebel at Large*, p. 156.

8. The quotations are from George Creel, *How We Advertised America*, pp. 16–17; and Creel, *Rebel at Large*, p. 157. See also "Preliminary Statement to the Press of the Committee on Public Information," Box 3, Creel Papers; Creel, "Public Opinion as a War Measure," Box 23, Creel Papers; Creel, *How We Advertised America*, p. 70; and Mock and Larson, *Words That Won the War*, p. 11.

9. The quotation is from "Preliminary Statement to the Press," Box 3, Creel Papers. See also Wilson to Creel, 17 May 1917, ser. 4, file 3856, Wilson Papers (Library of Congress); Creel, *How We Advertised America*, pp. 16–23; James E. Pollard, *The Presidents and the Press*, pp. 665–66; and Mock, *Censorship, 1917*, p. 48. Of the three categories, the "doubtful" stories were the ones that caused the CPI the most difficulties because the requirement of prior submission for approval had the flavor of direct censorship. To avoid this stigma, Creel issued on 30 July a more specific statement of "What the Government Asks of the Press," which made it unnecessary for newspapermen to submit stories to the CPI for approval and which ended much of the criticism of the committee's censorship activities. Creel, *How We Advertised America*, pp. 20–23; Bean, "Creel and His Critics," pp. 76–77, 80.

10. Mock, *Censorship, 1917*, pp. 51–52, 139, 155; and Creel to David Lawrence, 10

August 1917, 1–A1, Box 16, Committee on Public Information Records, Record Group 63. Although Creel was satisfied with the results of his voluntary censorship, he soon found that this view was not shared by the president. In Wilson's opinion, "the matter should not be put in the hands of the very men we are feeling the need of regulating in some degree," and he refused to heed the advice of either Creel or Tumulty to move cautiously in the matter. As a result, censorship laws were passed during the war that gave the government more control over information than at any time in the nation's history and that placed a serious strain upon the administration's relations with the press. The quotation is from Wilson to Franklin Lane, 8 May 1917, ser. 4, file 3856A, Wilson Papers (Library of Congress); and see Tumulty to Wilson, 8 May 1917, Box 5, Tumulty Papers.

11. The quotations are from Creel, *How We Advertised America*, pp. 4, 71–72. See also *Report of the Chairman of the Committee on Public Information*, pp. 12–13, in Box 23, Creel Papers.

12. *Report of the Chairman*, pp. 12–14, Box 23, Creel Papers; and Creel to Wilson, 28 November 1917, Box 1, Creel Papers.

13. Creel, *How We Advertised America*, pp. 72–73. In the years before the war, presidents had employed a number of newspapermen to serve as secretaries and White House assistants, but none of these staff members had worked as exclusively with the press as the former reporters within the CPI. The problem of divided loyalties—almost always settled in favor of the president—became a more serious problem with the creation of the office of presidential press secretary, which has generally been filled by the appointment of journalists.

14. John Morton Blum, *Joe Tumulty and the Wilson Era*, pp. 133–34; and Tumulty to Wilson, 12 July, and 10 October 1917, and 21 January 1918, Box 5, Tumulty Papers.

15. Creel to Wilson, 8 June 1917, Box 1, Creel Papers.

16. Creel to Wilson, 16 May 1918, Box 2, Creel Papers.

17. The quotation is from Creel, *How We Advertised America*, p. 24. See also Bean, "Creel and His Critics," pp. 127–28; Creel, *How We Advertised America*, pp. 72–74; Daniels, *Cabinet Diaries*, p. 135; and Paul Moore to Lansing, 7 May 1917, Box 27, Lansing Papers.

18. Creel, *How We Advertised America*, pp. 28–29, 74–75.

19. *New York Times*, 4 July 1917; Bean, "Creel and His Critics," pp. 141, 159–60; and Daniels, *Cabinet Diaries*, p. 172.

20. Creel, *How We Advertised America*, pp. 28–34; Wilson to Creel, 2 August 1917, ser. 4, file 3856, Wilson Papers (Library of Congress); and Bean, "Creel and His Critics," p. 160.

21. The quotation is from Creel, *How We Advertised America*, p. 29.

22. The quotation is from Lansing, *War Memoirs*, p. 323. See also Graham H. Stuart, *The Department of State*, pp. 244–45; and Lansing, *War Memoirs*, pp. 322–24. It is ironic that Lansing, who became one of the CPI's chief detractors, should have been both one of the proposers and a member of the committee. He was apparently surprised by the scope that Creel quickly gave to the CPI and was certainly disenchanted by the chairman's determination to run it as a "one man office." Lansing, *War Memoirs*, p. 322.

23. The quotations are from Wilson to Lansing, 29 June 1917, and Wilson to Long, 20 November 1917, Box 1, Creel Papers. See also Long to Wilson, 19 November 1917, and Creel to Wilson, 28 November 1917, Box 1, Creel Papers; and Creel's remarks, apparently written in 1931, at the bottom of Wilson to Lansing, 29 June 1917, Box 1, Creel Papers.

24. The quotations are from Lansing, *War Memoirs*, p. 320; and Tumulty to Wilson,

8 May 1917, Box 5, Tumulty Papers. See also clipping, *New York Evening Sun*, 8 May 1917, and Lansing to Edward N. Smith, 14 May 1917, Box 27, Lansing Papers; Lansing, *War Memoirs*, pp. 320–21; and Stuart, *Department of State*, pp. 244–45.

25. U.S., Government Printing Office, *Register of the Department of State, 1918*, p. 30; Gibson to Warren D. Robbins, 6 July 1917, DSDF 763.72/6120; Patchin to Lansing, 10 November 1918, DSDF 763.72119/2559½; Lansing, *War Memoirs*, p. 319; and John S. Dickey, "The Secretary and the American Public," p. 143.

26. The quotations are from Lansing to Edward Smith, 14 May 1917, and Lansing to Paul Moore, 10 May 1917, Box 27, Lansing Papers. See also Tumulty to Wilson, 8 May 1917, Box 5, Tumulty Papers; Grant Squires to Lansing, 8 May 1917, Box 27, Lansing Papers; Lansing, *War Memoirs*, p. 322; and Daniels, *Cabinet Diaries*, p. 149.

27. The quotation is from Creel, *How We Advertised America*, p. 74. See also *Report of the Chairman*, p. 14, Box 23, Creel Papers; Mock and Larson, *Words That Won the War*, p. 91; and Wilson to Creel, 4 September 1917, ser. 4, file 1645C, Wilson Papers (Library of Congress).

28. Wilson to Creel, 27 April 1917, Box 1, Creel Papers; Wilson to Tumulty, undated but in July 1917, ser. 4, file 3856, Wilson Papers (Library of Congress); "Facts concerning Official Bulletin, Its Field and Function: How and Why Publication Was Authorized by the President," 5-A3, Box 152, CPI Records, Record Group 63; "The Official United States Bulletin, Daily Government Newspaper: An Explanation," 5-A3, Box 152, CPI Records, Record Group 63; *Report of the Chairman*, pp. 63–67, Box 23, Creel Papers; and Mock and Larson, *Words That Won the War*, pp. 92–93.

29. Wilson to Tumulty, undated but in July 1917, ser. 4, file 3856, Wilson Papers (Library of Congress); "Facts concerning Official Bulletin," 5-A3, Box 152, CPI Records, Record Group 63; and Creel, *How We Advertised America*, p. 208.

30. "Facts concerning Official Bulletin," 5-A3, Box 152, CPI Records, Record Group 63; *Report of the Chairman*, pp. 64–65, Box 23, Creel Papers; and Mock and Larson, *Words That Won the War*, pp. 93–94.

31. The quotation is from the *Official Bulletin*, 23 June 1917. See also E. S. Rochester, editor of the *Official Bulletin*, to John F. Mitchel, 16 October 1918, ser. 4, file 3856, Wilson Papers (Library of Congress); Wilson to Secretary of Commerce William Redfield, 18 November 1918, Rochester to Tumulty, 12 November 1918, Secretary of Labor William B. Wilson to Wilson, 23 November 1918, Redfield to Wilson, 29 November 1918, and Wilson to Redfield, 30 November 1918, ser. 4, file 3856, Wilson Papers (Library of Congress); Mock and Larson, *Words That Won the War*, pp. 94–95; and Bean, "Creel and His Critics," p. 58.

32. Creel, *How We Advertised America*, pp. 4–5, 99–102; Creel, Address to the City Editor's Association, Columbus, Ohio, 19 January 1918, Box 23, Creel Papers; and Harold D. Lasswell, *Propaganda Techniques in the World War*, p. 10.

33. The quotations are from *Report of the Chairman*, p. 15, Box 23, Creel Papers; and Creel, *How We Advertised America*, p. 101.

34. George Creel, "Propaganda and Morale," p. 349; and Guy Stanton Ford, "The Fight for Public Opinion," pp. 3–26. For an excellent discussion of the issues treated in this paragraph, see Carol S. Gruber, *Mars and Minerva*, pp. 141–57.

35. *Report of the Chairman*, pp. 15–19, Box 23, Creel Papers; "The Activities of the Committee on Public Information," 27 January 1918, Box 23, Creel Papers; Creel to Wilson, 14 June 1917, Box 1, Creel Papers; and Pamphlet Advertisement in 1-B1, Box 51, CPI Records, Record Group 63.

36. The quotation is from International Film Service to Tumulty, 15 December 1915, ser. 4, file 149, Wilson Papers (Library of Congress). See also H. A. Spaweth to

Wilson, 28 March 1913, and Spaweth to Tumulty, 1 April 1913, ser. 4, file 72, Wilson Papers (Library of Congress); and S. H. MacKean of International News Service to Tumulty, 18 February 1914, ser. 4, file 149, Wilson Papers (Library of Congress).

37. The quotation is from Memorandum, Wilson to Tumulty, attached to Fox to Tumulty, 4 March 1916, ser. 4, file 72, Wilson Papers (Library of Congress). See also J. Cohn to Tumulty, 30 October 1914, Universal Film Manufacturing Co. to Wilson, 5 March 1915, Juliet Barrett Rublee to Wilson, 26 March 1915, Fox to Tumulty, 4 March 1916, and Memorandum, Wilson to Tumulty, undated but April 1916, ser. 4, file 72, Wilson Papers (Library of Congress).

38. The quotation is from Memorandum, Wilson to Tumulty, undated but late April 1916, ser. 4, file 72, Wilson Papers (Library of Congress). See also Fox to Tumulty, 20 April 1916, Memorandum, Wilson to Tumulty, undated but April 1916, William A. Brady, World Film Corp., to Tumulty, 31 July 1916, and Memorandum, Wilson to Tumulty, 3 August 1916, ser. 4, file 72, Wilson Papers (Library of Congress). The kind of rivalry feared by Wilson caused Creel considerable problems during the war. Chief among these was the complaint that the Hearst organization, which had many former employees working for Creel, was receiving special treatment from the committee's Film Division. But despite the many charges made by competing newsreel companies, no evidence of favoritism was ever discovered. See Mock and Larson, *Words That Won the War*, pp. 148–50.

39. The quotation is from Laurence Rubel to Wilson, 24 May 1916, ser. 4, file 72, Wilson Papers (Library of Congress). See also Miranda to Tumulty, 12 February 1916, Memorandum, Wilson to Tumulty, undated but early April 1916, Memorandum, Tumulty to Wilson, 19 May 1916, and Memorandum, Wilson to Tumulty, undated but acknowledged 20 May 1916, ser. 4, file 72, Wilson Papers (Library of Congress).

40. The quotations are from Redfield to Wilson, 1 June 1917, and Wilson to Berst, 14 June 1917, ser. 4, file 4020, Wilson Papers (Library of Congress). See also Memorandum, Wilson to Tumulty, undated but early June 1917, and Frank Polk to Wilson, 12 June 1917, ser. 4, file 4020, Wilson Papers (Library of Congress).

41. The quotations are from Wilson to Berst, 11 August 1917, and MacFarland to Wilson, 23 August 1917, ser. 4, file 4020, Wilson Papers (Library of Congress). See also Berst to Wilson, 8 June 1917, Polk to Wilson, 11 August 1917, Berst to Wilson, 16 August 1917, Wilson to Berst, 21 August 1917, Lansing to Tumulty, 1 September 1917, Wilson to Tumulty, 6 September 1917, Memorandum, Wilson to Tumulty, undated but September 1917, Lansing to Tumulty, 4 October 1917, and Lansing to MacFarland, 4 October 1917, ser. 4, file 4020, Wilson Papers (Library of Congress).

42. The quotation is from Wilson to Brady, 28 June 1917, ser. 4, file 72, Wilson Papers (Library of Congress). See also Brady to Wilson, 22 June 1917, and Carl Laemmle of Universal Films to Wilson, 25 April 1917, ser. 4, file 72, Wilson Papers (Library of Congress); and Mock and Larson, *Words That Won the War*, pp. 151–52.

43. The quotation is from Creel to Frank Lockhart, 5 July 1918, 1-A1, Box 16, CPI Records, Record Group 63. See also Mock and Larson, *Words That Won the War*, pp. 144–47.

44. Creel, *How We Advertised America*, pp. 119–20; and *Report of the Chairman*, pp. 47–48, Box 23, Creel Papers.

45. The quotation is from Howard Herrick, Division of Films publicity manager, to T. D. Bonneville, 10 May 1918, 10A-A1, Box 156, CPI Records, Record Group 63. See also Manager, Feature Film Department, to Charles Aebli, 8 April 1918, Herrick to W. J. Benedict, 30 April 1918, Herrick to Archie Bell, 30 April 1918, and Hart to J. G. Barnes, 23 March 1918; 10A-A1, Box 155, CPI Records, Record Group 63.

46. Hart to James L. Hoff, 25 April 1918, 10A-A1, Box 155, CPI Records, Record Group 63; and Creel, *How We Advertised America*, pp. 123–24.

47. The quotation is from Creel to Tumulty, 18 April 1918, ser. 4, file 3856, Wilson Papers (Library of Congress). See also S. H. Symmers to Tumulty, 16 April 1918, ser. 4, file 3856, Wilson Papers (Library of Congress); Creel to Tumulty, 20 August 1918, ser. 4, file 72, Wilson Papers (Library of Congress); Creel to Tumulty, 16 September 1918, ser. 4, file 3856, Wilson Papers (Library of Congress); Tumulty to Wilson, 19 October, 1917, Box 5, Tumulty Papers; Wilson to Tumulty, 15 June 1918, ser. 4, file 541, Wilson Papers (Library of Congress); and William A. Brady to Tumulty, 5 June 1918, ser. 4, file 72, Wilson Papers (Library of Congress).

48. *Report of the Chairman*, pp. 21–24, Box 23, Creel Papers; and Four-Minute Men Bulletins, nos. 1 (22 May 1917) and 31 (27 May 1918), 11A-A1, Box 156, CPI Records, Record Group 63.

49. Creel to Wilson, 18 October 1918, Box 2, Creel Papers; School Bulletin, no. 4 (15 November 1918), 11A-A1, Box 156, CPI Records, Record Group 63; and Mock and Larson, *Words That Won the War*, p. 114.

50. Creel, *How We Advertised America*, pp. 212–21; Grosvenor Clarkson, secretary of the Council of National Defense, to Creel, 14 August 1917, ser. 4, file 1645L, Wilson Papers (Library of Congress); and Arthur Brisbane to Tumulty, 3 October 1918, Tumulty Papers.

51. *Report of the Chairman*, pp. 78–103, Box 23, Creel Papers; Creel, *How We Advertised America*, pp. 166–99; Wilson to Creel, 8 May 1918, Box 2, Creel Papers; Report of the Division of Foreign Publications, January 1918, and Report of the Foreign Language Division, October 1918, 1-B1, Box 51, CPI Records, Record Group 63.

52. The quotations are from Creel to Wilson, 18 June 1918, and Wilson to Creel, 21 July 1918, Box 2, Creel Papers. See also Wilson to Creel, 18 June 1918, and Creel to Wilson, 5 July 1918, Box 2, Creel Papers; and Creel, *How We Advertised America*, pp. 125, 127, 217.

53. Creel, *How We Advertised America*, pp. 4–5.

54. Report on the CPI by Military Intelligence, May 1918, 1-A1, Box 5, CPI Records, Record Group 63; and Bean, "Creel and His Critics," pp. 127–29.

Chapter 8

1. Passenger list for *George Washington*, ser. 4, file 501FF, Wilson Papers (Library of Congress); Arthur Brisbane to Tumulty, 19 November 1918; Tumulty to Creel, 27 November 1918; and Creel to Brisbane, 27 November 1918, 1-A1, Box 3, CPI Records, Record Group 63; Ray Stannard Baker, *Woodrow Wilson and World Settlement*, 1:119. In addition to Wilson, the peace commissioners were Secretary of State Robert Lansing, Edward M. House, General Tasker H. Bliss, and veteran diplomat Henry White.

2. The quotation is from Cary Grayson to Tumulty, 12 December 1918, Box 1, Tumulty Papers. See also Cary T. Grayson, *Woodrow Wilson*, p. 59; clippings sent from Tumulty to Wilson, 6 December 1918 and after, ser. 5B, Wilson Papers (Library of Congress); and James D. Startt, "The Uneasy Partnership," pp. 58–59.

3. The quotations are from Tumulty to Grayson, 16, 17 December 1918, ser. 5B, Wilson Papers (Library of Congress). See also Grayson to Tumulty, 16 December 1918, Box 1, Tumulty Papers; clippings sent from Tumulty to Wilson in December 1918, ser. 5B, Wilson Papers (Library of Congress); John M. Blum, *Joe Tumulty and the Wilson Era*, p. 171; and William A. White, *Woodrow Wilson*, pp. 391, 394–96.

4. Lansing Deskbook, 25, 29 November 1918, Lansing Papers; Grayson to Tumulty, 12 December 1918, Box 1, Tumulty Papers; George Creel, "Woodrow Wilson's Last Years," p. 11, *Rebel at Large*, p. 205, and *How We Advertised America*, pp. 401–10.

5. The quotations are from Tumulty to Creel, undated but about 10 December 1918, ser. 5B, Wilson Papers (Library of Congress). See also Creel, *Rebel at Large*, pp. 205–14, "Wilson's Last Years," p. 11, and *How We Advertised America*, pp. 409, 414; and Herman Kohlsaat, *From McKinley to Harding*, pp. 212–14. Enhancing the suspicions of American correspondents was the activity of the French censor, who read everything that went out over the Paris cable. See David Lawrence, *The True Story of Woodrow Wilson*, pp. 264–65.

6. The quotation is from Wilson to Tumulty, 19 December 1918, Box 5, Tumulty Papers. See also Philip Patchin to Joseph Grew, 23 June 1919, p. 184, DSDF 82/53; Creel to Wilson, 24 December 1918, ser. 5B, Wilson Papers (Library of Congress); Creel, "Wilson's Last Years," p. 11, *How We Advertised America*, pp. 412–13, and *Rebel at Large*, pp. 205–14. In addition, the CPI furnished biweekly editorial reviews from the United States to the American commission. See reviews in 1-B1, Box 51, CPI Records, Record Group 63.

7. The quotations are from Joseph Tumulty, *Woodrow Wilson as I Know Him*, p. 341; and Tumulty to Wilson, 21 November 1918, Box 5, Tumulty Papers. Tumulty's absence from the peace conference contributed greatly to the American commission's publicity difficulties. See Grayson to Tumulty, 16 December 1918 and 13 March 1919, Box 1, Tumulty Papers; and Grayson to Tumulty, 20 April 1919, ser. 5B, Wilson Papers (Library of Congress).

8. Press clippings, Tumulty to Wilson, 6 December 1918, and after, ser. 5B, Wilson Papers (Library of Congress); news items and editorial comment cabled from Tumulty to Wilson, December 1918, ser. 5B, Wilson Papers (Library of Congress); Grayson to Tumulty, 12, 16 December 1918, Box 1, Tumulty Papers; and Tumulty to Grayson, 16, 17, 22 December 1918, ser. 5B, Wilson Papers (Library of Congress). Later in the conference, Grayson's dual role as doctor and publicity agent would present something of a conflict of interest, as his concern for the president's health—always precarious—made him unwilling to push too hard for additional publicity efforts. Grayson to Tumulty, 10 April 1919, ser. 5B, Wilson Papers (Library of Congress).

9. The quotations are from Tumulty to Grayson (2), 16 December 1918, ser. 5B, Wilson Papers (Library of Congress). See also Tumulty to Grayson, 17 December 1918, ser. 5B, Wilson Papers (Library of Congress); and Grayson to Tumulty, 16 December 1918, Box 1, Tumulty Papers.

10. The quotations are from Grayson to Tumulty, 21 December 1918, and Tumulty to Grayson, 23 December 1918; ser. 5B, Wilson Papers (Library of Congress). See also Tumulty to Grayson, 22 December 1918, and Tumulty to Wilson, 24 December 1918 and 3 January 1919, ser. 5B, Wilson Papers (Library of Congress).

11. The quotations are from draft letter, Wilson to American Commissioners to Negotiate Peace, 16 December 1918, and Wilson to Tasker Bliss, 17 December 1918, ser. 5B, Wilson Papers (Library of Congress). See also House to Wilson, 22 October 1918, in U.S., Department of State, *Foreign Relations of the United States, 1919: The Paris Peace Conference*, 1:156; Confidential Secretary to the President to House, 17 December 1918, ser. 5B, Wilson Papers (Library of Congress); Baker, *World Settlement*, 1:119–20; Creel, *How We Advertised America*, p. 413.

12. The quotations are from Wilson to Bliss, 17 December 1918, ser. 5B, Wilson Papers (Library of Congress); and Journal, 17 December 1918, Box 132, Ray Stannard Baker Papers. See also Ray Stannard Baker, *American Chronicle*, pp. 373–75; and Wilson to Tumulty, 19 December 1918, Box 5, Tumulty Papers.

13. The quotations are from Journal, 20 May 1919, Box 132, Ray Stannard Baker

Papers. The emphasis is Baker's. See also Journal, 8 March and 31 May 1919, Box 132, Ray Stannard Baker Papers.

14. The quotation is from Journal, 20 December 1918, Box 132, Ray Stannard Baker Papers. See also Baker, *American Chronicle*, pp. 375–77; Journal, 26, 30 December 1918 and 30 April 1919, Box 132, Ray Stannard Baker Papers; and Wilson to Herbert B. Swope, 7 February 1919, ser. 5B, Wilson Papers (Library of Congress).

15. The quotations are from Journal, 23, 16 December 1918, Box 132, Ray Stannard Baker Papers. See also Journal, 19, 30 December 1918, Box 132, Ray Stannard Baker Papers; and Baker, *American Chronicle*, pp. 375–76.

16. Baker, *World Settlement*, 1:120, 123–24; Baker to Commission, 21 December 1918, DSDF, 184.52/5; and Creel, *How We Advertised America*, pp. 413–14. Cable space was apportioned by Baker as follows: 1,000 free words daily to each of the three press associations, with 3,000 words daily shared among the other correspondents. See Baker, *World Settlement*, 1:124. The CPI also helped by sending the text of documents and proclamations to a clearinghouse for American newspapers— "Compub"—in New York City. See Patchin to Grew, 23 June 1919, DSDF 184.82/53. So valuable did this service prove, in fact, that the commission decided to pay the cost of continuing the organization when congressional funding of the CPI ended on 30 June 1919. See Memorandum for Grew, 24 June 1919, DSDF, 184.82/55; and Memorandum from Grew, 2 July 1919, DSDF 184.82/59; and Lawrence Hill (chairman of the executive committee of American correspondents in Paris) to Frank Polk, 5 August 1919, in Department of State, *Foreign Relations, 1919: Peace Conference*, 11:628.

17. The quotations are from Journal, 26 December 1918, Box 132, Ray Stannard Baker Papers; and Baker, *World Settlement*, 1:131. See also Journal, 21, 23 December 1918, Box 132, Ray Stannard Baker Papers; Grayson to Tumulty, 19 May 1919, ser. 5B, Wilson Papers (Library of Congress); *World Settlement*, p. 130, and *American Chronicle*, pp. 378–83; and J. Frederick Essary, *Covering Washington*, p. 150. Ironically, House had authored with George Creel the proposal that the four commissioners meet jointly with the press. See Gilbert F. Close to House, 17 December 1918, and Wilson to the American Commissioners to Negotiate Peace, 16 December 1918, ser. 5B, Wilson Papers (Library of Congress).

18. The quotation is from Journal, Memorandum of 23 February 1919, Box 132, Ray Stannard Baker Papers. See also Baker, *American Chronicle*, pp. 375–76, and *World Settlement*, 1:130; and Startt, "Uneasy Partnership," p. 64.

19. The quotations are from Grew, executive secretary to the commission, to Sidney Mezes, director of the Intelligence Section, 17 January 1919, DSDF, 184.82/12; and Dulles to Grew, 20 January 1919, DSDF, 184.014/9. See also Grew to Isaiah Bowman, 9 January 1919, DSDF, 184.82/9; Baker, *American Chronicle*, pp. 375–76; Organization Chart of American Commission to Negotiate Peace, Box 9, Newton D. Baker Papers.

20. Baker, *American Chronicle*, p. 375; Journal, 21 December 1918, Box 132, Ray Stannard Baker Papers; List of Press Correspondents, 13 January 1919, ser. 5B, Wilson Papers (Library of Congress).

21. Executive Committee of the American Press Delegation to Members of the American Peace Commission, 15 January 1919, Box 97, Ray Stannard Baker Papers; Baker, *American Chronicle*, pp. 128–29.

22. Memorandum, Executive Committee of the American Press Delegation, 15 January 1919, Box 97, Ray Stannard Baker Papers.

23. The quotations are from Statement by Truman Talley, undated, DSDF, 184.82/25. See also excerpts from Minutes of American Commission Meeting, 15

February 1919, DSDF, 184.82/24, and 20 February 1919, DSDF, 184.82/28; and Memorandum to Commission from Correspondents' Executive Committee, 16 February 1919, DSDF, 184.82/26.

24. Memorandum, 23 February 1919, Box 132, Ray Stannard Baker Papers; Baker, *American Chronicle*, p. 377; Thomas A. Bailey, *Woodrow Wilson and the Lost Peace*, pp. 127–29.

25. The quotations are from Baker to Grew, 7 January 1919, DSDF, 184.82/6; Leland Harrison to Grew, 8 January 1919, DSDF, 184.82/7; and Statement by Associated Powers, 14 January 1919, ser. 5B, Wilson Papers (Library of Congress). See also Peace Conference Regulations, 18 January 1919, ser. 5B, Wilson Papers (Library of Congress).

26. Baker, *American Chronicle*, p. 377; Journal, 5 April 1919, Box 132, Ray Stannard Baker Papers; Bailey, *Lost Peace*, pp. 125–33.

27. The quotation is from Wilson to Tumulty, 20 January 1919, ser. 5B, Wilson Papers (Library of Congress). See also Journal, 8 March 1919, Box 132, Ray Stannard Baker Papers; Statement by Associated Powers, 14 January 1919, ser. 5B, Wilson Papers (Library of Congress); and Baker, *World Settlement*, 1:137–39. In meetings on 15 and 16 January, Wilson did argue on the side of enlarged publicity, but he was never willing to have the kind of open sessions desired by correspondents. See Department of State, *Foreign Relations, 1919: Peace Conference*, 3:543–52, 579–86, 609–21.

28. The quotations are from Baker, *World Settlement*, 1:117; and Journal, 8 March 1919, Box 132, Ray Stannard Baker Papers. See also Tumulty to Wilson, 18 January 1919, and Tumulty to Grayson, 16 January 1919, ser. 5B, Wilson Papers (Library of Congress); and Wilson to Lansing, 12 March 1918, in U.S., Congress, *Congressional Record*, 65th Cong., 2d sess., p. 7653.

29. Press correspondents to Wilson, 14 January 1919, ser. 5B,Wilson Papers (Library of Congress); Baker, *World Settlement*, 1:137; Lawrence, *True Story*, p. 348; Bailey, *Lost Peace*, pp. 125–27.

30. The quotations are from correspondents to Wilson, 14 January 1919, and Tumulty to Grayson, 18 January 1919, ser. 5B, Wilson Papers (Library of Congress). See also Resolutions of the Allied and American Press, mid-January 1919, ser. 5B, Wilson Papers (Library of Congress); Journal, Memorandum of 23 February 1919, Box 132, Ray Stannard Baker Papers; and Tumulty to Wilson, 16 January 1919, ser. 5B, Wilson Papers (Library of Congress).

31. Journal, Memorandum of 23 February 1919, Box 132, Ray Stannard Baker Papers; Baker to Grew, 29 January 1919, DSDF, 184.82/18; Grew to Baker, 30 January 1919, DSDF, 184.82/19; Wilson to Tumulty, 20 January 1919, ser. 5B, Wilson Papers (Library of Congress); Department of State, *Foreign Relations, 1919: Peace Conference*, 3:543–52, 609–21; Baker, *American Chronicle*, p. 377, and *World Settlement*, 1:121, 137, 139–41; Lawrence, *True Story*, pp. 254–58, 348; and Startt, "Uneasy Partnership," pp. 60–62.

32. Memorandum, Press Representatives to Peace Commissioners, 23 April 1919, Box 97, Ray Stannard Baker Papers; Baker to Close, 28 April 1919, ser. 5B, Wilson Papers (Library of Congress); General Secretariat of Peace Conference to General Secretariat of American Delegation, 29 April 1919, Box 97, Ray Stannard Baker Papers; Minutes of Council of Four, 30 April 1919, Box 97, Ray Stannard Baker Papers; Wilson to William A. White, 6 May 1919, ser. 5B, Wilson Papers (Library of Congress); Journal, 26 April, 1919, Box 132, Ray Stannard Baker Papers; and Baker, *American Chronicle*, pp. 424–26. Although Wilson proved instrumental in gaining Big Four approval for the admission of forty-five correspondents—five of whom were

American—for the treaty presentation, he agreed with the decision to ban any contact between the Germans and the press. See Minutes of Council of Four, 30 April 1919, Box 97, Ray Stannard Baker Papers.

33. The quotation is from Tumulty to Wilson, 13 January 1919, ser. 5B, Wilson Papers (Library of Congress). See also Tumulty to Grayson, 16 January 1919, and William A. White to Wilson, 22 January 1919, ser. 5B, Wilson Papers (Library of Congress); Journal, Memorandum of 23 February 1919, Box 132, Ray Stannard Baker Papers; Baker to Grayson, 5 February 1919, and Creel to Wilson, 3 February 1919, ser. 5B, Wilson Papers (Library of Congress).

34. Wilson to Tumulty, 16 January 1919, Box 1, Tumulty Papers; excerpts from Minutes of American Commission Meeting, 15 February 1919, DSDF, 184.82/24; White, *Wilson*, pp. 391, 394–96; and James E. Pollard, *The Presidents and the Press*, pp. 687, 683–84. One of Wilson's biographers has described the president's schedule thus: "After an eight o'clock breakfast, he did in two hours what in normal times might be thought a day's work at his desk. Then a conference or two before the morning meeting of the inner council; guests at lunch and sometimes at dinner; sessions all afternoon—sometimes two at once in adjoining rooms, with the President going back and forth and carrying in his mind the threads of the argument. In the evening a daily talk with Baker, then dinner—for which he no longer took time to dress—and afterwards another conference or study of maps and reports to prepare for the business of the morrow." Arthur Walworth, *Woodrow Wilson*, 2:296. See also Creel, *How We Advertised America*, p. 413.

35. The quotation is from Tumulty to Wilson, 7 January 1919, ser. 5B, Wilson Papers (Library of Congress).

36. Wilson to Tumulty, 7 January and 19, 20 February 1919, Tumulty to Grayson, 25 January 1919, Grayson to Tumulty, 25 January 1919, and Tumulty to Wilson, 27 January 1919, ser. 5B, Wilson Papers (Library of Congress).

37. The quotation is from Tumulty to Wilson, 30 January 1919, ser. 5B, Wilson Papers (Library of Congress). See also Tumulty to Wilson, 7 January and 5, 8 February 1919, and Attorney General Thomas Gregory to Wilson, 14 January 1919, ser. 5B, Wilson Papers (Library of Congress).

38. The quotation is from Tumulty to Wilson, 22 February 1919, ser. 5B, Wilson Papers (Library of Congress). See also Tumulty to Wilson, 7 January and 5, 8, 15 February 1919, Wilson to Tumulty, 7 January and 7, 9, 19 February 1919, Tumulty to Grayson, 17 February 1919, and Grayson to Peters, 20 February 1919, ser. 5B, Wilson Papers (Library of Congress); Alfred E. Smith to Wilson, 19 February 1919, ser. 4, file 501HH, Wilson Papers (Library of Congress).

39. Tumulty to Wilson, 15, 18, 19, 22 February 1919, ser. 5B, Wilson Papers (Library of Congress); Baker, *American Chronicle*, pp. 384–85; Blum, *Tumulty*, p. 183; Bailey, *Lost Peace*, pp. 197–98.

40. Wilson to Tumulty, 19, 20 February 1919, ser. 5B, Wilson Papers (Library of Congress); Journal, 7 March 1919, Box 132, Ray Stannard Baker Papers; Baker, *American Chronicle*, p. 385; Bailey, *Lost Peace*, pp. 198–99.

41. The quotations are from Baker, *American Chronicle*, p. 391; Tumulty to Grayson, 14 March 1919, and Tumulty to Wilson, 14 March 1919, ser. 5B, Wilson Papers (Library of Congress). See also Tumulty to Wilson, 13, 16, 25 March 1919, ser. 5B, Wilson Papers (Library of Congress).

42. The quotations are from Tumulty to Wilson, 13 March 1919, ser. 5B, Wilson Papers (Library of Congress); and Baker, *American Chronicle*, p. 392. See also Grayson to Tumulty, 13 March 1919, Box 1, Tumulty Papers; Tumulty to Wilson, 16 March 1919, ser. 5B, Wilson Papers (Library of Congress); Baker to Wilson, 15 March 1919, Box 97, Ray Stannard Baker Papers; and Baker, *World Settlement*, 1:311.

43. The quotations are from Baker, *American Chronicle*, p. 395; and Tumulty to Wilson, 28 March 1919, ser. 5B, Wilson Papers (Library of Congress). See also Tumulty to Wilson, 16, 25 March 1919, ser. 5B, Wilson Papers (Library of Congress); Journal, 28 March 1919, Box 132, Ray Stannard Baker Papers. Compub was the cable abbreviation for Combined Publishers in New York City, which served, under the auspices of the CPI, as a central clearing station for distribution of press releases and official statements to major newspapers and the three press associations in the United States. See Memorandum, Patchin to Grew, 23 June 1919, DSDF, 184.82/53.

44. The quotations are from Tumulty to Wilson, 30 March 1919, and Tumulty to Grayson, 5 April 1919, ser. 5B, Wilson Papers (Library of Congress). See also Tumulty to Wilson, 19, 29, 30 April 1919, and Tumulty to Grayson, 8 April 1919, ser. 5B, Wilson Papers (Library of Congress).

45. The quotation is from Journal, 28 March 1919, Box 132, Ray Stannard Baker Papers. This story is also related, with the quotation, in Baker, *American Chronicle*, p. 397.

46. The quotation is from Journal, 21 April 1919, Box 132, Ray Stannard Baker Papers. See also Baker, *World Settlement*, 1:xxxiii, 132; Journal, 5, 7, 12 April 1919, Box 132, Ray Stannard Baker Papers; Baker, *American Chronicle*, pp. 396–408; William A. White, *The Autobiography of William Allen White*, p. 554. The basis for Wilson's relationship with House, and perhaps with Baker, has been discussed in Sigmund Freud and William C. Bullitt, *Thomas Woodrow Wilson*, pp. 59–60, 77, 186–92, 201–3.

47. The quotation is from Tumulty to Wilson, 19 April 1919, ser. 5B, Wilson Papers (Library of Congress). See also White to Wilson, 16 April 1919, ser. 5B, Wilson Papers (Library of Congress); Tumulty to Rudolph Forster, 24 April 1919, Box 13, Tumulty Papers; Bailey, *Lost Peace*, pp. 227–37.

48. The quotation is from Wilson to Tumulty, 30 April 1919, ser. 5B, Wilson Papers (Library of Congress). See also Close to Baker, 30 April 1919, Box 125, Ray Stannard Baker Papers; Journal, 25, and 30 April 1919, Box 132, Ray Stannard Baker Papers.

49. The quotations are from Journal, 30 April and 1 May 1919, Box 132, Ray Stannard Baker Papers. See also Wilson to Tumulty, 30 April and 2 May 1919, and Tumulty to Wilson, 1, 2 May 1919, ser. 5B, Wilson Papers (Library of Congress); Baker, *American Chronicle*, pp. 411–18.

50. The quotation is from Lansing to Wilson, 12 April 1919, ser. 5B, Wilson Papers (Library of Congress). See also Journal, 17 April 1919, Box 132, Ray Stannard Baker Papers; Thomas A. Bailey, *Woodrow Wilson and the Great Betrayal*, pp. 3–4.

51. The quotations are from Wilson to Lansing, 3, 5 May 1919, ser. 5B, Wilson Papers (Library of Congress). See also Frank Polk to American Mission, 24 April 1919, and Lansing to Polk, 26 April 1919, ser. 5B, Wilson Papers (Library of Congress); and Baker, *American Chronicle*, pp. 430–31.

52. The quotation is from Tumulty to Wilson, 8 May 1919, ser. 5B, Wilson Papers (Library of Congress). See also American Mission to Secretary of State, 6 May 1919, ser. 5B, Wilson Papers (Library of Congress); Journal, 9 May 1919, Box 132, Ray Stannard Baker Papers; and Baker, *American Chronicle*, pp. 419–20. Baker also managed to master the "complicated" problem of sending maps along with the summaries. Journal, 2 May 1919, Box 132, Ray Stannard Baker Papers.

53. The quotations are from Tumulty to Wilson, 22 May 1919, Wilson to Tumulty, 24 May 1919, and Wilson to Lansing, 24 May 1919, ser. 5B, Wilson Papers (Library of Congress). See also Journal, 23 May 1919, Box 132, Ray Stannard Baker Papers; Tumulty to Wilson, 26 May 1919, Polk to Lansing, 4 June 1919, and Lansing to Wilson, 7 June 1919, ser. 5B, Wilson Papers (Library of Congress).

54. Lansing to Wilson, 7 June 1919, Box 43, Lansing Papers; Baker, *American*

Chronicle, p. 444; Polk to Lansing, 4, 5, 6 June 1919; Lansing to Wilson, 8 June 1919; Tumulty to Wilson, 4, 5 June 1919; Wilson to Tumulty, 7 June 1919, and Polk to Ammission (cable abbreviation for American Commission), 9 June 1919, ser. 5B, Wilson Papers (Library of Congress). Ultimately, the treaty was released for publication on 17 June by the CPI's Compub facilities in New York. Memorandum from Frederick A. Emery, August 1919, DSDF, 763.72119/6995.

55. The quotations are from Tumulty to Wilson, 21 November 1919, Box 5, Tumulty Papers; and Tumulty to Wilson, 16 June 1919, ser. 5B, Wilson Papers (Library of Congress). See also Close to Tumulty, 2 April 1919, Polk to Ammission, 31 May 1919, and Wilson to Tumulty, 18 December 1918, ser. 5B, Wilson Papers (Library of Congress).

56. The quotations are from Grayson to Tumulty, 12 December 1918, Box 1, Tumulty Papers; and Grayson to Tumulty, 23 December 1918, ser. 5B, Wilson Papers (Library of Congress). See also Polk to Lansing, 20 December 1918, and Baker to Grayson, 5 February 1919, ser. 5B, Wilson Papers (Library of Congress).

57. The quotations are from Journal, 21 December 1918, Box 132, Ray Stannard Baker Papers; and Tumulty to Grayson, 28 December 1918, ser. 5B, Wilson Papers (Library of Congress). See also Grayson to Tumulty, 31 December 1918, ser. 5B, Wilson Papers (Library of Congress).

58. The quotations are from Tumulty to Wilson, 14 January 1919, ser. 5B, Wilson Papers (Library of Congress); and Tumulty to Grayson, 18 May 1919, Box 1, Tumulty Papers. See also Grayson to Tumulty, 19 May 1919, ser. 5B, Wilson Papers (Library of Congress); Journal, 12 April 1919, Box 132, Ray Stannard Baker Papers; Tumulty to House, 25 June 1919, ser. 5B, Wilson Papers (Library of Congress).

59. Ammission to Secretary of State, 6 May 1919, and Polk to Lansing, 4, 5, 6, 9 June 1919, ser. 5B, Wilson Papers (Library of Congress); William Phillips to Lansing, 13 September 1919, Box 46, Lansing Papers; Baker, *American Chronicle*, pp. 424–25, 429.

60. The quotations are from Grayson to Tumulty, 10 April 1919, Box 1, Tumulty Papers; Grayson to Tumulty, 19 May 1919, and Wilson to Tumulty, 7 June 1919, ser. 5B, Wilson Papers (Library of Congress). See also Journal, 23 December 1918 and 12 April 1919, Box 132, Ray Stannard Baker Papers; White, *Autobiography*, p. 554.

61. Wilson to Tumulty, 19 December 1918, Box 5, Tumulty Papers; Creel to Wilson, 3 February 1919, ser. 5B, Wilson Papers (Library of Congress); Creel, *How We Advertised America*, pp. 410–13; Close to Foster, 18 December 1918, and List of Press Correspondents, 13 January 1919, ser. 5B, Wilson Papers (Library of Congress); Organization Chart, Box 9, Newton Baker Papers.

62. The quotations are from Wilson to Tumulty, 17 June 1919, and Wilson to Lansing, 24 May 1919, ser. 5B, Wilson Papers (Library of Congress).

63. The quotation is from Tumulty to Wilson, 29 April 1919, ser. 5B, Wilson Papers (Library of Congress). See also Tumulty to Wilson, 7 January and 13 June 1919, ser. 5B, Wilson Papers (Library of Congress); Wilson to Tumulty, 2 May 1919, in Tumulty, *Wilson*, p. 546; Tumulty, *Wilson*, pp. 434, 438; *New York Times*, 25 February 1919.

64. The quotations are from Tumulty to Wilson, 3, 9 June 1919, ser. 5B, Wilson Papers (Library of Congress). See also Memorandum, "Agenda for the Consideration of the Proposed Tour," June 1919, Box 6, Tumulty Papers; Tumulty to Wilson, 5, 17, 27 June 1919, Polk to Lansing, 1 June 1919, and former Ambassador William G. Sharp to Wilson, 21 June 1919, ser. 5B, Wilson Papers (Library of Congress).

65. The quotations are from Wilson to Tumulty, 16 June 1919, and Wilson to Lamont, 23 June 1919, ser. 5B, Wilson Papers (Library of Congress). See also Wilson to Tumulty, 5, 12 June 1919, ser. 5B, Wilson Papers (Library of Congress). Tumulty

was less than pleased by Wilson's inclusion of Lamont in what he regarded as his personal bailiwick. On 17 June he cabled the president that along with his other plans for a tour of the country he had already made contact with Taft's organization. See Tumulty to Wilson, 17 June 1919, ser. 5B, Wilson Papers (Library of Congress).

66. Tumulty to Wilson, 25 June 1919, Tumulty to Grayson, 27 June 1919, and Wilson to Tumulty, 27 June 1919, ser. 5B, Wilson Papers (Library of Congress).

67. The quotation is from Baker, *American Chronicle*, p. 457. See also *New York Times*, 9 July 1919; Wilson to Tumulty, 27 June 1919, ser. 5B, Wilson Papers (Library of Congress); Bailey, *Great Betrayal*, pp. 1–2.

68. The quotations are from Memorandum, Tumulty to Wilson, June 1919, and Tumulty to Wilson, 3 July 1919, ser. 5B, Wilson Papers (Library of Congress).

69. The message is in ser. 7B, Wilson Papers (Library of Congress). See also *Washington Post*, 11 July 1919; Bailey, *Great Betrayal*, pp. 4–7.

70. The quotations are from Tumulty to Wilson, 15 August 1919, Box 7, Tumulty Papers; House to Lansing and Wilson, 30 August 1919, Box 46, Lansing Papers. See also Creel to Tumulty, 28 August 1919, Box 14, Tumulty Papers; Grayson, *Wilson*, p. 95; Tumulty, *Wilson*, pp. 434, 438; James H. Dunn, *From Harrison to Harding*, pp. 382–83; Gene Smith, *When the Cheering Stopped*, pp. 57–59; Bailey, *Great Betrayal*, pp. 92–93.

71. Memorandum, "Agenda for the Consideration of the Proposed Tour," June 1919, Box 6, Tumulty Papers; Blum, *Tumulty*, p. 209; Tumulty, *Wilson*, p. 438; Smith, *When the Cheering Stopped*, p. 60; Bailey, *Great Betrayal*, pp. 101–3.

72. Scrapbooks, prepared by John R. Bolling, ser. 9, Wilson Papers (Library of Congress); Lawrence, *True Story*, pp. 104–7; Smith, *When the Cheering Stopped*, pp. 60–67; Bailey, *Great Betrayal*, pp. 105–9.

73. Scrapbooks, ser. 9, Wilson Papers (Library of Congress); Vance McCormick to Tumulty, ser. 4, file 470, Wilson Papers (Library of Congress). It can be argued, of course, that the real heart of enemy territory was the Northeast, which Tumulty had decided from the first to avoid on the president's speaking tour. The secretary apparently believed there was no hope of influencing opposition senators from that section of the country and decided to concentrate on the seemingly more tractable westerners. He chose to eliminate the South for the opposite reason. See Memorandum, "Agenda for the Consideration of the Proposed Tour," June 1919, Box 6, Tumulty Papers.

74. The quotation is from Tumulty to Wilson, 24 September 1919, Box 7, Tumulty Papers. See also Tumulty to Forster, 6 September 1919, ser. 4, file 470, Wilson Papers (Library of Congress); Tumulty to Wilson, 12, 19, 20, 24 September 1919, Box 7, Tumulty Papers; and Blum, *Tumulty*, pp. 210–13.

75. The quotation is from *New York Times*, 21 September 1919. See also Journal, 21 September 1919, Box 125, Ray Stannard Baker Papers; Scrapbooks, ser. 9, Wilson Papers (Library of Congress); Lawrence, *True Story*, pp. 275–81; Smith, *When the Cheering Stopped*, pp. 76–77; Bailey, *Great Betrayal*, pp. 110–12.

76. The conclusion of Wilson's speech is quoted in Smith, *When the Cheering Stopped*, p. 82. See also Scrapbooks, ser. 9, Wilson Papers (Library of Congress); Tumulty, *Wilson*, p. 449; Bailey, *Great Betrayal*, pp. 113–14. Despite Wilson's brilliance at Pueblo, the fact that he stumbled over one sentence in the speech has provoked a malicious legend about his coherence at the time. See Lillian Rogers Parks, *My Thirty Years Backstairs at the White House*, p. 154; Edmund W. Starling, *Starling of the White House*, p. 152. For the opposite viewpoint, see Scrapbooks, ser. 9, Wilson Papers (Library of Congress); Tumulty, *Wilson*, p. 449.

77. The quotation is from Woodrow Wilson, *Constitutional Government in the*

United States, pp. 139–40. See also Scrapbooks, ser. 9, Wilson Papers (Library of Congress); Tumulty to Wilson, 30 September 1919, ser. 5B, Wilson Papers (Library of Congress); Charles E. Morris to Tumulty, 1 October 1919, Box 14, Tumulty Papers; Bailey, *Great Betrayal*, pp. 93–97, 120–21, 266–70.

78. The quotation is from Baker, *American Chronicle*, p. 462. See also Lawrence, *True Story*, pp. 340–41.

Conclusion

1. The quotation is from J. Frederick Essary, *Covering Washington*, p. 83. Essary was the Washington correspondent of the *Baltimore Sun* during this period. See also Elmer E. Cornwell, Jr., "Presidential News," pp. 275–85.

2. The quotations are from Hans H. Gerth and C. Wright Mills, *From Max Weber*, pp. 246ff. For an example of a work citing Roosevelt as the originator of self-conscious presidential publicity, see Sidney Warren, *The President as World Leader*, pp. 20–23.

3. See Robert W. Desmond, *The Press and World Affairs*, pp. 63, 96–98.

4. The quotation is from Arthur M. Schlesinger, Jr., *The Imperial Presidency*, p. 208.

5. The quotation is from Graham Wallas, *Human Nature in Politics*, pp. 98–113. See also Edward A. Ross, *Social Control*; Herbert Croly, *The Promise of American Life*, pp. 265–300, 399–454; Richard T. Ely, "Progressivism, True and False," pp. 209–11; Walter Lippmann, *A Preface to Politics*, pp. 228–30, 235–37, 317, and *Public Opinion*, pp. 253–316, 358–65, 398–418. For a contemporary counterweight to Lippmann, see Abbott Lawrence Lowell, *Public Opinion in War and Peace*, pp. 40, 96–99.

6. The quotations are from V. O. Key, *Public Opinion and American Democracy*, p. 414; and Douglas Cater, "The President and the Press," p. 55.

7. The quotation is from Melvin Small, "Historians Look at Public Opinion," p. 14.

8. The quotation is from Bernard C. Cohen, "The Relationship between Public Opinion and Foreign Policy Maker," p. 68.

9. See Key, *Public Opinion*, pp. 293–405; James N. Rosenau, *Public Opinion and Foreign Policy*, pp. 45–92; and Elihu Katz and Paul Lazarsfield, *Personal Influence*. For a discussion of presidential support in time of crisis, see Nelson W. Polsby, *Congress and the Presidency*, pp. 25–26.

10. The quotation is from Walter Lippmann, *The Public Philosophy*, p. 48. See also Dexter Perkins, *Foreign Policy and the American Spirit*, chap. 4.

Bibliography

Manuscript Collections

Princeton, N.J.
  Firestone Library
    Charles L. Swem Papers
    Charles W. Thompson Papers
    Woodrow Wilson Papers
Fremont, Ohio
  Rutherford B. Hayes Memorial Library
    Rutherford B. Hayes Papers
Washington, D.C.
  Library of Congress
    Chester A. Arthur Papers
    Newton D. Baker Papers
    Ray Stannard Baker Papers
    Thomas F. Bayard Papers
    Grover Cleveland Papers
    George B. Cortelyou Papers
    George Creel Papers
    Hamilton Fish Papers
    James A. Garfield Papers
    Ulysses S. Grant Papers
    Walter Q. Gresham Papers
    Benjamin Harrison Papers
    Philander Knox Papers
    Robert Lansing Papers
    William McKinley Papers
    Richard Olney Papers
    Whitelaw Reid Papers
    Theodore Roosevelt Papers
    Elihu Root Papers
    William Howard Taft Papers
    Joseph P. Tumulty Papers
    Woodrow Wilson Papers
  National Archives
    William J. Bryan Papers
    Committee on Public Information Records
    Correspondence of Secretary of State Bryan with
      President Wilson, 1913–15
    State Department Records
    War Department Records
Collegeville, Pa.
  Ursinus College
    Francis M. Huntington Wilson Papers

Published Documents

U.S. Congress. *Congressional Record*.
U.S. Department of State. *Foreign Relations of the United States*.
U.S. Government Printing Office. *Register of the Department of State*.
————. *Spanish Diplomatic Correspondence and Documents, 1896–1900: Presented to the Cortes by the Minister of State*. 1905.

Published Journals, Diaries, and Papers

Bryan, William Jennings. *The Memoirs of William Jennings Bryan*. Edited by Mary Bryan. Philadelphia: John C. Winston Co., 1925.
Butt, Archie. *Taft and Roosevelt: The Intimate Letters of Archie Butt, Military Aide*. 2 vols. Garden City, N.Y.: Doubleday, Doran, 1930.
Daniels, Josephus. *The Cabinet Diaries of Josephus Daniels, 1913–1921*. Edited by E. David Cronon. Lincoln: University of Nebraska Press, 1963.
Dawes, Charles G. *A Journal of the McKinley Years*. Chicago: Lakeside Press, 1950.
Garfield, James Abram. *The Works of James Abram Garfield*. 2 vols. Edited by Burke A. Hinsdale. Boston: James R. Osgood and Co., 1882–83.
Harrison, Benjamin, and Blaine, James G. *The Correspondence between Benjamin Harrison and James G. Blaine, 1882–1893*. Edited by Albert T. Volwiler. Memoirs of the American Philosophical Society, vol. 14. Philadelphia: American Philosophical Society, 1940.
House, Edward M. *The Intimate Papers of Colonel House*. 4 vols. Edited by Charles Seymour. Boston: Houghton Mifflin Co., 1926.
Long, John Davis. *America of Yesterday: As Reflected in the Journal of John Davis Long*. Edited by Lawrence Shaw Mayo. Boston: Atlantic Monthly Press, 1923.
McKinley, William. *The Speeches and Addresses of William McKinley from March 1, 1897, to May 30, 1900*. New York: Doubleday and McClure, 1900.
Reid, Whitelaw. *Making Peace with Spain: The Diary of Whitelaw Reid, September–December, 1898*. Edited by H. Wayne Morgan. Austin: University of Texas Press, 1965.
Roosevelt, Theodore. *The Letters of Theodore Roosevelt*. 8 vols. Edited by Elting E. Morison. Cambridge, Mass.: Harvard University Press, 1951.
Washington, George, et al. *A Compilation of the Messages and Papers of the Presidents, 1789–1905*. 11 vols. Edited by James D. Richardson. Washington, D.C.: Government Printing Office. 1905.
Wilson, Woodrow. *The Public Papers of Woodrow Wilson*. 6 vols. Edited by Ray S. Baker and William E. Dodd. New York: Harper and Brothers, 1925–27.

Iowa Newspapers

Bloomfield Republican
Boone County Democrat
Saturday Evening Post (Burlington)
Burlington Weekly Hawk-Eye
Carroll Herald
Carroll Sentinal
Cedar Rapids Evening Gazette

Clinton Age
Clinton Herald
Council Bluffs Nonpareil
Davenport Daily Democrat
Davenport Daily Gazette
Denison Review
Des Moines Daily News
Des Moines Leader
Dubuque Daily Telegraph
Dubuque Daily Times
Dubuque Herald
Eldora Herald
Weekly Northern Vindicator (Estherville)
Greenfield Transcript
Iowa Citizen (Iowa City)
Iowa State Press (Iowa City)
Jefferson Bee
Keokuk Daily Gate City
Lansing Mirror and Chronicle
Maquoketa Excelsior
Marengo Republican
Evening Times-Republican (Marshalltown)
North Iowa Times (McGregor)
Monticello Express
Mount Vernon Hawk-Eye
Oskaloosa Weekly Herald
Ottumwa Courier
Sioux City Daily Journal
Sioux City Tribune
Spencer Daily Reporter
Storm Lake Pilot-Tribune
Vinton Review
Washington Press
Waterloo Daily Reporter
Waukon Standard
West Branch Times
West Union Republican Gazette
Winnebago Summit

Published Sources

Abbott, Lawrence F. *Impressions of Theodore Roosevelt*. Garden City, N.Y.: Double-
    day, Page and Co., 1919.
Baker, Ray Stannard. *American Chronicle: The Autobiography of Ray Stannard
    Baker*. New York: Charles Scribner's Sons, 1945.
_____. "Wilson." *Collier's* 58 (7 October 1916): 5–6.
_____. *Woodrow Wilson and World Settlement*. 3 vols. Garden City, N.Y.: Doubleday,
    Page and Co., 1922.
Barry, David S. *Forty Years in Washington*. Boston: Little, Brown and Co., 1924.
_____. "News-Getting at the Capital." *Chautauquan* 26, no. 3 (December 1897).

Benson, Allan L. "The Politics of Preparedness." *Pearson's Magazine*, February 1916.

Blaine, James G. *Twenty Years of Congress: From Lincoln to Garfield*. Norwich, Conn.: Henry Bill Publishing Co., 1884.

Blythe, Samuel G. "A Talk with the President." *Saturday Evening Post* 186 (9 January 1915): 3–4, 37–38.

Cleveland, Grover. *The Venezuela Boundary Controversy*. Princeton, N.J.: Princeton University Press, 1913.

Cole, Cyrenus. *I Remember I Remember: A Book of Recollections*. Iowa City: State Historical Society of Iowa, 1936.

Colman, Edna M. *White House Gossip: From Andrew Johnson to Calvin Coolidge*. Garden City, N.Y.: Doubleday, Page and Co., 1927.

Creel, George. *How We Advertised America*. New York: Harper and Brothers, 1920.

_____. "Propaganda and Morale." *American Journal of Sociology* 47 (November 1941).

_____. *Rebel at Large: Recollections of Fifty Crowded Years*. New York: G. P. Putnam's Sons, 1947.

_____. "Woodrow Wilson's Last Years." *Saturday Evening Post* 203, no. 28 (10 January 1931).

_____. "Woodrow Wilson: The Man behind the President." *Saturday Evening Post* 203, no. 39 (28 March 1931).

Croly, Herbert. *The Promise of American Life*. New York: Macmillan Co., 1909.

Davis, Oscar King. *Released for Publication: Some Inside Political History of Theodore Roosevelt and His Times, 1898–1918*. Boston: Houghton Mifflin Co., 1925.

Dunn, Arthur W. *From Harrison to Harding: A Personal Narrative Covering a Third of a Century, 1888–1921*. 2 vols. New York: G. P. Putnam's Sons, 1922.

Ely, Richard T. "Progressivism, True and False: An Outline." *Review of Reviews* 51 (February 1915).

Essary, J. Frederick. *Covering Washington: Government Reflected to the Public in the Press, 1822–1926*. Boston: Houghton Mifflin Co., 1927.

Ford, Guy Stanton. "The Fight for Public Opinion." *Minnesota History Bulletin* 3 (February 1919).

Garrison, Lindley M. "Reasonable Preparation." *Independent* 82 (16 August 1915).

Grayson, Cary T. *Woodrow Wilson: An Intimate Memoir*. New York: Holt, Rinehart and Winston, 1960.

Grew, Joseph. *Turbulent Era: A Diplomatic Record of Forty Years, 1904–1945*. 2 vols. London: Hammond, 1953.

Halford, E. W. "Family Life in the White House." *Leslie's Weekly* 129, no. 3341 (20 September 1919).

Halstead, Ablert. "The President at Work: A Character Sketch." *Independent* 53, no. 2753 (5 September 1901).

Heaton, John L. *Cobb of "The World": A Leader in Liberalism*. New York: E. P. Dutton, 1924.

Hoar, George F. *Autobiography of Seventy Years*. 2 vols. Boston: Charles Scribner's Sons, 1903.

Hoover, Irwin Hood. *Forty-Two Years at the White House*. Boston: Houghton Mifflin Co., 1934.

Houston, David F. *Eight Years with Wilson's Cabinet, 1913–1920*. 2 vols. Garden City, N.Y.: Doubleday, Page and Co., 1926.

Huntington Wilson, Francis M. *Memoirs of an Ex-Diplomat*. Boston: B. Humphries, 1945.

Kohlsaat, Herman H. *From McKinley to Harding: Personal Recollections of Our Presidents*. New York: Charles Scribner's Sons, 1923.

Lansing, Robert. *The War Memoirs of Robert Lansing*. New York: Bobbs-Merrill Co., 1935.

Lawrence, David. *The True Story of Woodrow Wilson*. New York: George H. Doran Co., 1924.

Link, Arthur S., ed. *The Papers of Woodrow Wilson*. 30 vols. Princeton, N.J.: Princeton University Press, 1966–79.

Lippmann, Walter. *A Preface to Politics*. New York: Kennerley, 1913.

———. *Public Opinion*. New York: Macmillan Co., 1922.

———. *The Public Philosophy*. Boston: Little, Brown and Co., 1955.

Lodge, Henry Cabot. *The Senate and the League of Nations*. New York: Charles Scribner's Sons, 1925.

Lowell, Abbott Lawrence. *Public Opinion in War and Peace*. Cambridge, Mass.: Harvard University Press, 1923.

Lowry, Edward G. *Washington Close-ups: Intimate Views of Some Public Figures*. Boston: Houghton Mifflin Co., 1921.

———. "What the President Is Trying to Do for Mexico." *World's Work* 27 (January 1914):261–66.

Marcosson, Isaac. *Adventures in Interviewing*. New York: John Lane, 1919.

Markham, Edwin; Lindsey, Benjamin; and Creel, George. *Children in Bondage*. New York: Hearst's International Library Co., 1914.

Norton, C. B. *The President and His Cabinet*. Boston: Cupples and Howard, 1888.

Parker, George F. *Recollections of Grover Cleveland*. New York: Century Co., 1909.

Parks, Lillian Rogers. *My Thirty Years Backstairs at the White House*. New York: Fleet Publishing Co., 1961.

Poore, Benjamin Perley. *Perley's Reminiscences of Sixty Years in the National Metropolis*. 2 vols. Philadelphia: Hubbard Brothers, 1886.

Roosevelt, Nicholas. *Theodore Roosevelt: The Man as I Knew Him*. New York: Dodd, Mead and Co., 1967.

Roosevelt, Theodore. *Autobiography*. New York: Charles Scribner's Sons, 1913.

Ross, Edward Allsworth. *Social Control: A Survey of the Foundations of Order*. New York: Macmillan Co., 1901.

Smith, Charles Emory. "McKinley in the Cabinet Room." *Saturday Evening Post*, 11 October 1902.

Smith, Ira T. *Dear Mr. President: The Story of Fifty Years in the White House Mail Room*. New York: Julian Messner, 1949.

Starling, Edmund W. *Starling of the White House*. New York: Simon and Schuster, 1946.

Stealey, Orlando O. *Twenty Years in the Press Gallery*. New York: Publishers Printing Co., 1906.

Steffens, Lincoln. *The Autobiography of Lincoln Steffens*. New York: Harcourt, Brace, and Co., 1931.

Sumner, Charles. *Republicanism vs. Grantism*. Washington, D.C.: Rives and Bailey, 1872.

Taft, William H. *Our Chief Magistrate and His Powers*. New York: Columbia University Press, 1916.

Tarbell, Ida. "A Talk with the President of the United States." *Collier's Weekly* 58 (28 October 1916): 5–6, 40.

———. "President McKinley in War Times." *McClure's Magazine* 11, no. 3 (July 1898).

Thompson, Charles Willis. *Presidents I've Known and Two Near Presidents*. Indianapolis: Bobbs-Merrill Co., 1929.

Tumulty, Joseph P. "In the White House Looking Glass." *New York Times*, 31 December 1921.

_____. *Woodrow Wilson as I Know Him*. Garden City, N.Y.: Doubleday, Page and Co., 1921.

Wallas, Graham. *Human Nature in Politics*. London: Constable, 1908.

White, William Allen. *The Autobiography of William Allen White*. New York: Macmillan Co., 1946.

Wilson, Henry Lane. *Diplomatic Episodes in Mexico, Belgium, and Chile*. New York: Doubleday, Page and Co., 1927.

Wilson, Woodrow. *Congressional Government: A Study in American Politics*. New York: World Publishing Co., 1885.

_____. *Constitutional Government in the United States*. New York: World Publishing Co., 1908.

Books and Articles

Allport, Floyd H. "Toward a Science of Public Opinion." *Public Opinion Quarterly* 1, no. 1 (January 1937).

Almond, Gabriel. *The American People and Foreign Policy*. New York: Harcourt, Brace and Co., 1950.

Anderson, Donald F. *William Howard Taft: A Conservative's Conception of the Presidency*. Ithaca, N.Y.: Cornell University Press, 1973.

Auxier, George. "Middle-Western Newspapers and the Spanish-American War, 1895–1898." *Mississippi Valley Historical Review* 26, no. 4 (March 1940).

Bailey, Thomas A. *The Man in the Street: The Impact of American Public Opinion on Foreign Policy*. New York: Macmillan Co., 1948.

_____. *Theodore Roosevelt and the Japanese-American Crises*. Palo Alto, Cal.,: Stanford University Press, 1934.

_____. *Woodrow Wilson and the Great Betrayal*. New York: Macmillan Co., 1945.

_____. *Woodrow Wilson and the Lost Peace*. New York: Macmillan Co., 1944.

Baker, Ray Stannard. *Woodrow Wilson: Life and Letters*. 8 vols. Garden City, N.Y.: Doubleday, Doran and Co., 1931.

Beale, Howard K. *Theodore Roosevelt and the Rise of America to World Power*. Baltimore: Johns Hopkins University Press, 1956.

Beisner, Robert L. *From the Old Diplomacy to the New, 1865–1900*. New York: Thomas Y. Crowell Co., 1975.

_____. *Twelve against Empire: The Anti-Imperialists, 1898–1900*. New York: McGraw-Hill, 1968.

Benson, Lee. "An Approach to the Scientific Study of Past Public Opinion," *Public Opinion Quarterly* 21, no. 4 (Winter 1967–68).

Blum, John Morton. *Joe Tumulty and the Wilson Era*. Boston: Houghton Mifflin Co., 1951.

_____. *The Republican Roosevelt*. Cambridge, Mass.: Harvard University Press, 1954.

_____. *Woodrow Wilson and the Politics of Morality*. Boston: Houghton Mifflin Co., 1956.

Bobrow, Davis B. "Organization of American National Security Opinions." *Public Opinion Quarterly* 33, no. 2 (Summer 1969).

Brown, Charles H. *The Correspondents' War: Journalists in the Spanish-American War*. New York: Charles Scribner's Sons, 1967.

Bryant, Samuel W. *The Sea and the States: A Maritime History of the American People*. New York: Thomas Y. Crowell Co., 1947.

Busbey, L. White. *Uncle Joe Cannon: The Story of a Pioneer American*. New York: H. Holt and Co., 1927.

Califano, Joseph A., Jr. *A Presidential Nation*. New York: W. W. Norton and Co., 1975.

Canfield, Bertrand R. *Public Relations: Principles, Cases, and Problems*. Homewood, Ill.: Richard P. Irwin, 1956.

Carpenter, John A. *Ulysses S. Grant*. New York: Twayne Publishers, 1970.

Cater, Douglas. "The President and the Press." *Annals of the American Academy of Political and Social Science*, September 1956.

Chessman, G. Wallace. *Theodore Roosevelt and the Politics of Power*. Boston: Little, Brown and Co., 1969.

Childs, Harwood L. *Public Opinion: Nature, Formation, and Role*. Princeton, N.J.: D. Van Nostrand Co., 1965.

Chittick, William O. *State Department, Press, and Pressure Groups: A Role Analysis*. New York: John Wiley and Sons, 1970.

Cohen, Bernard C. *The Press and Foreign Policy*. Princeton, N.J.: Princeton University Press, 1963.

_____. "The Relationship between Public Opinion and Foreign Policy Maker." In *Public Opinion and Historians: Interdisciplinary Perspectives*, edited by Melvin Small. Detroit: Wayne State University Press, 1970.

Coletta, Paolo E. "Bryan, McKinley, and the Treaty of Paris." *Pacific Historical Review* 26 (May 1957).

_____. "Prologue: William McKinley and the Conduct of American Foreign Relations." In *Threshold to American Internationalism: Essays on the Foreign Policies of William McKinley*, edited by Paolo Coletta. New York: Exposition Press, 1970.

_____. "The Peace Negotiations and the Treaty of Paris." In *Threshold to American Internationalism: Essays on the Foreign Policies of William McKinley*, edited by Paolo Coletta. New York: Exposition Press, 1970.

_____. *The Presidency of William Howard Taft*. Lawrence: University of Kansas Press, 1973.

Cornwell, Elmer E., Jr. *Presidential Leadership of Public Opinion*. Bloomington: University of Indiana Press, 1965.

_____. "Presidential News: The Expanding Public Image." *Journalism Quarterly* 36 (1959).

_____. "The Press Conferences of Woodrow Wilson." *Journalism Quarterly* 39 (1962).

Cortissoz, Royal. *The Life of Whitelaw Reid*. 2 vols. New York: Charles Scribner's Sons, 1921.

Cutlip, Scott M., and Center, Allen H. *Effective Public Relations*. Englewood Cliffs, N.J.: Prentice-Hall, 1964.

Dafoe, John W. "Public Opinion as a Factor in Government." In *Public Opinion and World Politics*, edited by Quincy Wright. Chicago: University of Chicago Press, 1973.

De Fleur, Melvin L. *Theories of Mass Communication*. New York: David McKay Co., 1966.

Dennett, Tyler. *John Hay: From Poetry to Politics*. New York: Dodd, Mead and Co., 1933.

Desmond, Robert W. *The Press and World Affairs*. New York: D. Appleton-Century Co., 1937.

Dickey, John S. "The Secretary and the American Public." In *The Secretary of State*, edited by Don K. Price. Englewood Cliffs, N.J.: Prentice-Hall, 1960.

Doob, Leonard. *Public Opinion and Propaganda*. 2d ed. Hamden, Conn.: Archon Books, 1966.

Dulebohn, George Roscoe. *Principles of Foreign Policy under the Cleveland Administrations*. Philadelphia: University of Pennsylvania Press, 1941.

Dulles, Foster Rhea. *The Imperial Years*. New York: Thomas Y. Crowell Co., 1956.

―――. *Prelude to World Power: American Diplomatic History, 1860–1900*. New York: Macmillan Co., 1965.

Freidel, Frank. "Dissent in the Spanish-American War and the Philippine Insurrection." In Samuel Eliot Morrison, Frederick Merk, and Frank Freidel, *Dissent in Three American Wars*. Cambridge, Mass.: Harvard University Press, 1970.

Freud, Sigmund, and Bullitt, William C. *Thomas Woodrow Wilson*. Boston: Houghton Mifflin, 1967.

George, Alexander L., and George, Juliette L. *Woodrow Wilson and Colonel House: A Personality Study*. New York: Dover Publications, 1956.

Gerth, Hans H., and Mills, C. Wright. *From Max Weber: Essays in Sociology*. New York: Oxford University Press, 1958.

Gillis, James Andrew. *The Hawaiian Incident: An Examination of Mr. Cleveland's Attitude toward the Revolution of 1893*. Reprint. Books for Libraries Press, no date.

Grant, Ulysses S., III. *Ulysses S. Grant: Warrior and Statesman*. New York: William Morrow and Co., 1969.

Grieb, Kenneth J. *The United States and Huerta*. Lincoln: University of Nebraska Press, 1969.

Gruber, Carol S. *Mars and Minerva: World War I and the Uses of Higher Learning*. Baton Rouge: Louisiana State University Press, 1975.

Haber, Samuel. *Efficiency and Uplift: Scientific Management in the Progressive Era, 1890–1920*. Chicago: University of Chicago Press, 1964.

Harrington, Fred H. "The Anti-Imperialist Movement in the United States, 1898–1900." *Mississippi Valley Historical Review* 22, no. 2 (September 1935).

Hays, Samuel P. *Conservation and the Gospel of Efficiency: The Progressive Conservation Movement, 1890–1920*. Cambridge, Mass.: Harvard University Press, 1959.

Hennessey, Bernard C. *Public Opinion*. 2d ed. Belmont, Calif.: Wadsworth Publishing Co., 1970.

Hill, Norman L. *Mr. Secretary of State*. New York: Random House, 1963.

Hofstadter, Richard. *The American Political Tradition and the Men Who Made It*. New York: Alfred A. Knopf, 1948.

―――. "Manifest Destiny and the Philippines." In *America in Crisis*, edited by Daniel Aaron. New York: Alfred A. Knopf, 1952.

Hovland, Carl I.; Janis, Irving L.; and Kelley, Harold H. *Communication and Persuasion: Psychological Studies of Opinion Change*. New Haven, Conn.: Yale University Press, 1953.

Hulen, Bertram D. *Inside the Department of State*. New York: McGraw-Hill, 1939.

Hunt, Gaillard. *The Department of State of the United States: Its History and Functions*. New Haven, Conn.: Yale University Press, 1914.

Jessup, Philip. *Elihu Root*. 2 vols. New York: Dodd, Mead and Co., 1938.

Kaplan, Justin. *Lincoln Steffens: A Biography*. New York: Simon and Schuster, 1974.

Katz, Elihu, and Lazarsfield, Paul. *Personal Influence*. Glencoe, Ill.: Free Press, 1955.

Key, V. O. *Public Opinion and American Democracy*. New York: Alfred A. Knopf, 1961.

———. "Public Opinion and the Decay of Democracy." *Virginia Quarterly Review* 37, no. 4 (1961).

———. *The Responsible Electorate: Rationality in Presidential Voting, 1936–1960.* Cambridge, Mass.: Harvard University Press, 1966.

La Feber, Walter. *The New Empire: An Interpretation of American Expansion, 1860–1900.* Ithaca, N.Y.: Cornell University Press, 1963.

Langley, Lester D. *The Cuban Policy of the United States: A Brief History.* New York: John Wiley and Sons, 1968.

Lasch, Christopher. "The Anti-Imperialists, the Philippines, and the Inequality of Man." *Journal of Southern History* 24, no. 3 (August 1958).

Lasswell, Harold D. *Propaganda Techniques in the World War.* London: Kegan Paul, Trench, Trubner and Co., 1927.

Lazarsfield, Paul F. "The Historian and the Pollster." In *Common Frontiers of the Social Sciences*, edited by Mirra Komarovsky. Glencoe, Ill.: Free Press, 1957.

Leech, Margaret. *In the Days of McKinley.* New York: Harper and Brothers, 1959.

Levin, N. Gordon, Jr. *Woodrow Wilson and World Politics: America's Response to War and Revolution.* Oxford: Oxford University Press, 1968.

Levine, Lawrence W. *Defender of the Faith, William Jennings Bryan: The Last Decade, 1915–1925.* Oxford: Oxford University Press, 1965.

Link, Arthur S. *Wilson: Campaigns for Progressivism and Peace, 1916–1917.* Princeton, N.J.: Princeton University Press, 1965.

———. *Wilson: Confusions and Crises, 1915–1916.* Princeton, N.J.: Princeton University Press, 1964.

———. *Wilson: The Road to the White House.* Princeton, N.J.: Princeton University Press, 1947.

———. *Wilson: The Struggle for Neutrality.* Princeton, N.J.: Princeton University Press, 1960.

———. *Wilson the Diplomatist: A Look at His Major Foreign Policies.* Baltimore: Johns Hopkins University Press, 1957.

———. *Woodrow Wilson and the Progressive Era, 1910–1917.* New York: Harper and Brothers, 1954.

Markel, Lester. *Public Opinion and Foreign Policy.* New York: Harper and Brothers, 1959.

May, Ernest R. *American Imperialism: A Speculative Essay.* New York: Atheneum, 1968.

———. *Imperial Democracy: The Emergence of America as a Great Power.* New York: Harcourt, Brace and World, 1961.

McCain, William D. *The United States and the Republic of Panama.* Durham, N.C.: Duke University Press, 1937.

McCormick, Thomas J. *China Market: America's Quest for Informal Empire, 1893–1901.* Chicago: Quadrangle, 1967.

McQuail, Denis. *Towards a Sociology of Mass Communications.* London: Collier, Macmillan, 1969.

Millis, Walter. *The Martial Spirit: A Study of Our War with Spain.* Boston: Houghton Mifflin Co., 1931.

Mock, James R. *Censorship, 1917.* Princeton, N.J.: Princeton University Press, 1941.

Mock, James R., and Larson, Cedric. *Words That Won the War: The Story of the Committee on Public Information, 1917–1919.* Princeton, N.J.: Princeton University Press, 1939.

Morgan, H. Wayne. *America's Road to Empire: The War with Spain and Overseas*

Expansion. New York: John Wiley and Sons, 1965.

———. *From Hayes to McKinley: National Party Politics, 1877–1896*. Syracuse, N.Y.: Syracuse University Press, 1969.

———. *William McKinley and His America*. Syracuse, N.Y.: Syracuse University Press, 1963.

Mowry, George. *The Era of Theodore Roosevelt and the Birth of Modern America, 1900–1912*. New York: Harper and Row, 1958.

———. *Theodore Roosevelt and the Progressive Movement*. New York: Hill and Wang, 1946.

Nevins, Allan. *Grover Cleveland: A Study in Courage*. New York: Dodd, Mead and Co., 1933.

———. *Hamilton Fish: The Inner History of the Grant Administration*. 2 vols. Rev. ed. New York: Frederick Ungar Publishing Co., 1957.

Nichols, Jeannett P. "The United States Congress and Imperialism, 1861–1897." *Journal of Economic History* 21, no. 4 (December 1961).

Olcott, Charles S. *The Life of William McKinley*. 2 vols. Boston and New York: Houghton Mifflin Co., 1916.

Peck, Harry T. *Twenty Years of the Republic, 1885–1905*. New York: Dodd, Mead and Co., 1919.

Perkins, Dexter. *Foreign Policy and the American Spirit*. Ithaca, N.Y.: Cornell University Press, 1957.

Pike, Frederick B. *Chile and the United States, 1880–1962*. Notre Dame, Ind.: University of Notre Dame Press, 1963.

Plesur, Milton. *America's Outward Thrust: Approaches to Foreign Affairs, 1865–1890*. De Kalb: Northern Illinois University Press, 1971.

Pletcher, David M. *The Awkward Years: American Foreign Policy under Garfield and Arthur*. Columbia: University of Missouri Press, 1962.

Pollard, James E. *The Presidents and the Press*. New York: Macmillan Co., 1947.

Polsby, Nelson W. *Congress and the Presidency*. Englewood Cliffs, N.J.: Prentice-Hall, 1964.

———. "The Institutionalization of the U.S. House of Representatives." *American Political Science Review* 62 (1968).

Pratt, Julius W. *Expansionists of 1898: The Acquisition of Hawaii and the Spanish Islands*. Baltimore: Johns Hopkins University Press, 1936.

———. "The Coming War with Spain." In *Threshold to American Internationlism: Essays on the Foreign Policies of William McKinley*, edited by Paolo Coletta. New York: Exposition Press, 1970.

Pringle, Henry F. *Theodore Roosevelt: A Biography*. New York: Harcourt, Brace and World, 1931.

———. *The Life and Times of William Howard Taft*. 2 vols. New York: Farrar and Rinehart, Inc., 1939.

Quirk, Robert E. *An Affair of Honor: Woodrow Wilson and the Occupation of Veracruz*. Lexington: University of Kentucky Press, 1962.

Rhodes, James Ford. *The McKinley and Roosevelt Administrations, 1897–1909*. New York: Macmillan Co., 1927.

Roper, Elmo. "Foreword." In Elihu Katz and Paul Lazarsfield. *Personal Influence*. Glencoe, Ill.: Free Press, 1955.

Rosenau, James N. *Public Opinion and Foreign Policy: An Operational Formulation*. New York: Random House, 1961.

Ryden, George Herbert. *The Foreign Policy of the United States in Relation to Samoa*. New Haven, Conn.: Yale University Press, 1933.

Salmon, Lucy Maynard. *The Newspaper and the Historian*. New York: Oxford University Press, 1923.

Sauerwein, Jules Auguste. "The Molders of Public Opinion." In *Public Opinion and World Politics*, edited by Quincy Wright. Chicago: University of Chicago Press, 1933.

Schirmer, Daniel B. *Republic or Empire: American Resistance to the Philippine War*. Cambridge, Mass.: Schenkman Publishing Co., 1972.

Schlesinger, Arthur M., Jr. *The Imperial Presidency*. Boston: Houghton Mifflin Co., 1973.

Schmitt, Bernadotte E. "The Relation of Public Opinion and World Affairs before and during the First World War." In *Studies in Diplomatic History*, edited by A. O. Sarkissian. London: Longmans, Green and Co., 1961.

Scholes, Walter V., and Scholes, Marie V. *The Foreign Policies of the Taft Administration*. Columbia: University of Missouri Press, 1970.

Shankman, Arnold M. "Southern Methodist Newspapers and the Coming of the Spanish-American War." *Journal of Southern History* 39, no. 1 (February 1973).

Sievers, Harry J. *Benjamin Harrison, Hoosier President: The White House and After, 1889–1901*. Indianapolis, Ind.: Bobbs-Merrill Co., 1968.

Small, Melvin. "Historians Look at Public Opinion." In *Public Opinion and Historians: Interdisciplinary Perspectives*, edited by Melvin Small. Detroit: Wayne State University Press, 1970.

Smith, Gene. *When the Cheering Stopped: The Last Years of Woodrow Wilson*. New York: William Morrow and Co., 1964.

Smith, Joe Patterson. *Republican Expansionists of the Early Reconstruction Era*. Chicago: University of Chicago Press, 1930.

Smith, Paul A. "Opinions, Publics, and World Affairs in the United States." *Western Political Quarterly* 14, no. 3 (September 1961).

Startt, James D. "The Uneasy Partnership: Wilson and the Press at Paris." *Mid-America* 42 (January 1970).

Stern-Rubarth, Edgar. "The Methods of Political Propaganda." In *Public Opinion and World Politics*, edited by Quincy Wright. Chicago: University of Chicago Press, 1933.

Stevens, Sylvester. *American Expansion in Hawaii*. Harrisburg, Pa.: Archives Publishing Co., 1945.

Stoddard, Henry L. *As I Knew Them: Presidents and Politics from Grant to Coolidge*. New York: Macmillan Co., 1927.

Strayer, Joseph R. "The Historian's Concept of Public Opinion." In *Common Frontiers of the Social Sciences*, edited by Mirra Komarovsky. Glencoe, Ill.: Free Press, 1957.

Strum, Philippa. *Presidential Power and American Democracy*. Pacific Palisades, Calif.: Goodyear Publishing Co., 1972.

Stuart, Graham H. *The Department of State: A History of Its Organization, Procedure, and Personnel*. New York: Macmillan Co., 1949.

Taylor, John M. *Garfield of Ohio: The Available Man*. New York: W. W. Norton and Co., 1970.

Tyler, Alice Felt. *The Foreign Policies of James G. Blaine*. Minneapolis: University of Minnesota Press, 1927.

Walworth, Arthur. *Woodrow Wilson*. 2 vols. New York: Longmans, Green and Co., 1958.

Warner, Lucien. "The Reliability of Public Opinion Surveys." *Public Opinion Quarterly* 3 (July 1939).

Warren, Sidney. *The President as World Leader*. Philadelphia: J. B. Lippincott Co.,
    1964.
White, David Manning. "The 'Gatekeeper': A Case Study in the Selection of News." In
    People, Society, and Mass Communications, edited by Lewis A. Dexter and David
    M. White. Glencoe, Ill.: Free Press, 1964.
White, Leonard D. *The Republican Era: A Study in Administrative History, 1869–*
    1901. Glencoe, Ill.: Free Press, 1965.
White, William A. *Woodrow Wilson*. Boston and New York: Houghton Mifflin Co.,
    1924.
Wilkerson, Marcus M. *Public Opinion and the Spanish-American War: A Study in*
    War Propaganda. Baton Rouge: Louisiana State University Press, 1932.
Wilson, Francis G. *A Theory of Public Opinion*. Chicago: Henry Regnery Co., 1962.
Wisan, Joseph E. *The Cuban Crisis as Reflected in the New York Press, 1895–1898*.
    New York: Columbia University Press, 1934.

Dissertations

Bean, Walton, E. "George Creel and His Critics: A Study of the Attacks on the
    Committee on Public Information, 1917–1919." Ph.D. dissertation, University of
    California, 1941.
Offner, John L. "President McKinley and the Origins of the Spanish-American War."
    Ph.D. dissertation, Pennsylvania State University, 1957.
Rinn, Fanueil J. "The Presidential Press Conference." Ph.D. dissertation, University
    of Chicago, 1960.

Index

Publication of Supplementary Volumes to *The Papers of Woodrow Wilson* is assisted from time to time by the Woodrow Wilson Foundation in order to encourage scholarly work about Woodrow Wilson and his time. All volumes have passed the review procedures of the publishers and the Editor and the Editorial Advisory Committee of *The Papers of Woodrow Wilson*. Inquiries about the Series should be addressed to The Editor, Papers of Woodrow Wilson, Firestone Library, Princeton University, Princeton, N.J. 08540.

Raymond B. Fosdick, *Letters on the League of Nations: From the Files of Raymond B. Fosdick* (Princeton University Press, 1966).

Wilton B. Fowler, *British-American Relations, 1917–1918: The Role of Sir William Wiseman* (Princeton University Press, 1969).

John M. Mulder, *Woodrow Wilson: The Years of Preparation* (Princeton University Press, 1978).

George Egerton, *Great Britain and the Creation of the League of Nations: Strategy, Politics, and International Organization, 1914–1919* (University of North Carolina Press, 1978).

Stephen Vaughn, *Holding Fast the Inner Lines: Democracy, Nationalism, and the Committee on Public Information* (University of North Carolina Press, 1979).

Robert C. Hilderbrand, *Power and the People: Executive Management of Public Opinion in Foreign Affairs, 1897–1921* (University of North Carolina Press, 1980).